God's blessing upon the Diocese of Sydney in the election of Howard Mowll as its sixth Diocesan Bishop in 1933 is clearly evident in these pages. Despite the inadvertent loss of his personal papers, the authors of this fine anthology provide an insightful and informative account of the ministry of Archbishop Mowll across four continents. These scholarly chapters provide a rich tapestry of the outstanding leadership of Mowll not only in the Diocese of Sydney but throughout Australia and beyond. His zeal for a robust theological education, energetic evangelism and a vision for youth ministry made a formidable impact on evangelical Anglicanism in Sydney. This book is long overdue in celebrating the legacy of Howard Mowll, arguably the most significant and effective Archbishop of Sydney of the twentieth century.

Glenn N Davies, Archbishop of Sydney 2013 – 2021

From its earliest days, mission and CMS have been an integral part of the Anglican church in Sydney and throughout Australia. Through engaging and insightful explanations of the personal involvement of Archbishop and Mrs Mowll in cross-cultural mission at all stages of their ministry life, this book reminds the reader of the critical place of world-wide mission in the life of the individual Christian, the local church, and the structures and institutions that serve the church.

Rev. Canon Peter Sholl, International Director – CMS Australia

HOWARD AND DOROTHY MOWLL

GLOBAL ANGLICAN PIONEERS

EDITED BY ERIN MOLLENHAUER

The Latimer Trust

Howard and Dorothy Mowll: Global Anglican Pioneers © Erin Mollenhauer. All rights reserved.

ISBN 978-1-906327-84-2 Published by the Latimer Trust October 2023.

Cover Image: Howard and Dorothy Mowll with the Niemollers. Taken for Truth and Daily Mirror, 1949. (Public Domain)

CONTENTS PAGE

Preface

Howard West Kilvinton Mowll and his wife Dorothy were the subjects of Moore College's Library Day on 13 March 2021, a successful and well-attended event at which most of the papers in this volume were presented.

The Moore College Library lectures have had a distinguished history, focusing on highly influential figures such as T. C. Hammond, Samuel Marsden, Deaconess Mary Andrews and D. Broughton Knox. The Mowlls are certainly no exception to this tradition, and their adventurous lives provide the scope for a book with a broad global focus.

Peter Jensen's introduction provides an overview of Mowll's life, from the perspective of one of his successors as Archbishop. The volume opens and closes with chapters on Mowll's spiritual and personal development, with **Tom Habib** outlining his studies at Cambridge and formative experience with the Cambridge Inter-Collegiate Christian Union (Chapter 1), and **Stuart Piggin** interpreting the marginalia in his Bibles (Chapter 12).

The international scope of his career is highlighted firstly by **Michael Gladwin's** exploration of Mowll's experiences as a chaplain in the First World War (Chapter 2), and later by **Mark Earngey** who describes his influence on the Church of England in South Africa (Chapter 8). Unfortunately, this volume was not able to include any in-depth detail of Howard Mowll's career in China.

Mowll's long and highly influential term as Archbishop of Sydney is the focus of this volume. **Edward Loane** investigates the events surrounding his election in 1933 (Chapter 3), followed by **Geoffrey Treloar's** analysis of the archbishop in the 1930s (Chapter 4) and **Colin Bale's** inquiry into his activities during the Second World War (Chapter 5). Soon after the war, the Red Book Case arose and this incident is explored by **Robert Tong** (Chapter 6). The current Principal of Moore College, **Mark Thompson**, analyses Mowll's influence on the College in Chapter 7, and Dean of Women at Youthworks College, **Ruth Lukabyo**, writes about his development of youth ministry in Chapter 9. Dr Treloar returns in Chapter 10 to provide insight into Mowll's term as Primate of Australia.

Dorothy Mowll was a remarkable woman in her own right, and **Jane Tooher's** paper details her early life as a single missionary in China as well as her later role in the development of retirement villages in Sydney (Chapter 11).

The Mowlls – as the focus of a historical study – are a fascinating example of archival silence.[1] A frequent lament from the historians involved in this project, was the unfortunate destruction of Howard Mowll's papers. Initially believed to have been caused by Marcus Loane, Mowll's biographer, at Mowll's request, a handwritten note by Loane dated 15 August 1998, states that it was in fact a secretary sent by Bishop W. G. Hilliard who had destroyed the papers on her own initiative.[2] This was highly unethical, and resulted in the significant loss of primary sources.

Similarly, Dorothy's diaries, which would provide valuable insight into her personal life and thoughts, are nowhere to be found. The authors of these papers have therefore had to rely very heavily on printed sources.

The archives held by Moore College Library were created predominantly throughout the 20th century. Despite there being only a handful of folders created by Mowll himself, his name appears frequently in documents included elsewhere – minutes of the Moore

---

[1] 'The unintentional or purposeful absence or distortion of documentation of enduring value, resulting in gaps and inabilities to represent the past accurately' Society of American Archivists, *Dictionary of Archives Terminology*, https://dictionary.archivists.org/entry/archival-silence.html (Accessed 5 November 2021).

[2] 'It is false to say that "A/b Mowll left instructions to burn his papers". They were burnt – but not on his instructions. Bishop Hilliard as Commissary sent Miss Huntley, one of the Archbishops' secretaries, out to Bishopscourt to sort things out. She burnt the papers without advice or supervision.' M. L. Loane, 15 August 1998, hand written note in the Diocesan Archives.

Theological College committee, photographs from the Australian Church Record, the sermon Mowll preached at the funeral of R. B. S. Hammond, documents relating to the Church of England in South Africa, material collected by the Church of England Historical Society. He can be found in numerous places because the scope of his activities was so broad, and he was such a leading public figure.

As a librarian and archivist, I am new to the publishing world, and am particularly grateful for the people who have assisted with this project: Ed Loane who advised me on the editing process; Geoff Treolar who provided invaluable proof reading assistance; the publishing team at Latimer Trust; and the Library, events and kitchen teams at Moore College who helped the event come together. Also, many of the contributors to this volume could not have written their chapters without the generous assistance of Sydney Diocesan Archivist Dr Louise Trott, whom I would like to thank on their behalf.

Erin Mollenhauer

Team Leader, Library and Archives, Moore College

Contributors

Rev Dr Colin Bale is an Emeritus Faculty member of Moore Theological College. He previously served as Vice-Principal and Head of Church History. He is the author of *A Crowd of Witnesses: Epitaphs on First World War Australian War Graves* (Longueville, 2015).

Rev Dr Mark Earngey is the Head of Church History and Lecturer in Christian Thought at Moore Theological College. His research interests include ecclesiastical history, historical theology, and systematic theology, with special focus on the European Reformations.

Dr Michael Gladwin is Senior Lecturer in History at St Mark's National Theological Centre in the School of Theology, Charles Sturt University. He is also a research fellow in CSU's Public and Contextual Theology (PaCT) research centre. A graduate of the ANU and the University of Cambridge, his research focuses on the religious, cultural, and intellectual history of Australia in the context of modern British and European history, as well as on the relationship between religion and war in Australian history. He also edits *St Mark's Review*, one of Australia's longest-running theological journals.

Rev Tom Habib was appointed to the Faculty of Moore Theological College in 2022, and has just completed doctoral studies at Cambridge University on moral characterisation in the Gospel of John.

The Rt Rev Dr Peter Jensen was Principal of Moore Theological College from 1985 – 2001, and the eleventh Archbishop of Sydney from 2001 – 2013.

Rev Dr Edward Loane is the Warden of St Paul's College at the University of Sydney, and is an Adjunct Lecturer in Church History at Moore Theological College. His research interests include Anglican, reformation and evangelical history, ecclesiology, atonement, revelation, and preaching.

Dr Ruth Lukabyo is Senior Lecturer and Dean of Women at Youthworks College and completed her PhD in church history at Macquarie University. She is author of *From a Ministry for Youth to a*

Ministry of Youth: Aspects of Protestant Youth Ministry in Sydney 1930 – 1959 (Wipf & Stock, 2020).

Associate Professor Stuart Piggin has published more than 100 academic articles and seven books, notably *Evangelical Christianity in Australia: Spirit, Word and Work* (OUP, 1996). He was Master of Robert Menzies College at Macquarie University from 1990 to 2004. He was the founding Director of the Macquarie Christian Studies Institute, and the founding Chairman of the Australian Christian Heritage Foundation.

Rev Canon Dr Mark Thompson is the Principal of Moore Theological College. He is the Chair of the Sydney Diocesan Doctrine Commission and has been involved with the GAFCON movement from its beginning. His most recent publication is *The Doctrine of Scripture: An Introduction* (Crossway, 2022).

Jane Tooher is the Director of Moore College's Priscilla and Aquila Centre, which encourages the ministries of women in partnership with men. She also lectures in ministry and church history, and is the co-author (with Graham Beynon) of *Embracing Complementarianism: Turning Biblical Convictions into Positive Church Culture* (Good Book Company, 2022).

Dr Robert Tong AM is a lawyer and Deputy Chancellor of the Diocese of Sydney. He has been active in lay ministry and in church government for more than 40 years. He was an Australian representative on the Anglican Consultative Council (1995 – 2000), and a Member of the Archbishop of Canterbury's Panel of Reference (2005 – 2008). In 2010, he was appointed a Member of the Order of Australia in the Australia Day Honours list.

Dr Geoffrey Treloar is Reader in the History of Christianity at the Australian College of Theology and Visiting Fellow in History in the School of Humanities and Languages at the University of New South Wales. He is the author or editor of numerous books and articles, notably *The Disruption of Evangelicalism: The Age of Torrey, Mott, McPherson and Hammond* (Inter-Varsity Press, 2016).

Introduction: Howard West Kilvinton Mowll and Dorothy Mowll

Peter F Jensen

Archbishop and Mrs Mowll made an immense contribution to Christian work. This is especially the case in Sydney, where they served together from 1934 to 1958. It is very fitting that we should remember them.

I have been given the honour of writing a foreword to this book. What I am about to say is not based on independent research. It is merely aimed at introducing us to the Archbishop and Mrs Mowll and sketching an outline of their lives.

I begin with an event which may not have happened, but which should have. It is the night of the Archbishop's enthronement in St Andrew's Cathedral. There is a crowd, bustle, splendour as the Archbishop gets ready to enter, from his shoulders flowing a cloak with a long train, choir boys getting ready to carry it.

It is 13 March 1934, in the midst of the Great Depression. A man much affected by drink passes by, and, seeing the throng, asks what is going on. On being told that it was the welcome to the new Archbishop from England, he makes a classic Aussie crack: 'with so many out of work here, why do we have to import a bloody Pommie as Archbishop?'

Well you may ask.

Sydney did not elect its first local Archbishop until 32 years later, so strong was the nature of the commitment to king and church and empire. The Archbishop came, swathed with a pre-existent glory, Cambridge educated, always in love with his alma mater, consecrated in Westminster Abbey, one of a recognisable leadership elite, not averse to exercising authority in a very direct way, commanding in stature and in voice. But was he a fit choice for Sydney?

Although he was indisputably English in speech and manner, he had not spent the previous years in a comfortable vicarage at home looking up occasionally from *The Times* crossword puzzle. Aged only 43, Mowll had already been a Bishop for eleven years, serving in West China. Before that, from 1913 until 1922 (with a brief time as an army chaplain in France), he was a member of the faculty of Wycliffe College in Toronto. Both in Canada and in China, his time was marked by travel, adventure and peril for the sake of the gospel, whether visiting the far-flung graduates of Wycliffe in the vastness of Canada, or journeying to the clergy and churches in China. He and his wife Dorothy endured kidnap, assault and bullets. At the same time, they gave themselves unstintingly to the ministry of the gospel, to building up the churches, to advancing local leadership. 'We preach not ourselves,' was the text of his first sermon in Sydney, 'but Christ Jesus the Lord; and ourselves your servants for Jesus' sake.'

Dorothy Mowll was born in June 1890, just six months after Howard. But, whereas he was born and grew up in Dover in a prosperous middle-class home, she was the daughter of Church Missionary Society (CMS) missionary parents and spent the first four years of her life in China, experiencing the language and the culture. After her education in England, which included teaching and medical work, she fulfilled her ambition to be a missionary and returned to the land of her birth. Her vigour and enthusiasm were remarkable. It appears that it was not obvious to her that they should marry; but it *was* obvious to Howard Mowll, and he pursued this ambition with characteristic zeal. They were married in October 1923 and over the next 33 years, their ministries and their personalities complemented each other, with joint achievements which have had a lasting effect. They had no children, but even more than usual, when thinking of an episcopal ministry, it is not possible to think of one without the other. To this day, we benefit from that joint ministry.

In the election, the liberal evangelicals, such as the Principal of Moore College and the Dean of Sydney, were understandably keen to secure the election of one like themselves, Archdeacon J W Hunkin. However, those whose tradition went back to Nathaniel Jones and Bishop Barker supported Bishop Mowll, and they won the day, not without some bitterness and later repercussions. It was hotly contested; rightly, as we can now see, because the result of that election set the course for the Diocese of Sydney until the present day. But the Archbishop of Canterbury, Cosmo Gordon Lang, had told Mowll that 'he possessed neither the gifts nor the training which the See of Sydney required'[1] and pivotal though the moment was, it did not necessarily mean that the right choice had been made. After all, he had tried to learn Chinese but made little progress. Could he learn Australian?

Who was this man? He was imposingly tall, like Bishop Barker, with a voice which could fill any hall. He seems to have relied on others, not least Dorothy, for a number of the ordinary things of life. Sir Marcus Loane tells us that he was courteous but reserved in manner, although he was also the sort of man around whom stories would cluster, and there was no doubting his will and purpose and energy and strength. Is this what Sydney needed?

Some of what we are looking for goes back to those Cambridge days, for he was shaped by his student experience. For a record five terms he was president of the Cambridge Inter-Collegiate Christian Union, immediately after the great split with the Student Christian Movement over the absolute centrality of the cross of Christ understood as a penal substitution. At that time, he was merely 21 years of age, but true to the evangelical ethos of the time, through missions, beach missions, open air preaching and personal evangelism he learned the skills which made him such a formidable leader. Central to that was, of course, powerful evangelical conviction, for only those who are deeply conservative can be truly innovative.

Those convictions prepared him to stand for the truth of the gospel in the midst of debate. They also drove him to new and lasting work to promote the same gospel. He was not merely a cultural Anglican, but first and foremost an evangelical Christian with a world-wide vision. One of the first things he did on arrival in Australia was to get on to

---

[1] Marcus Loane, *Archbishop Mowll: The Biography of Howard West Kilvinton Mowll, Archbishop of Sydney and Primate of Australia* (London: Hodder and Stoughton, 1960), 133.

the Council of the interdenominational Katoomba Christian Convention and work with them over the years, especially on the Mission Evenings. He was a mission-driven evangelical Anglican, evangelical first, Anglican second.

Let me come clean. Was he the right man for mid-twentieth century Sydney? Absolutely. Bishop Barker was a great Bishop. You can form your own opinion as you read this book as to whether Mowll also falls into that rare category. Naturally Jane Barker and Dorothy were integral to whatever success their husbands had. Dorothy died in December 1957; Howard, ten months later, in October 1958.

As you read this book, you will learn more about their accomplishments. But, just as the legacy of the Barkers included Moore College, the Church Society (now Anglicare) and St Catherine's School, so the legacy of the Mowlls included the Youth Department and the Church of England National Emergency Fund (CENEF), the Anglican Retirement Villages, as well as the rejuvenation of Moore College and the Home Mission Society and widespread church planting. I ought to include his ability to choose and advance the leaders of the next generation, notably Graham Delbridge, Clive Kerle and Marcus Loane. And his willingness to put T C Hammond at Moore College and to work with him.

But pre-eminently Mowll did what every Archbishop of Sydney should do, make the Diocese more evangelical than he found it. Not for party political reasons, but for the sake of the preaching of the gospel and the salvation of souls. He was not alone in doing this – the Diocese was not absolutely subservient to him by any means, and he suffered losses on the floor of Synod and elsewhere. This is Sydney after all! People stood up to him, dissented from him and were critical of him. But without him, the pivot away from liberal evangelicalism would not have occurred, and we would not be sitting here today. You need only to trace the history of Moore College to see that.

He worked with energy and an eye for detail in the Diocese. He did not delegate easily. He did not allow criticism to deter him from his great evangelical passion. Both Dorothy and he worked with energy and enthusiasm during the war days, doing all that could be done to look after the members of the armed forces on leave or training in Sydney. In those days, the Archbishop was a national figure and it is indicative of how well he was known and respected that we are told that there were 150,000 people lining the streets at his funeral.

But as well, as time went on and his leadership capacity was recognised, he was made the Primate of Australia, overcoming an earlier hostility and in spite of having to weather the Red Book Case. As Primate, he travelled and visited extensively around the nation. And, especially after the war, he and Dorothy engaged in much overseas travel, not least to China, and he became involved in the early stages of the World Council of Churches. It is not surprising that from his base in far-away Sydney he became a global figure, especially in evangelical circles. I myself wonder whether his extended absences from the Diocese were in its best interests.

His agreement with the Constitution of the Australian Church was fundamental to its success, as was the support of T C Hammond. That meant that the doubts of people like D B Knox and Donald Robinson were overcome in the Synod. But even here, Mowll only approved the Constitution because it safeguarded what he called 'the Protestant and Reformed character of the Church of England', a viewpoint which he saw as 'the tradition of the Diocese' which he was bound to protect.

Was this Pommie the right man?

In 1954, as was the custom in those days, there was an award ceremony in the Chapter House, where children who had done well in the Diocesan Sunday School exams received a certificate. The person who handed out the awards was the Archbishop. My brother Phillip received an award and so did I. I can remember only that as I was given the certificate, I stuck my hand up vertically above my head so that the huge, mountainous man could shake it. I cannot forget that moment. And it was a moment in which, strangely, that present moment shook hands with the remote future and looked down from a great height with a kindly if totally unsuspecting eye.

But between that moment and the long, in the distance future, was the Billy Graham Crusade in which my infant faith became real and living and salvation arrived. Without the Archbishop, Billy Graham would not have received such a welcome to Australia. Other Anglicans opposed the invitation, but such was the respect with which Mowll was held that he united and inspired the Protestant Churches and, although he did not live to see the results, the 1959 Crusade was the consequence.

In 2012, a friend showed me an email he had received from Jerry Beaven, one of Billy Graham's team. He recalled that in 1957, when initial discussions were being held about the Crusade, he dined at Bishopscourt, and afterwards prayed in the chapel with Dr Mowll. 'As we knelt there he said, "Pray for me, Brother Jerry." Me – a 38-year-old Southern Baptist being asked to pray for perhaps the strongest Evangelical voice in the world. It is a moment I can never forget...'

We are right to spend time thinking about the Archbishop and Mrs Mowll. Remember this, however: at the heart of everything he did and accomplished was a deep piety, discernible if you read the marginalia of his Bible. Whether he was a great Archbishop (and I believe that he was the second of only two), we also know that both he and Dorothy knew that they (like the rest of us) were miserable sinners. Their faithfulness, zeal and energy arose first and foremost from the assurance they received as they trusted the Christ who died in their place on the cross. We will give thanks for them both and rightly so. We will learn from them. But if they were here today they would say to us, remember, 'We do not preach ourselves, but Christ Jesus as Lord, with ourselves as your servants, for Christ's sake' (2 Cor 4:5).

1. The Cambridge Years: 1909 – 1912[2]

Tom Habib

Walking old paths in perilous times: Mowll's first year at Cambridge

In the middle of Cambridge, next door to Holy Trinity Church, stands Henry Martyn Hall. The hall was named after a missionary, Henry Martyn, who arrived in Cambridge to study in 1797. Whilst studying, Martyn came under the influence and teaching of Charles Simeon. Forsaking a promising academic career, Martyn first served as Simeon's curate at Holy Trinity before embarking on the mission field in India and Persia. He died in 1812, aged only 31. Almost a century later, Howard Mowll sat in the hall named after Martyn, listening to a long and heated debate over whether the Christian Inter-Collegiate Christian Union (CICCU) should disaffiliate from the Student Christian Movement (SCM).

Over the previous years, CICCU members had grown increasingly concerned with the changing doctrine and practice of the Student Christian Movement. They believed that the SCM had embraced higher criticism and questioned central doctrines including the inspiration of Scripture, the penal view of the atonement, and the divinity of Christ.[3] Moreover, SCM's interest in apologetics and social action was believed to be dampening the 'aggressive Christian

---

[2] This chapter focuses on Mowll's time in the CICCU (Cambridge Inter-Collegiate Union) from 1909-1912. See Loane, *Archbishop Mowll,* for details on his time at Ridley College.

[3] Basil F.C. Atkinson, *Old Paths in Perilous Times,* 2nd ed. (London, 1932), 8. Cf. Tissington Tatlow, *The Story of the Student Christian Movement of Great Britain and Ireland* (London: Student Christian Movement Press, 1933), 384. Tatlow, the leader of the SCM, identified the same doctrinal issues as the cause of division, though he argued that in their zeal CICCU misrepresented the SCM position.

evangelism' that CICCU prided itself on.[4] Perhaps most painfully of all, the SCM had replaced Keswick (an annual summer conference), 'the spiritual birthplace'[5] of many of its leaders, with conferences that platformed High Churchmen and non-conformists over evangelical speakers.[6] Many CICCU members believed that they were walking away from the truths that Simeon had lived for and Henry Martyn had died for.[7] In March 1910 CICCU voted in favour of disaffiliation, 17 votes to five. Howard Mowll had only just signed his membership with CICCU a few months before.

This was not an easy time to join. A few years later a booklet entitled *Old Paths in Perilous Times* was published, defending CICCU's decision. Mowll was one of its six signatories. The booklet recalls:

> It seemed *indeed* presumption for 250 men to differ – and to differ so emphatically from 152,000 students in the World's Universities; it seemed, indeed the height of misguided enthusiasm for this handful of young men to isolate themselves from so colossal and inspiring a federation of students. No wonder that on all sides were raised voices of warm entreaty, indignant remonstrance and even violent protest. [8]

CICCU was isolated and unpopular. It was seen by some as 'a small select club of saved men'[9] and others as a 'handful of brainless undergraduates.'[10] Liberalism was on the rise and the general

---

[4] Atkinson, *Old Paths in Perilous Times*, 7. Cf. David Goodhew, 'The Rise of the Cambridge Inter-Collegiate Christian Union, 1910-1971,' *Journal of Ecclesiastical History* 54.1 (2003): 65.

[5] Atkinson, *Old Paths in Perilous Times*, 9.

[6] 'Puzzled', *The English Churchman and St James Chronicle* (February 1, 1909), as cited in Steve Bruce, 'The Student Christian Movement and the Inter-Varsity Fellowship: A Sociological Study of Two Student Movements', PhD thesis (University of Stirling, 1980), 186.

[7] John Pollock, *A Cambridge Movement* (London: Murray, 1953), 172.

[8] Atkinson, *Old Paths in Perilous Times*, 11.

[9] Pollock, *A Cambridge Movement*, 176.

[10] SCM Papers, Box 20, 'S. Donnithorne to T. Tatlow', 17 September 1911, Orchard Learning Centre, Westhill College, Birmingham, as cited in Bruce, 'The Student Christian Movement and the Inter-Varsity Fellowship,' 184.

consensus was that 'old fashioned evangelicalism' had no future.[11] Following the disaffiliation, Richard Pelly, a former CICCU president who had supported the SCM, wrote, 'I'm afraid poor old CICCU is bound to go down ... in these days a society which clings (as I suppose it now will cling) to verbal inspiration is doomed.'[12] The SCM began its own branch in Cambridge and grew steadily while CICCU's membership declined. This was the context into which Howard Mowll joined the CICCU. Yet Mowll had come up to Cambridge with strong evangelical convictions, and CICCU's conservative theology and focus on evangelism aligned squarely with his own beliefs. In the face of growing opposition, Mowll, 'was never in doubt as to where his duty would lie.'[13]

Mowll immediately became involved in CICCU life and walked the old paths that the Union had now preserved. On his first night at Cambridge, he was invited by Cecil Hyde Hills to Colin Kerr's rooms over at Parker's Piece for prayer and Bible study.[14] Each weekday that year Mowll would head to the Henry Martyn Hall for the daily prayer meetings, kneeling with fellow members in a new spirit of devotion.[15] Every Sunday he would again walk over to Henry Martyn Hall for the weekly Bible reading, where a range of well-known evangelical speakers were invited to give a 'Keswick talk', addressing Christians on the spiritual life and its practical problems. Students would pray informally with one another afterwards over tea and coffee.[16] In the evening, Mowll would attend the weekly evangelistic sermon, which had once again become the focus of CICCU life.[17] CICCU also provided Mowll with the opportunity to cut his teeth on ministry and

---

[11] Oliver R. Barclay and Robert M. Horn, *From Cambridge to the World: 125 Years of Student Witness* (Leicester: Inter-Varsity, 2002), 80.

[12] SCM papers, Box 20, 'R. Pelly to T. Tatlow', 12 March 1910, Orchard Learning Centre, Westhill College, Birmingham as cited in Goodhew, 'The Rise of the Cambridge Inter-Collegiate Christian Union, 1910-1971,' 65.

[13] Loane, *Archbishop Mowll*, 45.

[14] Loane, *Archbishop Mowll*, 42.

[15] Loane, *Archbishop Mowll*, 45.

[16] CICCU Records and Papers, 'Basil's Recollections,' Cambridge University Library, Cambridge.

[17] Pollock, *A Cambridge Movement*, 176.

evangelism. His first opportunity to speak was teaching a Bible class in Barnwell, a village on the outskirts of town. He and his best friend, Arthur Pitt-Pitts, would regularly teach there on a Sunday afternoon before the CICCU sermon in the evening.[18] Mowll felt awkward during his first experience of open-air preaching, but he was soon speaking regularly on Sunday evenings beneath a lamppost in Parker's Piece or in the marketplace in town. His voice was so strong that people would have to close their windows to avoid hearing him speak.[19] And so, Mowll walked the well-worn paths of Cambridge men like Charles Simeon and Henry Martyn. He finished his first year in July 1910 joining his fellow CICCU members at the newly reformed Cambridge camp at Keswick. He would attend each summer after that, organising his final camp in 1914.[20]

Getting back to evangelism: Mowll's presidency & the Torrey Mission

In the new academic year (October 1910), Howard Mowll joined the executive of CICCU. Following the turmoil of the past year, the Executive were keen for the Union to turn their focus back to evangelism. They discussed the possibility of organizing a full-scale mission to the university and decided to invite Dr R A Torrey, an American revivalist to lead their mission the following November. At the start of the new term Mowll was appointed president, and he set out to prepare for the mission.

Mowll began with prayer, organising prayer slips, printed on expensive India paper, to be sent to thousands of friends throughout the world. Students would meet and pray long into the night in each other's rooms. One student wishing to attend a meeting in another college had to convince his tutor to let him stay out past midnight. 'Sir,' he said, 'you would grant it for a May week ball, wouldn't you?'[21] Colin Kerr, who had met Mowll on his first night at Cambridge a year earlier, remarked, 'It was as natural to go into a man's rooms and suggest

---

[18] Loane, *Archbishop Mowll*, 56.
[19] Loane, *Archbishop Mowll*, 57.
[20] Loane, *Archbishop Mowll*, 45, 57.
[21] Pollock, *A Cambridge Movement*, 183.

prayer as to talk about the boats or the debates at the Union.'[22] Along with prayer, Mowll was convinced that the mission must depend on the Word of God alone. Torrey had often travelled with a singer, Charles Alexander, but the executive decided not to invite him. Mowll later wrote of this decision:

> [The disaffiliation] mainly turned upon what attitude was adopted towards Holy Scripture and how it was used in Christian witness. The CICCU Executive therefore planned for a mission to be conducted in the University which would rely only on the power of the Word of God, without any other aids to attract an audience or to lead to the conversion of souls.[23]

Relying on prayer and the word, Mowll made preparations on a remarkable scale.[24] Colin Kerr was in charge of publicity, and one hundred pounds was spent on printing alone.[25] Huge 2.5 metre posters were displayed in front of King's and St. Catherine's College, as well as in the market and throughout the town, whilst smaller posters were displayed across colleges and shop windows. Months in advance, Mowll organised for invitation cards to be printed and sent to all resident graduates and undergraduates and sent a second card closer to the date. Every undergraduate in the university was allocated to a CICCU member and special classes were run to train them in how to invite these people to the mission.

By the start of Michaelmas term (October 1911) everyone in Cambridge knew that Dr Torrey was coming. Of course, not everyone was happy about it. Scorned as an 'American revivalist', Torrey was also disliked for his opposition to higher criticism. There was so little outside support for him coming that CICCU had trouble finding a meeting place or a don willing to chair the meeting. Shortly before the mission,

---

[22] Pollock, *A Cambridge Movement*, 183.

[23] Pollock, *A Cambridge Movement*, 182.

[24] The following details of Mowll's preparations are drawn from Pollock, *A Cambridge Movement*, 182-3 and Loane, *Archbishop Mowll*, 47-48.

[25] Pollock, *A Cambridge Movement*, 183. This would be the equivalent of about £11,000 today.

CICCU members discovered a plot to kidnap Dr Torrey from the train station and hold him in a hotel in Royston until the mission was over. The plan was for someone to impersonate Torrey and leave with the CICCU members whilst other kidnappers would welcome the real Torrey and drive him to the hotel. Upon hearing this, Colin Kerr suggested that they should kick Torrey in the shin when they meet him: 'If he does not swear, he is Torrey!'[26] After being escorted from the train station by a large contingent of CICCU students, Torrey began the mission.

Even his most ardent critics could not deny the impact. A few days before the mission started, Torrey spoke to CICCU members and a man who was brought along by a friend was converted. The man was an alcoholic, and Mowll later recalled, 'He often declared that from that moment all desire for drink left him. For many years he has rendered devoted and outstanding service as a missionary.'[27] Two of C T Studd's daughters reported that during one of Torrey's sermons some men had stink bombs in their pockets but had been converted before they could throw them.[28] The mission was so successful that Torrey stayed a second, and then a third week. Many were converted, with a hundred Scofield Reference Bibles given out to men who had professed faith.[29] Mowll oversaw the follow up to the mission, gathering the names of everyone converted during the mission and organising CICCU members to read the Bible with them in their rooms. He himself read the Bible with one man in his rooms at King's. Reflecting on the mission years later, Mowll recalled,

> I have reason to know that the conversions were not only numerous but lasting...When I look at the College War memorials of the First World War I find there are so many names of men who came to the Lord just before they gave their lives for their country.[30]

---

[26] Pollock, *A Cambridge Movement*, 184.
[27] Pollock, *A Cambridge Movement*, 185.
[28] Pollock, *A Cambridge Movement*, 186.
[29] Barclay and Horn, *From Cambridge to the World*, 85.
[30] As quoted in Pollock, *A Cambridge Movement*, 189.

A burning heart: Mowll's passion for mission

In his first year at Cambridge, Mowll joined the Cambridge Volunteer Union (CVU), the missionary wing of CICCU.[31] This group existed to enrol students in the call to go abroad and to make the pledge: 'It is my purpose if God permit to become a foreign missionary.'[32] At the end of his first year at Cambridge, Arthur Pitt-Pitts invited him to take part in the CMS Exhibition at the Agricultural Hall in London. He was put in charge of the stall for China. That week Mowll's heart for mission grew as he gave talks to crowds gathered around his stall.[33] During his presidency the following year, Mowll led the CVU prayer meetings each week at 7.30am in the Henry Martyn Hall, followed by a missionary breakfast at Dorothy Café.[34] At the end of that summer in 1911, just before the Torrey Mission, Mowll took part in the Cambridge University Missionary Campaign in Liverpool. Seventy men helped run meetings in eighty-five parish churches. At the final meeting in the Philharmonic Hall on October 2nd, Mowll spoke and explained his reasons for wishing to go abroad.[35]

During this campaign, Mowll met C T Studd. Studd was one of the Cambridge Seven who joined Hudson Taylor and the China Inland Mission in 1885. In 1910, Studd went to Sudan and saw the need for missionary work in central Africa. He returned to England to raise support and missionaries to set up the Heart of Africa Mission, and met Mowll at the Cambridge University Missionary Campaign. Mowll 'soon fell beneath the spell of his intrepid leadership.'[36] Studd was invited by Mowll to speak at the Torrey Mission where he called for a 'Cambridge Seventy' to join him in Africa. Alfred Barclay Buxton, who would leave his studies to join Studd, said at the time, 'It was a most solemn meeting, and from what we have heard since, God's clear call

---

[31] At that time, it was called the Student Volunteer Missionary Union (SVMU) but reformed as the Cambridge Volunteer Union (CVU) following CICCU's disaffiliation with the SCM.
[32] Loane, *Archbishop Mowll*, 51.
[33] Loane, *Archbishop Mowll*, 53.
[34] Loane, *Archbishop Mowll*, 52.
[35] Loane, *Archbishop Mowll*, 53.
[36] Loane, *Archbishop Mowll*, 53.

was heard by many a man.'[37] Mowll was conflicted. He had considered leaving with Studd too, but was advised by his father to stay, complete his studies, and be ordained. At the end of his third year at Cambridge, Studd wrote to Mowll:

> You have the great opportunity of a lifetime and of a century. Does not your heart and spirit burn within you? Did I not love you so dearly, I could not again write you on the subject; I hardly like writing now. You set your face steadfastly to go to Jerusalem. Let nothing and nobody hinder you... You and everyone best honour parents by doing the will of God and storming the devil's breaches. I verily believe that if you fling away your present opportunity, you will regret it all your life, and so will many others. You can if you will be a leader for Christ; be not like dumb, driven cattle. Gamble with your life, and all you have, for Christ's sake.[38]

Mowll, with great difficulty and disappointment, followed his father's advice and said no to Africa. But he did not say no to mission. As his third year drew to a close, Mowll and his close friends from CICCU wanted to remain connected and support one another in their future missionary endeavours. They formed the Cambridge Missionary Band, which would publish news from its members twice a year and raise £200 a year to support one member as a missionary. Of Mowll's CICCU friends, Loane wrote, 'no friendships in his later life could ever displace them in his heart or could enrich him half so much.'[39] Among them were Arthur Pitt-Pitts, Mowll's closest friend (who would later die in East Africa); Harold Earnshaw Smith (missionary to West Africa); Alfred and Murray Buxton (missionaries to Congo and Japan); A. C. Stanley Smith and Leonard Sharp (pioneer missionaries to Rwanda); and T. H. Somervell (missionary to India).[40] Mowll too never

---

[37] Loane, *Archbishop Mowll*, 53.
[38] As quoted in Loane, *Archbishop Mowll*, 54.
[39] Loane, *Archbishop Mowll*, 55.
[40] Loane, *Archbishop Mowll*, 55.

lost his passionate heart for mission, a passion that led him across the seas to Canada, West China and Sydney.

The legacy of Cambridge

Mowll came up to Cambridge with firm evangelical convictions – he most likely would not have joined CICCU without them. Yet it was in the CICCU that he found his home. He thrived under its strong biblical preaching, tight fellowship and devotional culture. It was CICCU that offered Mowll his first experiences in ministry and evangelism, work that would continue for the rest of his life. The opposition CICCU faced no doubt strengthened Mowll's resolve to never compromise on his evangelical convictions. At the same time, the Torrey mission was a clear demonstration of the power of the word in the face of opposition. As President of CICCU, Mowll came under the strong influence of evangelical leaders such as Stuart Holden and C T Studd. But it was perhaps the deep friendships that he made that formed him most of all. Mowll's time at Cambridge had given him an example and vision of undivided service to Christ. The notes from a talk Mowll gave while at Cambridge perhaps best describe how this time had grown him. The talk was entitled, 'Wanting to Join',[41] and the three points were as follows:

1. Nothing but all.

2. No time but now.

3. No one but me.

---

[41] Loane, *Archbishop Mowll*, 56.

2. 'Our Padre': A future Archbishop as First World War Army chaplain

Michael Gladwin

Howard Mowll's experience as chaplain with the British Expeditionary Force (BEF) on the Western Front during 1918–19 remains one of the least explored aspects of his life and legacy. This is due in part to a lack of extant sources and in part to Mowll's biographer (Anglican Primate and Sir) Marcus Loane devoting only one page of his biography to Mowll's chaplaincy role.[1] In recent years, however, an efflorescence of scholarship on Anglican chaplaincy has provided new background information with which to better reconstruct and contextualise Mowll's chaplaincy experience. Although a major difficulty with any study of Mowll is the fact that his private papers were destroyed after his death, a modest cache of new extant sources has recently come to light, notably Mowll's Royal Army Chaplains Department (RAChD) recruitment documents. Taken together, these new extant sources shed a little more light on this little-known phase of Mowll's life and, in turn, its impact on his character and ministry.

Pre-war years

In the years just prior to the outbreak of the war Howard Mowll was reading history at King's College, Cambridge. He took his BA in 1912 (which, following traditional Oxbridge practice, was upgraded to an MA in 1916). Mowll had demonstrated his leadership credentials while at Cambridge, where he was president of the firmly evangelical Cambridge Inter-Collegiate Christian Union (CICCU) during 1911–12. In that capacity he had, as historian Ken Cable pithily put it, 'battled the liberal Student Christian Movement, emerging as a doughty leader and controversialist'.[2] Mowll undertook theological training with

---

[1] Loane, *Archbishop Mowll*, 79.
[2] K. J. Cable, 'Mowll, Howard West Kilvinton (1890–1958)', in *Australian Dictionary of Biography*, National Centre of Biography, Australian National

around fifty other ordinands at Ridley Hall during 1913–14 (Ridley Hall being the training college in Cambridge for evangelical Anglican graduates, whereas those of higher or broader churchmanship tended to train at Westcott House).[3]

Around this time a clerical acquaintance of Mowll's mentioned the aspiring young clergyman's name to Canon T R O'Meara, principal of Wycliffe College, a leading Canadian evangelical theological college based in the University of Toronto. Not long afterwards, on a trip to England, O'Meara invited Mowll to call on him in London. Expecting O'Meara to ask him about CICCU work, O'Meara instead invited an astonished Mowll to take up duties as lecturer in church history at Wycliffe. Mowll accepted and on 21 September 1913, having reached the canonical age of 23 at which one could be ordained, Mowll was deaconed for colonial service by the evangelical bishop of Manchester, Edmund Arbuthnott Knox. This followed a longstanding practice, that stretched back to the passing of the so-called Colonial Clergy Act (1819), which gave authority to the Bishop of London to ordain men solely for service in the colonies and not in England (under English and canonical law such men were unable to officiate in the UK without testimonials from the bishop to whose diocese they had been licenced). After 1848, in the wake of a tussle between the bishop of London and the then colonial secretary, bishops beyond London had been given the authority to ordain men for the colonies.[4] Mowll arrived at Wycliffe in 1913, where he served as a tutor until 1916 and then as professor of history (1916–22).

University, https://adb.anu.edu.au/biography/mowll-howard-west-kilvinton-11189/text19943 (accessed 18 June 2021).

[3] These arrangements still prevailed (with Anglican evangelical ordinands going to Ridley and non-evangelicals to Westcott House) when this author was studying at Cambridge University during 2007–10.

[4] Loane, *Archbishop Mowll*, 63–64. For the 'Colonial Clergy Act', see Michael Gladwin, *Anglican Clergy in Australia, 1788–1850: Building a British World* (Woodbridge, Suffolk: Boydell Press, 2015), 185–86. The full title of the Act is the *Ordination for the Colonies Act, 59 Geo III, c.60*.

Application and recruitment for chaplaincy

Mowll was in Toronto when heard the news, on 4 August 1914, that Britain had declared war on Germany.[5] Like many young Anglican clergymen of the day, Mowll felt the strong pull of national and religious duty. He submitted his name immediately to be considered for chaplaincy with the Royal Army Chaplains' Department (RAChD). Bishop John Taylor Smith, a former missionary bishop to Sierra Leone and royal chaplain, was the RAChD's Chaplain General, responsible for the recruitment of Anglican chaplains. Taylor Smith had known Mowll through Cambridge and CICCU circles, but this worked to Mowll's disadvantage because the bishop was determined to keep talented men like Mowll in key posts such as Wycliffe College. Consequently the bishop rejected Mowll's application, stating plainly that his duty was to return to his Canadian post. Mowll wrote again in 1917, but the reply was once more negative. On a return trip to England in 1917, Mowll approached Taylor Smith in person, enjoying a 'long evening' at the bishop's home in Northwood on the north-western outskirts of London. Mowll stayed with the bishop again on 21 December. There is little doubt that Mowll's chaplaincy aspirations were discussed during these visits. Yet Taylor Smith remained implacable, dissuading Mowll once more from applying.[6]

Larger forces and events, however, would play a decisive role in Mowll's fourth application for chaplaincy in 1918. On 21 March of that year the German commander, General Erich Ludendorff, launched the first offensive of what has come to be known as the 'Spring Offensive'. It was the German army's last throw of the strategic dice. The aim of the offensive was for a decisive victory – in short, to kill enough Allied men to force the *Entente* powers to sue for peace – before the USA, with its titanic material and industrial capacity, was able to disgorge

---

[5] Details on Mowll's Wycliffe years are still sketchy. There is, unfortunately, scant material relating to Mowll in Wycliffe College's archives. Secondary sources also say little about Mowll's time there. Loane's biography still provides the fullest account of Mowll during these years. I am grateful to Wycliffe College archivist, Dr Tom Power, for conducting a detailed search of those archives on my behalf.

[6] Loane, *Archbishop Mowll*, 68–69, 78.

hundreds of thousands of fresh Allied soldiers on to the Western Front. The German offensive, which concentrated shock troops and tactics such as advancing infantry under 'creeping' artillery barrages, experienced immediate success. The German army thrusted forward, creating bulges in the Allied lines and inflicting 300,000 Allied casualties within a month. This created a crisis for the *Entente* powers, who faced the real possibility of running out of men to counter the German offensive.

This was to some extent because of their 'extravagant' squandering of manpower resources during the preceding years and significant losses of men that had not been made up. The offensive also exposed profound inefficiencies in British and French manpower policy and execution, as well as strategic British errors in trying to prosecute the war further east against the crumbling Ottoman Empire or principally through naval contributions. By 1918 Germany had also come to terms with Russia and was able to deploy large numbers of troops (forty-four more divisions) to the Western Front. All the *Entente* countries, but especially Britain, had to maintain a difficult balance between having sufficient specialist workers at home – in the merchant ships, engineering works, coalmines, and munitions factories – and still be able to send a sufficient number of reinforcements to the front to be able to hold on until US troops arrived. Churches and church leaders such as Bishop Taylor Smith had to walk the same tightrope, balancing the need for clergy at home with the increasing demands of the armed forces. In 1916 Britain had introduced conscription, requiring all males aged between eighteen and forty-one years to serve (excepting those working in essential industries, with eighteen year olds not being sent overseas).[7] In the new circumstances of April 1918, however, British Prime Minister Lloyd George brought in a new 'Man Power Bill', extending the ages for men liable to conscription for overseas service to those between eighteen and fifty-five. 355,000 British men were dispatched to France within a month.[8] Knowing that many more

---

[7] Elizabeth Greenhalgh, 'David Lloyd George, Georges Clemenceau, and the 1918 Manpower Crisis', *The Historical Journal* 50, 2 (2007): 397–421, at 397–99, 402, 404–5.
[8] Greenhalgh, 'David Lloyd George', 404.

chaplains would now be needed to minister to the influx of new recruits, Mowll saw his chance and, once more, put in his fourth application for chaplaincy.[9] This time his perseverance paid off and he was granted an interview.

On 30 April 1918 Mowll travelled from his place of residence in Malden, Surrey, to the War Office in London for an interview. In the event, it was Bishop Taylor Smith himself who interviewed Mowll (as evidenced by Taylor Smith's distinctive handwriting on the record cards that were created for each applicant).[10]

Prospective Anglican chaplains were quizzed on a number of different topics. For example, Mowll was asked whether he could preach with or without notes – an important consideration for chaplains who often had to improvise sermons at short notice and for myriad different contexts, whether during a formal parade, in dugouts, at impromptu services or behind the lines. Mowll responded in the affirmative and 'Extempore' was subsequently noted on his record card. He was also asked if he could ride a horse, although the result of that question is not clear from the card entry.[11]

Recruiters were also interested in churchmanship and theological persuasion. The 'parties' or 'wings' of Anglican clergy at that time ranged widely across a spectrum: conservative evangelical, liberal evangelical, broad church, Anglo-Catholic, and High Church. Mowll was of course a committed evangelical, as attested by Taylor Smith's

---

[9] Loane, *Archbishop Mowll*, 74–75. See the Hansard discussions in the British House of Commons, which note specifically the need for more ministers of religion: 'Military Service Bill', House of Commons (HC), Deb. 10 April 1918, vol. 104, cc1475–606, https://api.parliament.uk/historic-hansard/commons/1918/apr/10/military-service-bill (accessed 4 July 2021).
[10] Loane, *Archbishop Mowll*, 78–79; 'Mowll, Herbert', RAChD recruitment card MS, RAChD Museum, available online at: https://chaplains-museum.co.uk/archive/record-cards/220189-mowll-hwk-01jpg. 'Herbert' appears to have been a clerical error.
[11] 'Mowll, Herbert', RAChD recruitment card MS.

inscription of 'Evan' on his recruitment card (Taylor Smith was himself one of England's leading evangelical churchmen).[12]

Inscribed on Mowll's card were 'good', 'manly', and 'student'.[13] Doubtless 'student' was shorthand for Mowll's experience of working with students at Cambridge, with which Taylor Smith was well acquainted. Recruiters were also concerned to attract chaplains who were 'in touch' with younger men and could 'mix it' with them relatively naturally. 'Manly' attributes and character qualities were also eagerly sought in chaplaincy candidates. Declining numbers of men – not least working men – in the pews during the nineteenth century had led to an emphasis in some quarters on a 'muscular Christianity' that stressed sporting and physical prowess in an effort to bridge the fissure of class that stood between the predominantly middle-class clergy and the mainstream culture of non-religious men, especially those of the *petit bourgeoise* or working classes.[14] As one Australian chaplain put it in relation to Australian soldiers, a chaplain was determined to do his best to keep the 'decent things before the digger[']s mind' and to gain his goodwill by being 'a man, and all things to all men'.[15] Another trooper observed that if a chaplain was 'a man's man and a soldier of Christian character, few troopers troubled about his particular denomination'.[16] Mowll certainly cut a manly figure. Standing at 6 feet 4 inches (193 cm), he was a big man with a big voice. A contemporary photograph shows him looking a little like a young Stephen Fry, close-cropped hair slicked back atop a stocky build, a wide face with

---

[12] 'Mowll, Herbert', RAChD recruitment card MS.
[13] 'Mowll, Herbert', RAChD recruitment card MS.
[14] On 'muscular Christianity' and the 'man problem' in Victorian churches, see Hugh McLeod, *Piety and Poverty: Working Class Religion in Berlin, London and New York, 1870–1914* (London: Holmes and Meier, 1996); Sarah Williams, *Religious Belief and Popular Culture in Southwark, c. 1880–1939* (Oxford: Oxford University Press, 1999); Dominic Erdozain, *The Problem of Pleasure: Sport, Recreation and the Crisis of Victorian Religion* (Woodbridge, Suffolk: The Boydell Press, 2010).
[15] J. Hennessy, Australian War Memorial, Canberra, J. Hennessy Papers, 1/DRL/635, f. 1.
[16] Henry Gullett, *The A.I.F. in Sinai and Palestine, 1914-1918* (St. Lucia, Qld: University of Queensland Press and Australian War Memorial, 1984), 551.

determined jaw, and wearing the full clerical collar of the Edwardian era (rather than the 'tabbed' dog collar characteristic of Anglican clergy today).

Figure 1: Howard Mowll, circa 1918.

Mowll had gained some experience of ministering to soldiers while at Wycliffe College. He had preached to soldiers during his travels through Canada in 1915 – at the fort in Halifax and at the military camp in Niagara, where some 13,000 men prepared for action on the Western Front in a virtual tent city; and in Sarcee, where 20,000 troops were in camp.[17]

In the event, Mowll was accepted as a chaplain and stamped medically fit 'for War' (rather than for merely auxiliary work in Britain). He was gazetted for chaplaincy duties on 21 May 1918, although he did not officially enter chaplaincy for the forces until 15 July 1918. Two months later, on 16 September 1918, he was sent overseas to serve with the BEF.[18]

[17] Loane, *Archbishop Mowll*, 73–74, 76.
[18] 'Mowll, Herbert', RAChD recruitment card MS. The card notes Mowll's date for overseas service as 'BEF 16/9/1918'.

Army chaplaincy during the First World War

Mowll was joining a chaplains' department that had expanded massively over the course of the war from 117 commissioned chaplains in its early stages to more than 5,000 temporary commissions (given to clergymen of eleven denominations) by November 1918. 60 per cent of these were Anglican, 20 per cent Roman Catholic, 10 per cent Presbyterian and, along with a handful of Jews, the balance was made up by English and Welsh Nonconformists. Their prescribed duties differed little across the Western Front and in other campaigns. In accordance with the 1864 Geneva Convention, chaplains were classed as hospital and ambulance personnel. The 'King's Regulations' stipulated their duties in terms of conducting the army's religious services and burying its dead, but in reality their duties were far more wide-ranging. Although a 1916 War Office ban was imposed on their free-range access to the front-line trenches on the Western Front, senior Catholic and Anglican churchmen protested against it; in any case many chaplains ignored the ban by serving with battalions up in the front lines as well as behind the lines in hospitals, where they knew their presence and ministry was most appreciated, and where the respect and affection of soldiers was most strongly fostered. By the summer of 1916, in preparations for the Somme offensive, the ban was lifted and chaplains were deployed wherever senior chaplains saw fit, even in offensive operations such as those on the Somme. This led to a rise in casualties among chaplains, including 100 fatalities by November 1918. Members of the Chaplains Department earned three Victoria Crosses (all Anglican), 250 Military Crosses and hundreds of other mentions in despatches, mostly for assisting wounded men under fire (another crucial role for chaplains in the front lines).

The army's verdict on the chaplains was positive. The leading historian of British Army chaplaincy, Michael Snape, records the official British war historian's assessment of Army chaplains in 1932: 'Nothing can be truer than that the troops liked having chaplains with them ... they were a potent influence in the domain of morale, and often a useful link between the man in the ranks and his officer.' Snape also quotes the verdict of F. R. Barry, a chaplain on the Western Front during 1916–18 who noted the conduct of Anglican chaplains as dispelling a great deal of anticlerical prejudice:

> The chaplains were allowed to move freely everywhere and when the units 'went up' we went with them. Several were awarded VCs, and a substantial number were killed in action ... We would give Holy Communion in the dugouts, minister to the wounded and dying, share, so far as we might, in what the troops endured ... We did what we could to serve them in Christ's name – and surely the distribution of cigarettes was a relevant form of the cup of cold water – and they understood that this was why we were doing it. They did not regard us just as welfare officers. In some dim way they discovered that they needed what the ministry of the Church sought to offer.[19]

Mowll joined the BEF in the war's late stages and at a time when the tide had turned in favour of Allied forces. By April 1918 twelve American divisions had arrived in France, and the trickle soon turned into a stream of 300,000 men per month. Further German attacks in June had created three large wedges in the Allied lines, but these had penetrated too far and too long without severing any vital rail artery, while using up the bulk of German reserves. A massive French counterattack, begun on 18 July with massed light tanks and infantry,

---

[19] F. R. Barry, quoted in Michael Snape, 'Church of England Army Chaplains in the First World War: Goodbye to "Goodbye to All That"', *The Journal of Ecclesiastical History* 62, 2 (2011): 318–45 (at 322). The substance of this paragraph is drawn from pp. 320–22 of Snape's article. For detailed studies of British Army chaplains in the First World War, see Michael F. Snape, *The Royal Army Chaplains' Department, 1796-1953: Clergy Under Fire* (Woodbridge, Suffolk: Boydell & Brewer, 2007). For Anglican chaplains and chaplaincy specifically, see Edward Madigan, *Faith Under Fire Anglican Army Chaplains and the Great War* (Basingstoke: Palgrave Macmillan, 2011); Linda Parker, *The Whole Armour of God: Anglican Army Chaplains in the Great War* (Havertown: Helion & Company, 2013). For an Australian comparison see Michael Gladwin, *Captains of the Soul: A History of Australian Army Chaplains* (Sydney: Big Sky Publishing, 2013).

forced exhausted German soldiers in the Champagne sector into a retreat. But it was not until 8 August 1918, in what became known as the Battle of Amiens, that the decisive Allied hammer blow was struck. The French 1st Army and the British 4th Army (which included Canadian and Australian corps, 600 tanks, 2,000 aircraft, and 'creeping barrage' tactics) sent the German army reeling, with many German divisions collapsing and tens of thousands taken prisoner. German General and military strategist Erich Ludendorff described 8 August as the 'black day of the German Army in the history of this war'. A string of further Allied offensive successes led finally to the collapse of the German army and the conclusion of the war on 11 November 1918.[20]

Opportunities for work on the frontlines were diminishing by the time Mowll arrived in France, but there was still an urgent need for chaplains within what is known as the 'care chain of command', especially in the casualty clearing stations and base hospitals to which thousands of wounded BEF, dominion, and American soldiers—and even German prisoners—were streaming. It was to one of the latter that Mowll was posted: in Trouville-sur-Mer, one of the most popular and frequented French seaside resorts and ports on the English Channel and northwestern Normandy coast (Claude Monet's painting, *The Beach at Trouville*, had famously captured something of its seaside charm back in 1870).[21]

Chaplaincy at the British Base Hospital, Trouville-sur-Mer

Base Hospitals were part of what was known as the casualty evacuation chain and situated further back from the front lines than the forward Casualty Clearing Stations that initially triaged and treated the wounded. Base Hospitals were very large facilities often sited in pre-war buildings such as seaside hotels or casinos and were assisted by

---

[20] For a more detailed overview of these events see Michael Howard, *The First World War* (Oxford: Oxford University Press, 2002). This is still probably the best single-volume introduction to the First World War.

[21] Loane, *Archbishop Mowll*, 79, has 'Abbéville', but it appears from the RAChD recruitment and posting cards that this is incorrrect. See 'Mowll, Herbert', RAChD recruitment card MS.

voluntary and auxiliary organisations such as the Red Cross and YMCA. They were situated adjacent to railway lines or canals to allow the wounded to be transported efficiently – and close to the coast and ports so that men needing longer-term treatment could be evacuated to the permanent hospitals in Britain. There were two types of Base Hospital: Stationary and General hospitals. The hospital at Trouville was a General Hospital. General Hospitals typically contained around 1,000 beds and a staff of around 40 officers (which included chaplains), 75 nurses and 200 or so other ranks drawn from the medical corps.[22] A British surgeon posted to Trouville recorded his impressions of the base hospital there:

> after a wait of four days in Boulogne ... I was posted to a large Base hospital at Trouville. Here I remained till the beginning of July ... The hospital was full of the wastage of war – men sent down from the Front, suffering from the ordinary diseases of civil life, which should have precluded their enlistment. The Front knocked them out almost at once, and they came to be patched up, to convalesce, and return. The mess was full of rather war-weary men, who had endured much, and were glad of an easy berth. I had plenty of operating on ordinary civil-life disabilities, and, when not engaged in filling up 'forms', enjoyed myself in field expeditions to collect butterflies and flowers, but the distant sound of guns was often disturbing.[23]

---

[22] For useful information on general and base hospitals on the Western Front, see 'British Base Hospitals in France, https://www.longlongtrail.co.uk/army/regiments-and-corps/british-base-hospitals-in-france/ (accessed 1 June 2021); 'Australian Army Medical Corps in World War I', https://anzacportal.dva.gov.au/wars-and-missions/wwi/military-organisation/australian-imperial-force/army-medical-corps (accessed 2 June 2021).
[23] John A. Hayward. M.D., F.R.C.S., in *Everyman at War* (ed. C. B. Purdom; J. M. Dent: London, 1930), reproduced at https://www.firstworldwar.com/diaries/casualtyclearingstation.htm. Hayward was an Assistant-Surgeon (rank. Captain), April to November 1918, Temporary Captain R.A.M.C., B.E.F.

Mowll based himself at a YMCA canteen, which was located adjacent to the Soldiers' Christian Association (a British association for reaching soldiers that had been founded in 1887).[24] Here he put his pastoral and evangelistic mission experience to good use:

> He arranged for Gospel meetings, confirmation classes, prayer meetings and Bible readings; there were interviews with men and decisions for Christ.[25]

Loane adds that Mowll was 'never content until he could get a convert to pray aloud; audible prayer to him was the best sign of a sound conversion'.[26]

Like Mowll, many chaplains found hospitals to be fertile soil for ministry. Some chaplains, like the Anglican Sidney Beveridge, declared them to be the most intimate and satisfying context for ministry among the troops.[27] Another Anglican chaplain on the Western Front recalled that he was most useful in hospital wards between 10pm and midnight – a time when many men could not sleep, and when loneliness and pain could be acute. A 'wearied, jaded, tormented spirit [was] given a little rest', he wrote, 'maybe through the thought of a Divine Love that does not let go'.[28]

Burial constituted another of the chaplain's important but unenviable duties. Mowll recalled taking many funerals and to his surprise sometimes heard a confession – more typically the province of Roman Catholic chaplains and soldiers for whom confession comprised part of the sacrament of reconciliation. Mowll's diary entries for these days are not extant, but the 1917 diary entry of the Rev. Gerald Tucker, an

---

[24] It is now called the Soldiers and Airmen's Scripture Readers Association (SASRA).
[25] Loane, *Archbishop Mowll*, 79.
[26] Loane, *Archbishop Mowll*, 79.
[27] Sidney Beveridge, AWM, Canberra, Sidney Beveridge Papers, 1/DRL/618, ff. 6–7.
[28] Kenneth Henderson, *Khaki and Cassock* (Melbourne: Melville & Mullen, 1919), 37–39.

Australian Anglican chaplain on the Western Front, recounts an experience with which Mowll would have resonated:

'What time will suit you for the burial today, sir?' Ah, how often have I been asked this question during these months of active service! I arrange the time and corporal departs. I am about to lay to rest all that remains of one of Australia's sons. The boy had been brought in the previous day. Mortally wounded, in great pain, covered in mud, but oh, so plucky. There was little hope from the first. I went to him at once and he seemed glad to see the padre. I prayed with him and promised to write his mother. I told him to try to sleep and that I would see him later. I went again in the evening. He was worse, but welcomed me with a cheerful smile and told me that the pain was "not too bad." I reminded him that he was suffering as did his Master before him – he was bearing pain for others – for his dear ones at home, for Australia, for the Empire, for the world. I tried to prepare him for what I knew must be death. He faced death with no outward sign of emotion, but he did tell me of his longing to see dear ones again. I gave him the church's blessing, and left him for the night. I was awakened next morning before daylight by the orderly. The boy was dying. I put on a few clothes and went to him. He was only semi-conscious, and in a weak voice was talking of home. I heard the word "Mother" more than once, and also "Dick" and "Kate." Then he lapsed into silence. All was quiet save the sound of the weak and irregular breathing. I could see the end was near, and kneeling at the bedside I silently commended the brave lad to his Maker. When I opened my eyes the soul had fled ... At the appointed time I ... make my way to the tent that acts as a mortuary ... a corporal, two bearers and the bugler were already there. The body, wrapped, in a blanket, and covered with the flag for which the boy fought and died, was brought out. A few patients who were well enough to be about joined the little company, and the procession made its way silently and reverently to the adjoining field. It was drizzling with rain, some snow had fallen, and the path was a perfect quagmire. I read the opening sentences of the burial service. The flag was taken from the body, and all that remained of the boy was lowered into the ground. I concluded the service, and added a prayer for the mourners. The "Last Post" was sounded. We saluted and silently walked away ... I returned to my hut to take off my robes before visiting a newly arrived convoy of wounded.[29]

Also striking was the diversity of men to whom the chaplain ministered. A British Base Hospital commander recalled the assortment of patients he treated:

in the same ward one may see English, Scots, Irish, Canadians, Australians, New Zealanders, South Africans, Newfoundlanders, British West Indians and members of other overseas units. It is a most striking example of the Empire's 'far flung battle line'. The contact that exists between hospital patients offers an admirable opportunity for men of various dominions and the mother country to know and understand each other.[30]

Likewise, Mowll recounted ministering to men of all sorts, conditions, and nationalities ranging from Australian diggers to 'coloured troops from the Cape [South Africa], for whom he took regular services'.[31] He was actually kneeling with one of the latter in prayer on 11 November, when the bells of churches across France pealed to signal the signing of the Armistice. 'November 11th', recorded Mowll laconically in his diary, 'while joy bells ring at noon, Cornelius [a Cape soldier] surrendered to Christ'. Loane comments that it seemed to Mowll 'as

[29] G. K. Tucker, *As Private and Padre with the A.I.F* (Melbourne: The British-Australasian, 1919), 135–38.

[30] 'Base hospitals', https://anzacportal.dva.gov.au/wars-and-missions/wwi/military-organisation/australian-imperial-force/army-medical-corps#3.

[31] Loane, *Archbishop Mowll*, 79.

though the bells of peace on earth were all harmony with the bells of joy in heaven'.[32]

A 'chance to prove the Grace of God'

Although Mowll's war service as a chaplain has only been mentioned in passing in biographical accounts, it would have a lasting impact on the young clergyman and future archbishop. Mowll maintained a longstanding correspondence with some of his wartime converts from Trouville. He especially treasured their gift of an eight-stanza poem entitled 'Our Padre'.[33] Loane recalled that these men were 'amused by [Mowll's] youth and impressed by his earnestness', as suggested by one line of the poem: "This youth would make the world pause"'. There is a larger significance in this gift in that relatively few chaplains had poems written about them. Mowll's biographer added that although his tour of service lasted only six months (he was demobilised soon after Easter 1919) the 'experience gave him in after-life a point of contact with men that was invaluable'; moreover, Mowll 'had grown in stature' in the immediate post-war years and was 'in wide demand' for missions and meetings.[34] Chaplaincy had represented, after all, one of the biggest youth outreaches in the Church's history, and would only be rivalled in scope and scale by the Church's mobilisation of chaplains and Christian workers during the Second World War. And Mowll had played a part, albeit a modest one, in it. It was also, to some extent, a natural outlet for Mowll's strong sense of missionary vocation, previously demonstrated in his work as president of CICCU at Cambridge, his evangelistic missions across Canada while at Wycliffe College, and his work with the Children's Special Service Mission

---

[32] Loane, *Archbishop Mowll*, 79.

[33] For the origin of the term 'Padre' for chaplains, see Gladwin, *Captains of the Soul*, 3: '[T]he term "padre" (Italian, Spanish and Portuguese for "Father") was first associated with Roman Catholic missionaries in India. By the early 1800s padre was also being used to denote Anglican clergymen who served as salaried chaplains of the EIC [East India Company]. One returned EIC chaplain explained to English readers in 1827 that "padre" was a "term invariably applied to the Clergy by Europeans as well as natives". Padre has become the universal appellation of both British and Australian army chaplains since this period.'

[34] Loane, *Archbishop Mowll*, 79.

(CSSM). In fact, Mowll would later become president of the CSSM after the death of his mentor and reluctant recruiter for chaplaincy, Bishop John Taylor Smith.[35]

Loane nevertheless records Mowll's sense of reticence about his suitability for chaplaincy work in wartime. 'We know,' wrote Loane, that Mowll 'never felt "cut out" for the role of a Chaplain; his was not the type of rugged bulldog courage that excels in the rough and tumble of war.' And yet, adds Loane, 'it was his duty, and he would not shirk what duty required.' On that score, it should be noted that Mowll had tried to join as a chaplain as soon as war had broken out, thereby exhibiting a strong and abiding sense of duty to both church and nation. A character trait of perseverance – not unlike the parable of the persistent widow on which he occasionally preached – is also evident in his four attempts to apply for a chaplaincy position, despite being based on the other side of the Atlantic in Canada.[36]

That sense of duty, which was strong among the clergy of the Sydney diocese, would be expressed again during the Second World War when Mowll threw the weight of the diocese and its resources behind both chaplaincy and the larger war effort. When war broke out in 1939, Mowll moved rapidly to appoint chaplains and to set up a Church of England National Emergency Fund (CENEF). The Fund provided multiple recreation huts for servicemen, including one that was prominently (and symbolically) erected in front of St Andrew's Cathedral in Sydney. Just as Mowll had witnessed firsthand the value and necessity of wartime auxiliary services and hospitals, he saw the essential need for such agencies alongside frontline chaplaincy work and was swift to support them after 1939.

It is also interesting, in light of Mowll's chaplaincy aspirations being thwarted by a well-meaning mentor, that Mowll would do the same to his successor Marcus Loane during the Second World War. Loane was serving as a chaplain on the Kokoda Track in New Guinea when Mowll

---

[35] Loane, *Archbishop Mowll*, 68.
[36] Christ's parable of the persistent widow (or 'unjust judge') is recorded in Luke 18:1–8.

put 'relentless pressure' on him to become the principal of Moore Theological College in Sydney.[37]

On a broader view, Mowll's chaplaincy experience also entitled him to a degree of credibility and social cachet among the pre-1960s generations of Sydney Anglicans who were closely tied to the military and the establishment.

Mowll later felt that his chaplaincy experience was 'the chance to prove the Grace of God, for his own strength was quite inadequate in such circumstances'.[38] His character traits of humility, duty, and indefatigable commitment were much remarked on by his contemporaries. As other chapters in this book demonstrate, they would be expressed consistently in a wide variety of places, whether in China, Canada, Australia, or as a hospital chaplain behind the lines of the colossal killing grounds of the Western Front.

---

[37] Rodney W. Tippett, 'Australian Army Chaplains: South-West Pacific Area, 1942–1945', MA (Hons) thesis; University of New South Wales, 1989, 37, 60, 211.

[38] Loane, *Archbishop Mowll*, 79.

3. The Election of Archbishop Mowll

Edward Loane

This chapter was written in the study of the St Paul's College Warden's Lodge at an old wooden table. The table has a central pedestal which fans out and a hinge so it can stand upright. I have not seen another table like it. The table that this chapter was written on arrived in Sydney on 1 March 1934 with its owner – the new Archbishop of Sydney. The question this chapter seeks to answer is: how did the owner of that table come to be elected Archbishop of Sydney? The larger story of the significance of his archiepiscopate will be found in the remainder of this volume. We will concern ourselves with the election itself. The story involves a familiar cast of characters for those associated with Sydney Diocese today: an archbishop, a former archbishop, the Dean of Sydney, the Principal of Moore College, several keen clergy and laity as well as that perpetual misfit in the Diocese of Sydney: the Warden of St Paul's College.

To set the scene for the 1933 election we must go back and look at what had been going on in the episcopacy of Mowll's predecessor, Archbishop John Charles Wright (1909-1933). Prior to election as Archbishop, Wright had been appointed as the Archdeacon of Manchester by the evangelical Bishop E. A. Knox who, along with Bishop Francis Chavasse of Liverpool and Bishop Handley Moule of Durham, had taken up the mantle of evangelical leadership in the Church of England following the death of Bishop J C Ryle.[1] Perhaps unknown to Bishop Knox, Wright had become a leader in the emerging movement of liberal evangelicalism.[2] Wright's theological position had found expression in his foundational role and chairmanship of the

---

[1] E. A. Knox had been Wright's tutor at Oxford and he was also the Bishop that ordained H.W.K. Mowll deacon on 21 September 1913.

[2] For a brief introduction to Liberal Evangelicalism at the beginning of the century see Martin Wellings, *Evangelicals Embattled: Responses of Evangelicals in the Church of England to Ritualism, Darwinism and Theological Liberalism, 1890-1930* (Carlisle: Paternoster, 2003), 115-119.

Group Brotherhood.[3] This movement sought to restate traditional evangelical essentials such as the authority of the Bible and the atonement so they were more compatible with contemporary scholarship.[4] The Group Brotherhood began as a private fellowship which was somewhat secretive until it 'went public' and changed its name to the Anglican Evangelical Group Movement in the 1920s. It is uncertain that those electing Wright as Archbishop in Sydney had an inkling of what the Group Brotherhood stood for. However, in their history of Sydney Diocese, *Sydney Anglicans*, Stephen Judd and Kenneth Cable claim that Wright won the confidence of English conservative evangelicals by being appointed a trustee of the Simeon Trust.[5] On the contrary, the Simeon Trust had long been criticised by conservatives for moving away from the traditional evangelical position. Indeed, *The English Churchman* used Wright's appointment to the Trust as a case in point. It reported: 'considering Simeon's pronounced Evangelical convictions this appointment is scarcely an ideal one... we are unaware that he is an Evangelical and Protestant of that well defined stamp for the lack of which other qualifications do not compensate.'[6] Five years after becoming a Simeon Trustee, Wright was elected Archbishop of Sydney. Soon after his enthronement as Archbishop of Sydney, Wright filled two of the most influential offices within the diocese, Principal of Moore College (D J Davies, 1911) and Dean of the Cathedral (A E Talbot, 1912), with Group Brotherhood members.[7] These three became a significant triumvirate and they

---

[3] Wright was even responsible for the name of the movement. Wellings, *Evangelicals Embattled*, 289-292. Cf. Stephen Judd and Kenneth Cable, *Sydney Anglicans: A History of the Diocese* (Sydney: The Anglican Information Office, 1987), 160.

[4] T. Guy Rogers ed., *Liberal Evangelicalism: An Interpretation by Members of the Church of England* (London: Hodder and Stoughton, 1923), vi-vii; cf. Letter from V.F. Storr, 'Evangelical Group Movement', *English Churchman*. 17 May 1928, 259.

[5] Judd and Cable, *Sydney Anglicans*, 160.

[6] 'Simeon Trustees', *English Churchman*, 19 May 1904, 315.

[7] Stephen E. Judd, *'Defenders of Their Faith': Power and Party in the Anglican Diocese of Sydney, 1909-1938* PhD Thesis, University of Sydney, 1984, 130; cf. Marcus Loane, *A Centenary History of Moore Theological College* (Sydney: Angus and Robertson, 1955), 113-114.

ensured that both the leadership of the diocese as well as the training of clergy had an unmistakably liberal evangelical stamp.

While the changes that were occurring within evangelicalism were noticeable earlier than 1909, it was only in the years following that real differences in theological emphasis and direction between conservatives and liberals proved insurmountable and resulted in painful division.[8] The first official division was the result of a stand made by a relatively small group of evangelical students at Cambridge.[9] The Cambridge Inter-Collegiate Christian Union (CICCU) could not consent to the position the inter-varsity Student Christian Movement (SCM) was holding on basic Christian truths. After much angst, grief and consultation, in 1910 the CICCU ultimately decided it had to disaffiliate with the organisation it had originally founded. Although attempts were made at rapprochement over the next decade, the Cambridge students, along with other conservative evangelicals in different universities established a parallel organisation to the SCM called the Inter-Varsity Fellowship (IVF).[10] Similar divisions to those between CICCU and SCM soon appeared within large iconic Anglican evangelical societies. Perhaps most significant of these was the schism in the Church Missionary Society (CMS) in 1922. After a series of crucial meetings the conservatives concluded that differences between themselves and the authorities in the CMS were irreconcilable and a new society needed to be formed. This resulted in the formation of Bible Churchman's Missionary Society (BCMS) in October 1922.[11] When several of the leaders of the CMS published a book entitled

---

[8] 'Evangelicals in Transition', *The Guardian*, 27 January 1909, 140.

[9] Pollock, *A Cambridge Movement*, 159-174.

[10] Geraint Fielder, *Lord of the Years: Sixty Years of Student Witness* (Leicester: IVP, 1988), 19-65.

[11] Wellings, *Evangelicals Embattled*, 281-289; Cf. Roger Steer, *Church on Fire: The Story of Anglican Evangelicals* (London: Hodder and Stoughton, 1998), 263-264. Interestingly, the year before being elected Archbishop of Sydney, Daniel Bartlett offered Mowll the role of Principal of the BCMS College in Bristol. Even though Mowll was a CMS missionary (which he had been before the split), this offer clearly demonstrated which side of the Conservative/Liberal divide he was associated with. Loane, *Archbishop Mowll*, 123.

Liberal Evangelicalism in 1923, the founders of BCMS felt vindicated in their decision.[12] The publication of *Liberal Evangelicalism* along with its sequel *The Inner Life: Essays in Liberal Evangelicalism* coincided with the Group Brotherhood becoming a public movement and changing its name to the Anglican Evangelical Group Movement (AEGM).[13] This movement grew rapidly and had the specific aim of increasing the influence of liberal evangelicalism within the Church of England.[14] Indeed, the liberal evangelicals were coming to the height of their power at this time.

The 1920s also witnessed the culmination of two decades of tumult and controversy in the Church of England surrounding Prayer Book revision. This process was begun by Archbishop Randall Davidson in 1906 but by the second half of the 20s the controversy reached fever pitch. The implications were far reaching but this process only further exacerbated tensions between liberal and conservative evangelicals.[15] A leader in the opposition to Prayer Book revision was the aged stalwart E A Knox who had retired from being Bishop of Manchester in 1921 but took up his cudgels in defence of what he believed was the pillar of evangelical Anglicanism.[16] The acerbic Bishop of Durham described

---

[12] Cf. Rogers, *Liberal Evangelicalism* and T. Guy Rogers, ed. *The Inner Life: Essays in Liberal Evangelicalism* (London: Hodder and Stoughton, 1925); cf. *English Churchman* Review, 29 March 1923.

[13] Letter from V.F Storr, *English Churchman*, 17 May 1928, 259.

[14] Martin Wellings' chapter 'The Anglican Evangelical Group Movement' is an excellent account of this movement and its impact on the Church of England. Martin Wellings, 'The Anglican Evangelical Group Movement,' in *Evangelicalism and the Church of England in the Twentieth Century: Reform, Resistance and Renewal* (eds. Andrew Atherstone and John Maiden; Woodbridge: Boydell & Brewer, 2014), 68-88.

[15] Cf. J.G. Maiden, *National Religion and the Prayer Book Controversy, 1927-1928* (Woodbridge: Boydell & Brewer, 2009). The *English Churchman* from 1926-28 constantly refers to the difference amongst Evangelicals e.g. 'It is fairly plain that the bishops and their friends with the Liberal Evangelicals are the people who are most disturbed by the defeat of the measure', 5 January 1928, 2, or 'co-operation and fellowship between old evangelicals and new ones is impossible', 19 January 1928, 33.

[16] E.A. Knox, *Reminiscences of an Octogenarian: 1847–1934* (London: Hutchinson, 1935), 306.

the opposition as 'an army of illiterates generalled by octogenarians'.[17] Throughout these years another thing became obviously apparent – all of the evangelical bishops and the majority of other evangelicals having received preferment were of the liberal persuasion.[18] Such was the state of evangelicals in the Church of England that Adrian Hastings stated: 'Never was Evangelicalism weaker than in the 1920s – in vigour of leadership, intellectual capacity, or largeness of heart.'[19] In contrast, Martin Wellings has pointed out that while the traditional historiography portrays evangelicalism generally as in a moribund state at that time, liberal evangelicalism's experience 'was the inverse of the familiar trajectory'.[20] These English ecclesiastical affairs were to have a significant impact across the empire.

For the conservative evangelicals in Sydney, the anxiety caused by these trends within British evangelicalism were compounded by several local factors. Firstly, the Sydney liberal and conservative evangelicals had found themselves on different sides of the debate about an Australian national church constitution. In general, the liberals promoted the constitution but for the conservatives the centralisation of authority to an organisation dominated by non-evangelicals posed too many dangers.[21] Judd convincingly demonstrates that the constitutional debates of the late 20s delineated the two sides and the conservatives in Sydney held the numbers. Secondly, the Diocese of Melbourne, the second largest Australian diocese and a traditional evangelical ally to Sydney, in 1929 elected as archbishop the liberal evangelical, Frederick Head. Early conservative reports of Head holding to a 'diluted form of the Gospel' were apparently confirmed when news circulated of Head

---

[17] Owen Chadwick, *Hensley Henson: A Study in the Friction between Church and State* (Oxford: Clarendon, 1983), 193.
[18] *English Churchman* consistently draws attention to the lack of Conservative Evangelicals receiving preferment. They go so far as to claim 'not since the death of Bishop Ryle has there been an appointment to the bench of any strong representative of Evangelicalism', 9 August 1928, 433.
[19] Adrian Hastings, *A History of English Christianity, 1920-2000*, 4th ed. (London: SCM, 2001), 20.
[20] Wellings, 'The Anglican Evangelical Group Movement', 68.
[21] Judd, *'Defenders'*, 293-6.

choosing to wear a cope and mitre.[22] This was quite a departure from what evangelicals held to be appropriate Protestant ecclesiastical attire and appeared a capitulation to the forces of Anglo-Catholicism. To put it in context, the first Archbishop of Canterbury to wear a mitre since the Reformation was Cosmo Lang who was also enthroned in 1929.[23] Lang, however, was clearly aligned with the Anglo-Catholic party. Archbishop Head was a colleague and friend of D J Davies from Emmanuel College, Cambridge but his behaviour in the once evangelical stronghold of Melbourne would not have endeared the conservatives in Sydney to endorse Davies' judgment on Archbishops.[24] Another concern Sydney evangelicals had with Davies was the state of Moore Theological College. Under his principalship the college had floundered and by the 1930s it was heavily in debt, had low academic standards and had few students.[25] Of the students that did attend, news circulated of at least one student giving up their evangelical convictions and candidacy under the influence of non-evangelical forces within the college.[26] Sydney Anglicans had witnessed the devastating effects of liberal theology within the local Presbyterian Church.[27] This teaching was promulgated by its training college, St Andrew's, whose principal, Dr Samuel Angus, was a friend and theological discussion partner with Davies.[28] St Andrew's was literally down the road from Moore College on Carillon Ave Newtown, and the possibility of Moore following it down the road of liberalism seemed increasingly likely.

---

[22] 'New Archbishop of Melbourne', *English Churchman*, 12 September 1929, 461; *English Churchman* 3 September 1931, 454.

[23] Robert Beaken, *Cosmo Lang: Archbishop in War and Crisis* (New York: I.B. Tauris, 2012), 16, 173.

[24] John A. McIntosh, *Anglican Evangelicalism in Sydney 1897 to 1953: Nathaniel Jones, D.J. Davies and T.C. Hammond* (Eugene: Wipf & Stock, 2018), 137.

[25] Loane, *Moore.* 125-135.

[26] ACL Minutes, 19 December, 1930. ACL Archives. Moore Theological College.

[27] Stuart Piggin, *Evangelical Christianity in Australia: Spirit, Word and World* (Melbourne: OUP, 1996), 92-94.

[28] Judd, *'Defenders'*, 349-352.

In February 1933 Archbishop Wright went to New Zealand for a holiday to visit his daughter, but two weeks later he had died after an operation in Christchurch.[29] Although the Archbishop's health had been weak for some time, the death was unexpected and there was no obvious succession plan. Furthermore, the ordinance did not allow much time before the election of a successor needed to take place. In just six weeks members of synod needed to determine who might make a suitable archbishop, ascertain if that person would accept if elected, and promote the potential candidate. This was a pivotal moment for Sydney Diocese.

Wider contextual factors were also significant in the archbishop election debates. Through the early 1930s Australia was suffering from the devastating effects of the Great Depression with the unemployment rate up to 29%. In an age when the archbishop was also a civic statesman, it was argued that electing someone who could make a positive contribution to 'social questions' was vital.[30] Furthermore, the conservative evangelicals were concerned about the advance of Anglo-Catholicism which Hastings described as 'a vast tide, flowing in apparently almost irresistibly' until it became something of the 'new normative centre' in the Anglican Communion by the 1930s.[31] Sydney Diocese had seen Anglo-Catholics advance in other dioceses around Australia, even where evangelicalism had once been dominant. Furthermore, 1933 was the centenary of the Oxford Movement. The year was marked by Anglo-Catholics celebrating the success of their movement and conservative evangelicals attempting to reassert the Protestant heritage of Anglicanism.[32] In this cultural and ecclesiastical

---

[29] 'Death of Archbishop Wright After an Operation in New Zealand', *Sydney Morning Herald*, Saturday 25 February 1933, 14.
[30] E.g. 'Archbishopric: Appeal to Synod', *Sydney Morning Herald*, Tuesday 14 March 1933, 8; 'Evangelical Demanded for See of Sydney: Reform Meeting', *Sydney Morning Herald*, Saturday 25 March 1933, 13.
[31] Hastings, *History of English Christianity*, 82, 261.
[32] J.A. Moses, ed. *From Oxford to the Bush: Essays on Catholic Anglicanism in Australia* (Adelaide: SPCK Australia, 1997); Andrew Atherstone, 'Evangelicals and the Oxford Movement Centenary', *Journal of Religious History* 37.1 (2013): 98-117; cf. ACL Minutes. 22 April, 1932. ACL Archives. Moore Theological

milieu, the occasion of electing an Archbishop presented the diocese with a choice of what it would stand for and in which direction it would advance.

In the common historiography of Sydney Diocese, the 1933 archbishop election is presented as the contest between two relatively equal sides, the liberal and conservative evangelicals. Each had a nominee which presented alternate futures for the diocese and things could have gone either way.[33] The reality is that the election was somewhat more complicated than that. On 24 March, just two weeks before the election, the *Sydney Morning Herald* claimed that between 20 and 30 overseas and Australian clerics had been discussed as potential nominees.[34] The net was cast wide and there were many issues to consider.

One of the challenges for those promoting a nominee was trying to ascertain whether the particular cleric would accept if elected. For those nominees who were overseas, the distance and communication difficulties only made this issue more problematic. Sydney was still considered a long way away for Englishmen and very few of the potential nominees had ever travelled to Australia. Several very attractive choices, such as Christopher Chavasse, indicated that they would not accept if elected.[35] A number of people argued publicly that

College. *Australian Church Record* in 1933 has articles about this centenary in several editions.

[33] Marcia Cameron, *Phenomenal Sydney: Anglicans in a Time of Change, 1945-2013* (Eugene: Wipf & Stock, 2016), 29-30; Judd and Cable, *Sydney Anglicans*, 227; Donald Robinson, 'The Origins of the Anglican Church League', pages 125-152 in *Donald Robinson, Selected Works, Volume 4*, ed. Edward Loane (Sydney: ACR and Moore College, 2018), 148-149.

[34] 'The Archbishopric: Successor to Dr Wright. Prominent Candidates', *Sydney Morning Herald*, Friday 24 March 1933, 9

[35] 'Summary', *Sydney Morning Herald* Wednesday 29 March 1933, 1. Christopher Chavasse was the son of the second Bishop of Liverpool, Francis Chavasse, and with his twin brother Noel had been an Olympian and a decorated war hero. He was the Master of St Peter's Hall, Oxford and was considered an up and coming Evangelical leader in England. He went on to become a very influential Bishop of Rochester. D.R. Vicary, 'Chavasse,

an Australian should be elected.[36] By the end of March, it appeared that there were three candidates with some organised support.[37]

First, the young Australian Bishop of Armidale, John Moyes, was backed by the Sydney Diocesan Reform Association (SDRA) whose key drivers were Professor F A Bland, Rev H N Baker of St Thomas' North Sydney and Arthur Garnsey, Warden of St Paul's College. The SDRA was an organisation that had been set up in July 1932 following what was perceived to be an overbearing interference in the appointment of the rector of St Barnabas', Chatswood.[38] As its name suggests, this group was not happy with the evangelical dominance in Sydney Diocese and were attempting to broaden the perspectives represented.[39] As Garnsey wrote to his son, they wanted a man 'who is not only good at saving souls and talking about 'the Gospel', but interested in humanity – with knowledge, sympathy and a broad outlook.'[40] Moyes was originally from South Australia and he had been educated and ordained in Adelaide.[41] He was an advocate of the 'social gospel' and had been speaking in Sydney in the weeks leading up to the election. He gave what Garnsey described as 'a really excellent address' at a SCM meeting at Sydney University in the middle of March 1933.[42] The SDRA organised public meetings and wrote to the press

Christopher Maude (1884-1962)', *Oxford Dictionary of National Biography*, online ed. https://doi.org/10.1093/ref:odnb/32384

[36] E.g. 'Archbishopric: Method of Election: Dr Wright's Successor', *Sydney Morning Herald*, Monday 9 March 1933, 9; 'Letter to the Editor: The Archbishopric of Sydney', *Sydney Morning Herald*, Wednesday 1 March 1933, 8.

[37] 'The Archbishopric: Nomination Declined. The Three Parties', *Sydney Morning Herald*, Wednesday 29 March 1933, 13.

[38] 'Now St Barnabas', East Roseville. Judd, *'Defenders'*, 342.

[39] 'Sydney Diocese,' *Australian Church Record*, 2 March 1933, 11.

[40] Arthur Garnsey letter to David Garnsey, cited in David Garnsey, *Arthur Garnsey* (Sydney: Kingsdale, 1985), 134.

[41] Anne O'Brien, 'Moyes, John Stoward (1884-1972)', *Australian Dictionary of National Biography*, online ed. https://adb.anu.edu.au/biography/moyes-john-stoward-11190

[42] Arthur Garnsey letter to David Garnsey, cited in Garnsey, *Garnsey*, 135. Moyes had been president of the SCM when he was a student in Adelaide and

arguing their case for Moyes.[43] One key argument they pressed was the need to appoint an Australian and the importance of this for younger clergy.[44] After one meeting promoting Moyes at King's Hall, the *Australian Church Record* urged its readers to remember the diocesan evangelical and Protestant heritage and warned synodsmen to vote together and 'be on guard for the sinister cry of so-called "comprehensiveness".'[45]

Second, Joseph W. Hunkin, who has generally been portrayed as the major rival to Mowll.[46] He was the Rector of Rugby and Archdeacon of Coventry and also the chairman of the Anglican Evangelical Group Movement. However, Hunkin apparently came late to the race with the first mention of his name in the press being only nine days before the election.[47] Dean Talbot and Principal Davies were his nominators and they attempted to use their positions as President and Vice President of the Anglican Church League (ACL) to influence the vote. They believed that Hunkin would be 'a centre of unity' in a similar vein to Archbishop Wright.[48] Unfortunately, Hunkin has been portrayed in Sydney Diocesan historiography simply as 'a liberal' or 'a modernist',[49] but that is an inappropriate and pejorative description that does not do justice to his evangelical credentials. In England, Hunkin was a regular speaker at renowned evangelical conferences, (sharing the platform

---

was a supporter of the movement throughout his life. O'Brien, 'Moyes', *ADNB*.

[43] Judd, '*Defenders*', 343; Garnsey, *Garnsey*, 135.

[44] 'Archbishop: Election To-Morrow. Methods of Voting. Divided Opinions', *Sydney Morning Herald*, Monday 3 April 1933, 10.

[45] 'An Amazing Meeting,' *Australian Church Record*, Thursday 30 March 1933, 1; cf. 'Evangelical Demanded for See of Sydney: Reform Meeting', *Sydney Morning Herald*, Saturday 25 Mar 1933, 13.

[46] Cameron, *Phenomenal Sydney*, 29-30; Robinson, 'The Origins of the Anglican Church League', 148-149; Macintosh, *Anglican Evangelicalism in Sydney*, 183-184; Judd and Cable, *Sydney Anglicans*, 227.

[47] 'The Archbishopric: Nomination Declined. The Three Parties,' *Sydney Morning Herald*, Wednesday 29 March 1933, 13.

[48] D.J. Davies, 'Archdeacon Hunkin,' *Sydney Morning Herald*, Saturday 1 April 1933, 14.

[49] Cameron, *Phenomenal Sydney*, 23.

with T. C. Hammond at the 1930 Oxford Conference).[50] He had previously been Vice Principal of Wycliffe Hall, Oxford and had made scholarly contributions to various works, including the above mentioned *Liberal Evangelicalism*. Hunkin was an outstanding scholar as an undergraduate at Cambridge and he had been there at the same time as Talbot and Davies.[51] Unfortunately for his key backers, they got a doubtful response when they phoned to see if he would accept should he be elected, but it did not deter them from putting him forward anyway.[52] In the press, Davies argued that he was 'a definite Evangelical and a strong Protestant' and pointed to his connection to Christopher Chavasse and the platform appearance at the Oxford Conference in 1930 as commending his evangelical orthodoxy.[53]

The final prominent candidate was Bishop Mowll of West China. Archdeacon Langford-Smith later said that the 'most careful inquiries were made in England, Ireland, and Canada regarding Bishop Mowll.'[54] There were several factors that attracted the conservatives to Mowll. Firstly, he was definitely and uncompromisingly evangelical. From the King's School, Canterbury he went up to King's College, Cambridge in 1909. He became heavily involved in the CICCU just at the time of the decisive split with the SCM. In 1910 he became the president of the CICCU and served for an unprecedented five terms.[55] From a very young age Mowll had proved that he would stand up for central gospel issues and lead others in doing so. This was an attractive feature for the conservative evangelicals in Sydney.

---

[50] See list of speakers in Appendix 2 of *Evangelicalism and the Church of England in Twentieth Century*, 299-301.

[51] Alan Dunstan and John S. Peart-Binns, *Cornish Bishop* (Letchworth: Epworth, 1977), 27-29; McIntosh, *Anglican Evangelicalism in Sydney*, 133.

[52] Judd, '*Defenders*', 347. Dunstan and Peart-Binns claim 'it was clear Sydney was not for Hunkin and he withdrew his name before the election took place.' *Cornish Bishop*, 87.

[53] 'Archbishopric: Method of Election. Move to Amend Ordinance,' *Sydney Morning Herald*, Saturday 1 April 1933, 14.

[54] 'Bishop Mowll New Archbishop: Synod's Choice, Evangelical Party's Success,' *Sydney Morning Herald*, Friday 7 April 1933, 9.

[55] Pollock, *A Cambridge Movement*, 182-189; Loane, *Archbishop Mowll*, 41-61.

Interestingly, it is also possible that Mowll's connection to the CICCU at the time of the SCM split and his subsequent uncompromising leadership of the group could have been a significant factor for those promoting the other two main nominees. Davies was at Cambridge at the time of the split, but he sided with the SCM. Likewise, Garnsey was a strong supporter, with Davies, of SCM at Sydney University. This group, however, was challenged when in 1930, the CICCU aligned IVF travelling secretary, Dr Howard Guinness, came to Sydney and established the Evangelical Union (EU) on the University campus.[56] Potentially, the EU's establishment in the years before the archbishop election, along with Davies' previous experience in Cambridge, led him and others to take an 'anyone but Mowll' position to the election. This is a difficult motivation to establish with certainty. However, the timing and personalities that were involved both in Cambridge and Sydney make the University tensions a probable factor in the 1933 archbishop election.

Another factor that attracted the conservatives to Mowll was his experience in theological education. Following ordination he had taken up a position lecturing at Wycliffe College, Toronto.[57] This would have given him valuable insights into the inner workings and needs of theological colleges. These were assets for which Sydney was in desperate need. From his own theological studies at Ridley Hall, Cambridge, to his student focused faculty position at Wycliffe College, Toronto, Mowll obviously prioritised the importance of evangelical theological colleges. Furthermore, the Anglican 'colonial' experience in Canada was considered by some as a closer comparison to the needs of Sydney. R. B. S. Hammond, the inimitable rector of St Barnabas' Broadway argued in the *Sydney Morning Herald* that Canada was the best place to look for nominees because it was so similar to Australia.[58]

---

[56] Howard Guiness, 'Australia,' in *Christ and the Colleges: A History of the Inter-Varsity Fellowship of Evangelical Unions* (London: IVF, 1934), 169-188; John Prince and Moyra Prince, *Out of the Tower* (Sydney: ANZEA Publishers, 1987), 8-15.

[57] Loane, *Archbishop Mowll*, 63-83.

[58] 'Archbishopric: Suggestion about Canada: Canon Hammond's Views,' *Sydney Morning Herald*, Tuesday 28 March 1933, 9.

Mowll, who had preached at Hammond's church just twenty months earlier, fitted this mould.[59]

There was a risk of electing a man who had never exercised a ministry outside of England. Perhaps he, or his family, would not fit in to the antipodean environment. This had been the scenario fifty years earlier when Bishop Barry only lasted five years in Sydney before retreating 'home' to England.[60] Howard and Dorothy Mowll, on the other hand, had toured Australia in August 1931.[61] They came to visit the home churches of Australian missionaries serving in their Diocese of West China.[62] This tour included bookending their trip with weeks in Sydney where they stayed in Bishopscourt and Bishop Mowll preached at the Cathedral.[63] The electors could imagine Mowll as Archbishop because they had recently seen him behaving archiepiscopally. Throughout the tour he spoke to large audiences and proved to be very popular in Sydney just twenty months before the unexpected archiepiscopal election. During this tour, at the height of the Great Depression, the newspapers reported Howard's comments on potential wool trade with China and Dorothy's insistence on touring Sydney's industrial areas.[64] Howard Mowll spoke to the Deaconess

---

[59] 'The Churches,' *Sydney Morning Herald*, Saturday 1 August 1933, 5.

[60] K.J. Cable, 'Barry, Alfred (1826-1910)', *Australian Dictionary of National Biography*, online ed. https://adb.anu.edu.au/biography/barry-alfred-2944

[61] 'The Church and China: Bishop Mowll's Visit: Combating Soviet Propaganda,' *Queensland Times*, Friday 14 August 1931, 5.

[62] Of the 100 missionaries in his diocese 14 were from Australia. 'Bishop Mowll Tells How He Was Held to Ransom – Chinese Brigandage,' *Sydney Morning Herald*, Monday 3 August 1931, 9; 'Floods in China – Bishop Mowll's Address,' *Sydney Morning Herald*, Thursday 27 August 1931, 4.

[63] 'From the Pulpit: Habakkuk's Vision,' *Sydney Morning Herald*, Mon 3 Aug 1931, 8. This is an account of Mowll's sermon in the Cathedral on Sun 2 Aug 1931. 'Seized by Bandits – Missionaries in China,' *Sydney Morning Herald*, Sat 22 Aug 1925, 15.

[64] 'Bishop Mowll Tells How He Was Held to Ransom – Chinese Brigandage,' *Sydney Morning Herald*, Monday 3 August 1931, 9; 'Archbishopric: Method of Election. Move to Amend Ordinance,' *Sydney Morning Herald*, Saturday 1 April 1933, 14; 'New Archbishop's Career,' *Sydney Morning Herald*, Friday 7 April 1933, 13.

Institution about the significance of women missionaries in the Chinese church and to the ACL on 'The Present Evangelical Outlook'.[65] The significance of this address to the ACL should not be underestimated. Mowll's strongest supporters were Vice Presidents of the ACL.[66] At the same time, the Liberal Evangelical opposition to Mowll's election were also ACL officials with Talbot being President and Davies being a Vice President. Perhaps Mowll's 'Present Evangelical Outlook' polarised evangelical outlooks on his suitability to be Archbishop of Sydney. Whether this was the case or not the fact remained that unlike so many of the prospective archbishops, Mowll was a relatively well-known man who had been ministering in Sydney not long before the election.

A further compelling reason his promoters got behind him was because, in Mowll, they saw a valiant missionary with the evangelisation of the lost in his heart. He and his wife had been missionaries in the remote province of Szechwan for over a decade. They had travelled extensively preaching the Gospel and had faced many hardships, even being kidnapped and held hostage.[67] These adversities in remote China were reported in the Australian press and the *Sydney Morning Herald* gave extensive details in 1925 of the Mowlls' abduction and captivity for 24 days.[68] This was the subject of much interest during the Mowlls' 1931 tour and, when they were attacked on

[65] 'The Churches,' *Sydney Morning Herald*, Saturday 22 August 1931, 7; 'Deaconess Institution Annual Meeting,' *Sydney Morning Herald*, Wednesday 26 August 1931, 6.

[66] Mowll was a Vice President of the ACL's mother organisation, the National Church League (NCL) in England. In January 1931, just prior to his successful visit to Sydney, Mowll was a platform speaker at NCL events in London and the renowned Islington Clerical Conference. 'On the Eve of Islington,' *English Churchman*, 15 Jan 1931, 37; 'Report of Islington,' *English Churchman*, 15 Jan 1931, 27.

[67] For an account see Loane, *Archbishop Mowll*, 120ff.

[68] 'Seized by Bandits – Missionaries in China,' *Sydney Morning Herald*, Saturday 22 August 1925, 15; cf. *Australian Church Record*, Wednesday 26 November 1925, 1.

the way home from that tour, it was again reported widely in 1932.[69]
In the second assault, Howard was clubbed and stabbed and Dorothy,
while suffering a facial wound that left a life-long scar, sought to settle
the attackers down by getting them to sit down and have a cup of tea.[70]
These experiences gave Mowll an aura of being an imperturbable,
resilient, missionary leader. He was a man that had endured costly
discipleship. Indeed, these aspects of Mowll's Chinese ministry
resonated in Sydney such that in Archbishop Wright's final paragraph
of his final letter to the Diocese he spoke warmly about correspondence
from 'the heroic Bishop of West China'.[71] This commendation of the
late archbishop was quoted in the press before the 1933 election almost
as though it was a word of succession.[72] Certainly, no other nominee
had what appeared to be a recommendation from the former
archbishop as an aspect of their case for election. Moreover, Mowll
already had a decade of episcopal leadership behind him and,
significantly, more than a fortnight before the election, C R Walsh had
ascertained that Mowll would certainly consider the offer if elected.[73]
From very early on he was perceived to be the favourite to succeed
as archbishop.

The movement promoting the election of Mowll was led by
Archdeacon Langford-Smith and he was ably assisted by H. S. Begbie,
D. J. Knox and R. B. Robinson.[74] These three organised four group
meetings in parishes across the diocese to discuss the upcoming

---

[69] 'The Churches,' *Sydney Morning Herald*, Saturday 13 February 1932, 7; cf.
'The Attack on Bishop Mowll,' *Australian Church Record*, Wednesday 17 March
1932, 7.

[70] Loane, *Archbishop Mowll*, 121.

[71] 'Archbishopric: Bishop Mowll May Be Elected. At Least Six Nominees,'
Sydney Morning Herald, Thursday 30 March 1933, 9; 'New Archbishop's
Career,' *Sydney Morning Herald*, Friday 7 April 1933, 13; 'Archbishopric of
Sydney,' *Australian Church Record*, Thursday 30 March 1933, 3.

[72] 'Archbishopric: Bishop Mowll May Be Elected. At Least Six Nominees,'
Sydney Morning Herald, Thursday 30 March 1933, 9.

[73] Loane, *Archbishop Mowll*, 125.

[74] Marcus Loane, *Mark These Men: A Brief Account of Some Evangelical Clergy
in the Diocese of Sydney Who Were Associated with Archbishop Mowll* (Kambah,
ACT: Acorn, 1985), 25-26; Stuart Piggin, *Spirit of a Nation*, 129.

election and highlight the strengths of Bishop Mowll as a potential Archbishop.[75] Articles were written in *The Australian Church Record and The Sydney Morning Herald* to endorse Mowll.[76] The campaign was diligent and convincing. More than a week before the election *The Sydney Morning Herald* wrote that indications suggested Mowll 'will be elected to the vacant Archbishopric of Sydney by a substantial majority.'[77] The papers highlighted Mowll's height (6ft 4in), for which he later gained the nickname 'the High Priest'.[78] Unlike other candidates, he was the only one that had his photo printed in the paper.[79] Liberal evangelicals argued that an Archbishop was needed that would deal with the vital social problems of their time such as unemployment and pejoratively claimed that 'a missionary without parochial experience, who has lived his life in China, cannot possibly be capable of dealing with the highly complicated questions of modern life'.[80] The scene was set for what all parties believed was a high stakes election.

In the end, twelve nominations were received.[81] On the first day of Synod they adjourned at 11pm having discussed and voted on nine of them. Four had progressed to the next list, Mowll, Grenstead, Grant and Hunkin. John Moyes was left in the three names yet to be

---

[75] Judd, 'Defenders', 341.

[76] 'Reply to "Liberal Evangelical",' *Sydney Morning Herald,* Saturday 1 April 1933, 14; 'Archbishopric of Sydney,' *Australian Church Record,* Thursday 30 March 1933, 3.

[77] 'Archbishopric: Bishop Mowll May Be Elected. At Least Six Nominees,' *Sydney Morning Herald,* Thursday 30 March 1933, 9.

[78] 'Archbishopric: Bishop Mowll May Be Elected. At Least Six Nominees,' *Sydney Morning Herald,* Thursday 30 March 1933, 9.

[79] 'Archbishopric: Method of Election. Move to Amend Ordinance,' *Sydney Morning Herald,* Saturday 1 April 1933, 14. The *SMH* later stated that the 'surprising' defeat of Bishop Moyes was a 'vital factor in the final result'. 'New Archbishop: Election of Right Rev. H.W.K. Mowll. Proceedings in Sydney,' *Sydney Morning Herald,* Friday 7 April 1933, 13.

[80] 'The Archbishopric: Day of Prayer: Liberal Evangelicals' Case,' *Sydney Morning Herald,* Friday 31 March 1933, 11.

[81] 'Nominations for Archbishopric: Twelve Received. Voting To-night,' *Sydney Morning Herald,* Wednesday 5 April 1933, 13. Nominees included A.E. Talbot, S.J. Kirkby and W.G. Hilliard.

considered. The next day, it was decided that those final three nominees would not progress and they moved on to creating a select list of three from the four remaining candidates.[82] Before the election, *The Sydney Morning Herald* had declared that the two favourites were Mowll and Hunkin,[83] but as soon as the first votes had been tallied it was clear Mowll's position was strong as he had the highest number of votes, while Hunkin, even though progressing, had polled the least votes of the four.[84] As debate continued, Synodsmen pointed to Hunkin's contributions to *Liberal Evangelicalism* and the journal *The Modern Churchman* to demonstrate what they believed were his theological weaknesses.[85] When the select list was determined Hunkin did not progress. Of the final three candidates, Mowll was elected in a landslide, collecting more votes than the other candidates put together.[86] The election synod was completed by midnight on the second day.

There were calls in the synod to make the election unanimous, but twenty-one synodsmen would not support him. And certainly, some others only did so reluctantly. According to Garnsey, who would not back Mowll, the Dean sent him a note saying: 'As Dean I must stand, but you others pass the word along to do what you wish.'[87] Surprising people, however, were backing Mowll. The following day in the paper, Father John Hope of Christ Church St Laurence said, 'I voted for Bishop Mowll because I had every reason to believe, on the authority of men whose word I trust that he is a man of God and has done most

---

[82] Moyes only received 44 of 135 votes in House of Clergy and 67 of 225 votes in House of Laity.

[83] 'Nominations for Archbishopric: Twelve Received. Voting To-night,' *Sydney Morning Herald*, Wednesday 5 April 1933, 13.

[84] 'Archbishopric: Synod's Progress. Choice Narrowed,' *Sydney Morning Herald*, Thursday 6 April 1933, 9.

[85] Judd, *'Defenders'*,347-8. John McIntosh suggests that Hunkin's critique of premillennialism in *Liberal Anglicanism* would have led conservatives in Sydney to believe he was inclined towards Modernism. McIntosh, *Anglican Evangelicalism in Sydney*, 47.

[86] 115 of 135 votes in House of Clergy and 191 of 225 votes in House of Laity. 'Archbishopric of Sydney: Election of Bishop Howard Mowll, of Western China,' *Australian Church Record*, Thursday 13 April 1933, 3.

[87] Garnsey, *Garnsey*, 135.

praise-worthy and self-sacrificing work in western China, and that he is large-hearted and most approachable.'[88] Garnsey wrote to his son lamenting they had 'elected the "favourite"', because 'the folk calling themselves Evangelicals were too solid a mass to be seriously shaken by any appeals to reason, or liberalism, or anything'.[89] Despite some intransient opposition, the election result demonstrated widespread and overwhelming support for Mowll.

Historiographically, Talbot and Davies have been highlighted to demonstrate the division in the diocese following the election.[90] There is no doubt the election was a significant blow to them. They soon resigned their positions as President and Vice-President of the ACL.[91] They began a new organisation called The Anglican Fellowship with a few other men such as Garnsey. This has been described as a split in the ACL, an irreparable schism and a crisis for the breadth of evangelicalism.[92] My contention is, however, that such reactions were the exception with very few actually resigning their membership of the ACL.[93] Furthermore, Garnsey described the move of Talbot and Davies in a letter to his son and concluded: 'they have come over from them to us.'[94] In his mind, this was not a split in the ACL but a defection to a different group and stance entirely.

It was not only Talbot and Davies who were bitter about the election of Mowll. Rev. O. V. Abram, rector of Epping, claimed that there had been 'deliberate misrepresentation and poisoning of the mind of synod'.[95] Some other scurrilous accusations were made in the *Church Standard, Anglo-Catholic Quarterly* and *Challenge* newspapers to the effect that

---

[88] 'Bishop Mowll: Appointment Welcomed,' *Sydney Morning Herald*, Saturday 8 April 1933, 13.
[89] Garnsey, *Garnsey*, 135.
[90] Judd and Cable, *Sydney Anglicans*, 234-235.
[91] The ACL Archives include the resignation letter from Talbot, 10 May 1933, as well as much other correspondence about this issue and the minutes from meetings in 1933 where the resignations of Talbot and Davies were discussed.
[92] Judd, *'Defenders',* 336-337, 366.
[93] Cf ACL Archives. Moore Theological College.
[94] Arthur Garnsey letter to David Garnsey, cited in Garnsey, *Garnsey*, 137.
[95] O.V. Abram, Letter to the Editor – 'Campaign of Slander,' *Australian Church Record*, Thursday 15 May 1933, 11.

Mowll had declined to come to Sydney because he heard about the methods by which the majority vote was secured.[96] The *Australian Church Record* described this as 'an orgy of abuse'.[97] Even Garnsey described this as 'unscrupulous journalism' and 'throwing mud at the Evangelicals'.[98] Another disgruntled spectator was the Governor of NSW, Sir Philip Game. He wrote to the Archbishop of Canterbury, Cosmo Lang decrying 'the methods employed by the extreme Evangelical faction' which he described as 'a disgrace'.[99] No doubt these letters were a significant influence on Lang's discouraging farewell to Mowll as he set off to begin as archbishop. Lang told Mowll that 'he possessed neither the gifts nor the training which the See of Sydney required'.[100] Nevertheless, in the face of this animosity, those supporting Mowll defended their methods of promoting him as Archbishop,[101] and history would prove Lang wrong in his pessimism about Mowll's ability.

For the Diocese of Sydney, the twenty five years of Mowll's archiepiscopate were marked by growth, consolidation and new ventures. Stuart Piggin and Bob Linder described Mowll as 'the most effective of evangelical ecclesiastical leaders to emerge on the Australian scene between the wars, and his episcopate (1933-1958) turned out to be the most momentous in the history of the Sydney diocese.'[102] The rest of this book unpacks some of the extraordinary achievements of these years and Mowll's legacy which is still with us today. Arthur Garnsey, the Warden of St Paul's College may not have supported the election, but it resulted in a wooden table being

---

[96] E.g. 'All decency and dignity have been thrown to the winds.' 'Electing an Archbishop,' *Church Standard*, Friday 7 April 1933, 3.

[97] 'An Orgy of Abuse,' *Australian Church Record*, Thursday 4 May 1933, 1.

[98] Arthur Garnsey letter to David Garnsey, cited in Garnsey, *Garnsey*, 136.

[99] Sir Philip Game letter to Archbishop Cosmo Lang, 26 September 1933. Sydney, Archbishop of., Lang Papers, Lambeth Palace Archives.

[100] Loane, *Archbishop Mowll*, 133.

[101] E.g. R. B. Robinson, 'Campaign of Slander', *Australian Church Record*, Thursday 1 June 1933, 11.

[102] Stuart Piggin and Robert D. Linder, *Attending to the National Soul: Evangelical Christians in Australian History 1914-2014* (Melbourne: Monash, 2020), 136.

transported to Sydney which, ninety years later, would end up in the Warden's Lodge. Mowll's wooden table was used as his desk in the study of Bishopscourt and, perhaps, some of the innovative strategic ministry initiatives which have continued to influence Sydney Diocese were developed at it. Wherever these ideas were formed, there is no doubt that the election of Mowll has been of profound and lasting significance.

4. The New Archbishop
Geoffrey R Treloar[1]

Following his election the previous year, Howard Mowll arrived in Sydney to take up his position as the sixth Bishop/Archbishop of Sydney on March 1, 1934. Almost a fortnight later, on March 13, he was enthroned in St Andrew's Cathedral. The next day there was a civic reception which was followed over the next few weeks by a series of diocesan welcomes. Despite the fanfare and enthusiasm, feelings about the new Archbishop were mixed. Cosmo Lang, the Archbishop of Canterbury, had already told Mowll (not unfairly) that he was unsuitable for Sydney. In Sydney itself his supporters looked to Mowll to retrieve the diocese from the lassitude into which it had fallen in the last years of Archbishop Wright. Yet not even they could be sure that he would be able to do so. Others had more serious misgivings. Those who had opposed Mowll's election retained their reservations about the outcome. Mowll himself had his doubts too. Aware that it was time to leave China, he had been surprised to receive the call to Sydney and was still unsure about whether it was the right post for him.[2] In 1934 it remained to be seen what the new archbishop would be like in office. What he would do and achieve, what kind of leader he would be, and whether he would succeed in the new setting were open questions. Based mainly on Mowll's writings from the period, this chapter focuses on the first five years of Mowll's term to ascertain how these questions were answered. It argues that the application during this foundational

---

[1] I would like to thank Sarah Mayhew of the General Synod Office, Louise Trott of the Sydney Diocesan Archives and Erin Mollenhauer of Moore Theological College for their assistance in collecting the materials on which this chapter is based. I am also grateful for comments on an earlier draft of the chapter by Brian Dickey and David Hilliard, both of Adelaide.
[2] 'From Bishop Mowll,' *Church Standard* [cited hereafter as CS], 28 July 1933, 2. *Summary of Proceedings of the ... Twenty-Third Synod of the Diocese of Sydney ... 1934*, 265 [mindful that the Synod Proceedings are almost always published in the Year Book of the following year, Mowll's Synod addresses are cited hereafter as 'Sydney Synod' with the year of the Synod's occurrence].

period of the identity and corresponding mindset he brought to Sydney – before his aims and intentions were complicated by the outbreak of World War II (1939 – 1945) and accession to the Primacy (1947 – 1958) – determined the character and course of Mowll's episcopate.[3]

Multiple Identities

As he took up office, Mowll's first major challenge was to overcome the doubts about his appointment, establish his leadership and take control of the diocese. An adequate response would require speedy adjustment to the unfamiliar environment of Sydney and setting a course for his administration, in the process providing reassurance to supporters and allaying the fears of opponents. In contrast with his predecessor whose first synod charge outlined a policy,[4] Mowll chose not to announce how he intended to proceed in the form of a plan for the diocese. Instead, he began with an identity statement. The text of his enthronement sermon – 2 Corinthians 4:5 – declared: "We preach not ourselves, but Christ Jesus as Lord; and ourselves your servants for Jesus' sake."[5] Servanthood under the lordship of Christ was the declared aspiration of Mowll's leadership. His intention was to be 'ministerial', not 'magisterial'.

---

[3] The early years in Sydney are covered in Loane, *Archbishop Mowll,* chap. 7. Over half of Judd and Cable, *Sydney Anglicans,* chap. 14 is devoted to Mowll's early years in office. For an overview of the whole, see K. J. Cable, 'Howard West Kilvinton Mowll,' *Australian Dictionary of Biography,* at https://adb.anu.au/biography/mowll-howard-west-kilvinton-11189, and Brian Dickey, 'Mowll, Howard West Kilvinton,' in *Biographical Dictionary of Evangelicals,* ed. Timothy Larsen (Leicester: Inter-Varsity Press, 2003), 455 - 456.

[4] *Proceedings of the ... Fifteenth Synod of the Diocese of Sydney ... 1909* (Sydney, 1910), 36-39. For comment, see Stephen Judd, '"Defenders of Their Faith": Power and Party in the Anglican Diocese of Sydney, 1909-1938,' PhD thesis; University of Sydney, 1984, 127-129.

[5] 'Sermon by Archbishop of Sydney at his Enthronement,' *Australian Church Record* [cited hereafter as *ACR*], 22 March 1934, 6-8.

The prayer that followed elaborated what this meant:

> Oh, Thou Who art Heroic Love, keep alive in our hearts that adventurous spirit which makes men scorn the way of safety so that Thy Will may be done. For so only, O Lord, shall we be worthy of those courageous souls who, in every age, have ventured all in obedience to Thy call, and for whom the trumpets have sounded on the other side.[6]

Among the 'courageous souls' with whom Mowll claimed continuity were the previous Bishops/Archbishops of Sydney whose contributions he briefly reviewed, tellingly giving most attention to Bishop Barker. Like his predecessors, his aim was to work out the lordship of Christ in bold heroic service. Mowll's consciousness of possessing 'a gospel' and a commission 'to proclaim Christ Jesus as Lord' invoked as a second line of continuity the calling that had already taken him to a peripatetic ministry in Canada and then to China as a missionary bishop.[7] In an important moment of transition, the two continuities were brought together as Mowll announced the transfer of the ideal which had guided his ministry so far to a new sphere of life and action.[8] As he allayed his own doubts, the primary element in the mindset of the new Archbishop emerged as faithfulness to his primary identity and sense of vocation.

During his early days in office, Mowll brought the classical evangelical worldview that had shaped this identity and calling into sharp focus.[9] Representation of the Bible as 'the Word of God itself', the principal

---

[6] 'Sermon by Archbishop of Sydney at his Enthronement,' *ACR*, 22 March 1934, 6-8.

[7] Loane, *Archbishop Mowll*, chaps 4-6.

[8] On the importance of faithfulness to calling, see: 'Lay Readers' Association Annual Meeting,' *Sydney Diocesan Magazine* [cited hereafter as *SDM*] 1 July 1934, 9-11; *SDM*, 1 June 1935, 114-15; Sydney Synod 1939, 57.

[9] 'Evangelical Always, Declares New Archbishop,' *Daily Telegraph*, 3 February 1934, 12. Basic to this representation of Mowll's evangelicalism is, of course, the Bebbington quadrilateral, presented initially in David W. Bebbington, *Evangelicalism in Modern Britain* (London: Unwin Hyman, 1989) and strongly reaffirmed after thirty years of evaluation in David W. Bebbington, *The Evangelical Quadrilateral* (2 vols; Waco, Texas: Baylor University Press, 2021).

means of grace and superior to all other sources of knowledge and understanding, established his acceptance of the pre-eminence of the Scriptures.[10] Emphasis on the centrality of 'the message of the Cross' to Christian faith and life affirmed his crucicentrism.[11] The priority assigned to evangelism in the work of the Church, prayer for revival and insistence on justification by faith as the basis of the new birth demonstrated not only a strong commitment to conversionism but adherence to the traditions of the Reformation and the Evangelical Revival of the eighteenth century.[12] Frequent recollection of his experience in China gave promise that Mowll had brought 'a great impetus to the missionary work of the Church'.[13] The undertaking to engage with the municipal life of Sydney foreshadowed a marked social dimension in this activism.[14] Frequent appeals for the nurture of vital Christian experience brought Mowll's own vigorous pietistic spirituality into view. To the great satisfaction of many, from the outset, Mowll confirmed in word and deed that he had come to Sydney to be the evangelical leader his supporters had promised.[15]

The full significance of this for the church in Sydney emerges against the background of wider developments in the previous decade.[16] Following almost half a century of pluralization within the evangelical movement, a divide between 'neo-' and 'traditional' or 'conservative' evangelicals had produced a marked polarization within Anglican

---

[10] Sydney Synod 1937, 290. *SDM*, 1 June 1938, 87. Mowll's biblicism is illustrated by Stuart Piggin in chapter 12 below.

[11] Sydney Synod 1935, 305-6; 1937, 291; 1938, 244. *SDM*, 1 March 1938, 34.

[12] Sydney Synod 1934, 282-3; 1935, 310; 1938, 243-4, 246-7, 258; 1939, 46.

[13] *SDM*, 1 May 1934, 8-9. Cf. *SDM*, 1 October 1934, 2-3. Sydney Synod 1934, 276-7 and 1935, 310.

[14] 'Civic Reception to Archbishop Mowll,' *ACR*, 22 March 1934, 8.

[15] Eg. The fulsome response of the Rector of Hunter's Hill, Rev. M.G. Hinsby, in *ACR*, 5 April 1934, 8.

[16] This paragraph is based on Andrew Atherstone, 'Anglican Evangelicalism in the Twentieth Century: Identities and Contexts,' in *Evangelicalism and the Church of England in the Twentieth Century: Reform, Resistance and Revival*, ed. Andrew Atherstone and John Maiden (Woodbridge: Boydell Press, 2014), 1-47. For the background, Geoffrey R. Treloar, *The Disruption of Evangelicalism: The Age of Torrey, Mott, McPherson and Hammond* (London: Inter-Varsity Press, 2016), chaps 4 and 9.

evangelicalism.[17] As the election of 1933 showed – in effect a referendum between the two positions – the tensions between the old and the new were played out in microcosm in the Diocese of Sydney. Mostly out of England while these developments were taking place, Mowll (so far as is presently known) never took a public stand on the issues involved. However, while he continued to serve with the allegedly liberal Church Missionary Society through the 1920s,[18] his address to the Anglican Church League titled 'The Call to Evangelicals, or The Present Evangelical Outlook' delivered on a visit to Sydney in 1931 had convinced the local conservatives that he, like them, had remained aligned with the traditional evangelical outlook.[19] In office, opposition to theological innovation and marginalisation of its proponents not only reflected his own certitude but also made clear that, as the new archbishop, Mowll was determined, following a hiatus of half a century during which liberal evangelical tendencies had become increasingly influential, to restore traditional evangelicalism as the governing perspective of the diocese.[20]

For the mindset of the new archbishop as he took up office, the most important component of this heritage was its ecclesiology.[21] As an

---

[17] The standpoints of the two main outlooks were set out in two of the key position statements of these years. *Liberal Evangelicalism*, published in 1923, described the so-called 'neo-evangelicalism' of the Anglican Evangelical Group Movement, while *Evangelicalism* (1925), produced by the Fellowship of Evangelical Churchmen, pointedly claimed in its title to represent true evangelicalism.

[18] On which, see David W. Bebbington, 'Missionary Controversy and the Polarising Tendency in Twentieth-Century British Protestantism,' *Anvil* 13.2 (1996): 141-157.

[19] 'Sydney Anglican Church League. Address by Bishop Mowll,' *ACR*, 20 August 1931, 4. Unfortunately no copy of this address has been traced.

[20] Eg. Sydney Synod 1938, 267-269, and below on 'The Memorial'. The liberalism of Bishop Barry (1884-9) and Archbishop Wright (1910-33) are well established. For the incipient liberal evangelicalism of Archbishop Saumarez Smith (1890-1909), see G.R. Treloar, 'Smith, William Saumarez,' *Australian Dictionary of Evangelical Biography*, ed. Brian Dickey (Sydney: EHA, 1994), 345-7.

[21] For Anglican ecclesiology in general, see Paul Avis, 'Anglican Ecclesiology,' in *The Oxford Handbook of Ecclesiology*, ed. Paul Avis (Oxford: Oxford

alternative to the Anglo-Catholic ecclesiologies now at the peak of their influence in the Australian church, Mowll brought to Sydney the simply stated conviction that the church is 'a divinely appointed society for the extension of the Kingdom of God on earth'.[22] Unfortunately, he never made clear what he understood by 'the kingdom of God', a controversial doctrine which church people of all stripes embraced but interpreted in their own ways.[23] Nevertheless, for Mowll it had four main corollaries which had a marked bearing on his approach as he assumed the leadership of the Sydney church:

1. A summons to identify with the kingdom and to labour devotedly for its increasing realisation in the world;[24]
2. 'Witness' to the world of the lordship of Christ as the essential task in its service;[25]
3. The basis of a fellowship transcending differences of opinion and church culture in a unity of mutual caring and cooperation;[26] and
4. An historical framework that sustained purpose and hope by making every moment and activity meaningful as preparation for the climactic moment of Christ's second coming.[27]

As a view of what the church should be and do, these convictions do much to explain Mowll's seemingly indefatigable labours, emphasis on

---

University Press, 2018), 239-262. For the Antipodean context, see Stephen Pickard, '"Home Away From Home": Displacement, Identity and Anglican Ecclesiology in Australasia,' in *The Oxford Handbook of Anglican Studies*, ed. Mark D. Chapman, Sathianathan Clarke and Martyn Percy (Oxford: Oxford University Press, 2015), 205-217.

[22] Sydney Synod 1938, 243. On the wider Church, see Brian H. Fletcher, *The Place of Anglicanism in Australia: Church, Society and Nation* (Mulgrave: Broughton Publishing, 2008), chap. 5.

[23] Eg. Mowll's rival in 1933, J.W. Hunkin, 'The Kingdom of God,' in T. Guy Rogers, ed., *Liberal Evangelicalism: An Interpretation by Members of the Church of England* (London: Hodder and Stoughton, 1923), 174-193.

[24] Sydney Synod 1936, 273; 1938, 243-4.

[25] Sydney Synod 1934, 275-6; 1935, 305; 1936, 286; 1939, 48.

[26] Sydney Synod 1934, 268-9.

[27] *SDM*, 1 November 1936, 208; Sydney Synod 1938, 244.

personal interaction, irrepressible optimism and priorities in office. As he began his new ministry, he reflected, alluding to the words of 'Lawrence of Arabia' to Emir Feisal at the beginning of the Arab Revolt in 1916 in relation to the distance between Wadi Safra and Damascus, 'We are still far from the Kingdom of God'.[28] Mowll's overriding aim as Archbishop of Sydney was to bring it nearer.

Like all of his predecessors, Mowll also came to Sydney as an Englishman. Although he had spent most of his adult life abroad, he still regarded England as 'the homeland' and 'the mother country'.[29] Prizing in particular his status as a freeman of his birth-city, Dover, Mowll soon revealed a great pride in his British identity.[30] As it came to expression, his 'Britishness' incorporated exaltation of Britain as the embodiment of Christian civilization,[31] respect for the monarchy as the institutionalisation of Christian morality and duty,[32] advocacy of the Empire – a force for peace and good order in the world as well as progressive leadership of the 'backward peoples' in its domain – as an instrument of the kingdom of God,[33] and an insistent Protestantism.[34] Such quasi-jingoism was another source of reassurance for a community which still largely regarded itself as British and looked to

---

[28] Sydney Synod 1935, 290-1. For the background, Jeremy Wilson, *Lawrence of Arabia: The Authorised Biography of T.E. Lawrence* (London: Minerva, 1990), 311-16 (with the quotation on 312).

[29] *SDM*, 1 March 1938, 35-36. Sydney Synod 1936, 276.

[30] 'Civic Reception to Archbishop Mowll,' *ACR*, 22 March 1934, 8. Loane, *Archbishop Mowll*, chap. 1.

[31] Sydney Synod 1935, 316-31; 1937, 279-280; 1939, 37-38.

[32] Sydney Synod 1936, 275-6; *SDM*, 1 March 1937, 27. Mowll was deeply disappointed by the abdication of Edward VIII in 1937. Sydney Synod 1937, 278-279.

[33] *SDM*, 1 March 1938, 35-36 and 'Enthronement Sermon,' *ACR*, 22 March 1934, 7-8 with Sydney Synod 1935, 293; 1936, 304-5; 1937, 279-80; 1939, 40.

[34] Such an outlook was not uncommon in the British world at the time, especially among evangelicals. See Geraldine Vaughan, '"Britishers and Protestants": Protestantism and Imperial British Identities in Britain, Canada and Australia from the 1880s to the 1920s,' *Studies in Church History* 54 (2018): 359-373.

Britain for leaders in church and state.[35] It also explains why Mowll was intent upon developing the Sydney Church as 'an Imperial link' for 'the peace and welfare of the world'.[36] At the very beginning, Mowll told the people of Sydney that they should think 'imperially' like him.[37]

Part of this imperial thinking was a determination to make the most of the opportunities accruing to the Church of England as 'the Church of the British people'.[38] Of course, this commitment to Anglicanism was a further aspect of Mowll's English provenance. He had been raised in an Anglican family and nurtured in the parish church in Dover. At the King's School in Canterbury in the shadow of the cathedral, he was not only educated but also drawn into the traditions of the English church at the height of its imperial influence.[39] Together with an early commitment to a lifetime of service in its ministry, this formation left its mark in Mowll's enthusiasm for the Book of Common Prayer, love of Anglican worship, confidence in the Anglican formularies as a foundation of sound doctrine, and tendency to look to the Church in England as a guide to what to think and do.[40] Mindful of the authority and influence of the Anglican Communion flowing from these sources, Mowll readily embraced the responsibility as Archbishop of Sydney of seeing to it that the Church's manifest spiritual power and

---

[35] *SDM*, 1 January 1938, 7. On 'Britishness in contemporary Australia, see Stephen A. Chavura and Greg Melleuish, *The Forgotten Menzies: The World Picture of Australia's Longest-serving Prime Minister* (Carlton: Melbourne University Press, 2021).

[36] Mowll ardently led the Sydney community in making 'Empire Day' a day of celebration and thanksgiving for Australia's British heritage. 'Enthronement Sermon,' *ACR*, 22 March 1934, 7-8; 'Great Service in Centennial Park,' *SDM*, 1 June 1935, 123-5; *SDM*, 1 July 1936, 100; Sydney Synod 1936, 281-2.

[37] 'Enthronement Sermon,' *ACR*, 22 March 1934, 7-8.

[38] Synod 1936, 282-283.

[39] Loane, *Archbishop Mowll*, chaps. 1-2.

[40] Synod 1934, 280-281;1935, 302-303, 315-317; 1936, 294; 1937, 278-279, 291-294; 1938, 243-244. *SDM*, 1 September 1935, 204; 1 January 1937, 247-248; 1 August 1937, 106 and 122; 1 August 1938, 112. Mowll felt extremely let down by the Report of the Commission on Christian Doctrine in 1938. See Sydney Synod 1938, 267-269 and 1939, 46-47.

'wealth of tradition and historical background' were fully deployed in the life of the Diocese.[41]

The achievement of this aim depended upon provision of suitable episcopal leadership. Mowll's understanding of his role as a bishop also derived from his English Anglican background.[42] In line with the Anglican tradition, two main tasks were rolled into one. As the new archbishop, Mowll became at once the chief administrator of the diocese and also its chief pastor. In theory and practice, this conception was hierarchical, still conferring early in the twentieth century considerable power and authority for the discharge of the bishop's administrative and pastoral responsibility.[43] Mowll's particular interpretation of the role had been shaped by the bishops he had encountered in his early years – the Archbishop of Canterbury, Randall Davidson, the Bishop of Durham, Handley Moule, and John Taylor-Smith, the Chaplain-General to the Armed Forces during the Great War – all models in varying degrees of devotion to duty, efficient administration, pastoral effectiveness and deep personal piety.[44] But two stand out. One was Edward Knox, who, as Bishop of Manchester and subsequently in retirement, had been a resolute defender of the church's essential Protestantism in the face of encroaching Anglo-Catholicism.[45] The other was the first Bishop of Western China, William Cassels – described by his biographer as 'a humble and loving autocrat, one who ever disciplined himself and expected others to accept discipline also' – whom Mowll encountered in China as his diocesan.[46] In Cassels he observed a model of unremitting toil and firm leadership, a style which he, temperamentally disposed to taking

---

[41] Sydney Synod 1934, 282.

[42] On the tradition, see Sarah Rowland Jones, 'Episcopé and Leadership,' in Chapman, Clarke and Percy, *Oxford Handbook of Anglican Studies*, 451-463.

[43] For the limit imposed by the power of the diocesan Synod, see below.

[44] For Mowll on Taylor-Smith, see *SDM*, 1 March 1938, 36 and 1 April 1938, 51-52. See also Michael Gladwin, '"Our Padre" Howard Mowll: a future archbishop as First World War Army chaplain,' chapter 2 above.

[45] *SDM*, 1 February 1937, 4. Cf. T.C. Hammond, 'Bishop Knox: An Appreciation,' *SDM*, 1 February 1937, 22-24 and 1 March 1937, 38-9.

[46] Marshall Broomhall, *W. W. Cassels: First Bishop of Western China* (London: China Inland Mission, 1926), 358.

control in exercising leadership,[47] continued as the second Bishop of Western China and then brought to Sydney. As a servant-leader along these lines, Mowll would be a servant, but, in a marked change from the approach of Archbishop Wright, he would also definitely be the leader.[48]

Although being evangelical and British were the crucial elements of the identity he brought to Sydney, Mowll understood that, if he was to succeed, he would also have to develop an Australian persona as part of his transition to the new role. That he was expected to identify with his new setting was implied by the Lord Mayor at the civic reception when he thought that the Mowlls 'would learn to love Australia as they had always loved England'.[49] Mowll began his adaptation to the new environment by promising in response to take an active interest in the affairs of the Sydney community. Shortly afterwards, he shared with the youth of the diocese his appreciation of 'the great historic Church to which it is our privilege to belong', while with its people at large he claimed a 'family connection'.[50] Before the wider society, Mowll celebrated Sydney as a 'great city' of considerable stature as 'the second white city of the Empire'.[51] Impressed like many foreigners by Sydney's beauty and amenity, he could even joke that 'it must be a great temptation' to its people 'to do nothing but enjoy the magnificent climate and beautiful surroundings'.[52] All too soon, however, he recognised acute social needs and rising secularisation and indifference to Christianity as particular challenges to the dedicated community service he offered.[53] After a year in Sydney, Mowll still

---

[47] See Loane, *Archbishop Mowll*, chap. 3, esp. 60-61, and Tom Habib, 'The Cambridge Years: 1909-1912', chapter 1 above.

[48] On Wright, see Judd, "Defenders of Their Faith," 203-205. On Mowll's sense of himself as the leader, Stuart Barton Babbage, *Memoirs of a Loose Canon* (Brunswick East: Acorn Press, 2004), 58.

[49] *ACR*, 22 March 1934, 8.

[50] *SDM*, 1 March 1934, 5. Sydney Synod 1934, 265.

[51] Sydney Synod 1934, 282. Sydney Synod 1940, 44.

[52] *ACR*, 22 March 1934, 8. Sydney Synod 1935, 290-1.

[53] Peter Spearritt, *Sydney Since the Twenties* (Marrickville, NSW: Hale and Iremonger, 1978), 62-79.

described himself as 'a newcomer',[54] but, as he settled down, he grew in affection and respect for the city and its people.[55] The introduction of a special cathedral service for the city and enthusiastic participation in the 150th anniversary of NSW in 1938 showed that Mowll's connection with Sydney was well established.[56] Although the change from a wild frontier diocese in China to a developing western society was a big adjustment, after almost five years in office Mowll had credibly aligned with Sydney and Australia as the third layer of his identity as the new Archbishop of Sydney.

Building Up the Church

In the absence of a detailed plan, Mowll's first strategy for turning this mindset into action was to know, and be known by, the diocese. During the early months of his term, he took the time to familiarise himself with Sydney and its peculiar conditions.[57] Subsequently he conducted something of a general visitation along traditional English lines to ensure comprehensive and realistic supervision as a condition of the welfare of the diocese.[58]

The obverse of getting to know the diocese was to become known throughout its length and breadth.[59] This was why Mowll's very first measures included establishing personal contact with the people and clergy by means of a program of systematic visitation of all the Rural Deaneries, the first round of which he had completed within three months.[60] Before his increasingly crowded schedule made it unviable,

---

[54] Sydney Synod 1935, 317.

[55] Sydney Synod 1935, 290. For his admiration of the level of altruism in the Sydney community, Sydney Synod 1936, 285-6.

[56] For the special service, *SDM*, 1 January 1938, 4, and 1 February 1938, 19. For the 150th anniversary of NSW, *SDM*, 1 January 1938, 3-4, 7; 1 February 1938, 29-30; and 1 March 1938, 34.

[57] Sydney Synod 1934, 282. *SDM*, 1 April 1934, 4; 1 June 1934, 4; 27 June 1934, 2.

[58] Sydney Synod 1937, 291-296.

[59] Note as evidence of the ideal his commendation of Arnold Wylde as he became Bishop of Bathurst. *SDM*, 1 December 1936, 232.

[60] *SDM*, 1 June 1934, 4 and 27 June 1934, 2. Sydney Synod 1934, 268-269; 1935, 291.

he was also regularly 'at home' at Bishopscourt which was intended to function as 'the central home of the Diocese'.[61] An enactment of the fellowship principle, high visibility and ready accessibility were key aspects of servant leadership. They also began the process of centralising authority in the person of the new archbishop.

This purpose was furthered by the use Mowll made of the *Sydney Diocesan Magazine* established by his predecessor in 1911. Recognizing that it furnished a ready means of speaking to the diocese at large, each month Mowll wrote an 'Archbishop's Letter' of 2-3 pages in which he laid out his plans and commented on diocesan events. To this he added a list of his major engagements. In chronicling his own activities, Mowll placed himself at the centre of diocesan life and created the image of the archbishop providing clear and definite leadership and always at work in the service of the diocese.

Supporting this image was immediate commencement of the 'episcopal oversight' and administration Mowll took to be his basic task as the new archbishop. Comprised in its administrative component of 'organisation, machinery and methods', he held that such routine work was transformed by the realisation that it enabled the advancement of the kingdom of God.[62] Working out his own commitment to the kingdom by his diligence and attention to detail, Mowll's intention in administration was to build up the operational capacity of the Sydney church so that, as an organisation, it could rise to its more overtly spiritual and pastoral opportunities. As he indicated regularly, his standard was 'effectiveness' which quickly became something of a watchword for the diocese.[63]

Optimising the impact of its operations required some re-organization of the Sydney church. Mowll began in 1936 with the creation of the new archdeaconry of Redfern.[64] Another archdeaconry was added in

---

[61] *SDM*, 1 April 1934, 4; 1 April 1935, 67-8, 85. Sydney Synod 1934, 276.
[62] Sydney Synod 1934, 265.
[63] For early examples of 'effectiveness' as an ideal, see Sydney Synod 1934, 266, 268, 277; and *SDM*, 1 October 1934, 3; 1 January 1935, 2; 1 February 1935, 19.
[64] Sydney Synod 136, 278-279. *SDM*, 1 December 1936, 234-236.

the following year when, 'for the more effective work of the Diocese', the boundaries of the rural deaneries and the archdeaconries were also redrawn.[65] In these early years, Mowll also began to rationalise by bringing as many diocesan organisations as possible together in Church House. He defended his changes as a 'necessary part of administration' of an expanding and increasingly complex operation.[66] Given the tendency to bureaucracy and rational order in the modern world, his administrative reforms were manifestly important steps in the modernisation of the diocese.[67]

Enhancing the capacity of the diocese also required continuous fundraising. While he did not underestimate the difficulties of the Depression era, Mowll was frequently frustrated by the inadequacy of the church's financial resources for accomplishing his purposes.[68] Accordingly he set out to improve the position by developing consciousness of the importance of ethically defensible revenue raising.[69] To this end he pressed the responsibility of personal stewardship and promoted established schemes for regular direct giving to church work.[70] Nor was he ever afraid to ask for money to pay for specific undertakings. In fundraising Mowll was creative as well as persistent. One daring scheme involved alleviating the financial weakness of Moore College by its amalgamation with the relatively affluent city parish of St Philip's.[71] Another innovative scheme was his appeal late in 1937 for a million shillings annually for five years to pay

---

[65] Sydney Synod 1937, 281.

[66] Sydney Synod 1937, 291-296.

[67] On modernisation and modernity, and the rise of administration and bureaucracy, see C. A. Bayly, *The Birth of the Modern World 1780-1914: Global Connections and Comparisons* (Malden: Blackwell Publishing, 2004), 9-12 and 276-277.

[68] Eg. Sydney Synod 1935, 308-9; 1938, 251-2. *SDM*, 1 November 1935, 253-254; 1 December 1935, 271.

[69] 'Parish Finance,' *SDM*, 1 December 1936, 243-244. Sydney Synod 1938, 252. On the proper attitude to fundraising and management of property, 245.

[70] *SDM*, 1 June 1935, 114. Sydney Synod 1936, 285, 287-8. Cf his support for post war membership drives and fundraising schemes.

[71] Sydney Synod 1935, 311-313; 1937, 296.

for a speedy increase in the number of clergy.[72] Such measures increased the pressure on the already stretched financial resources of the Diocese, but they were envisaged as what was needed to enable the Church of England 'to be an effective instrument in upholding the cause of God in this great city'.[73]

While implementing these strategies, Mowll also took steps to strengthen his grip on the diocese. The first was to draw the Diocesan Synod into his purposes and program. The legislative arm of the diocese, Mowll had not previously encountered a body with this kind of power and assertiveness in church government.[74] From the first Synod over which he presided in 1934, Mowll set out to harness its energy and capacity. Ever the politician, he sought to win it over by acknowledging its members as 'fellow workers' and affirming the Synod's function as 'the Parliament of the Church'.[75] He also dignified its frequently mundane concerns as work (like his own) for the extension of the kingdom of God and a source of inspiration and leadership in the diocese.[76] Mowll played his own part, by delivering long, informative, agenda-setting addresses which were received as 'statesmanlike', and by firm and fair chairmanship of Synod deliberations.[77] Behind the scenes he worked closely with the Standing Committee, not only in dealing with routine business, but especially in maintaining the distinctive character of the diocese in relation to the

---

[72] Sydney Synod 1937, 302-3. *SDM*, 1 June 1937, 74; 1 July 1937, 90; 1 January 1938, 4-5; 1 June 1938, 87.

[73] Sydney Synod 1938, 252. On the proper attitude to fundraising and management of property, 245.

[74] Judd, "Defenders of their Faith," chap. 8. For a response to this political reality in Australian dioceses, see Mowll's contemporary, the Archbishop of Brisbane, William Wand, in his *Changeful Page: The Autobiography of William Wand Formerly Bishop of London* (London: Hodder & Stoughton, 1965), 139 - 140.

[75] Sydney Synod 1936, 305, and *SDM*, 1 November 1936, 206. Cf. Sydney Synod 1937, 278; 1939, 37-38.

[76] Sydney Synod 1934, 263-5, esp. 265; 1938, 242-5, esp. 244.

[77] R. Harley-Jones, 'An Epoch-Making Synod,' *SDM*, 1 October 1934, 9-11; 'Notes on the Twenty-Fourth Synod of the Diocese of Sydney,' *SDM*, 1 September 1938, 133-5, esp. 135 for the reference to the 'statesmanlike charge'.

new constitution proposed for the Australian church.[78] It is true that the Synod consisted mainly of his supporters, but appreciative responses indicate that Mowll was adept at winning its support.[79]

The second step in this respect was the use of patronage to secure a united and coherent diocesan leadership. While Mowll tactfully recognised the calibre and contribution of the leadership team he inherited, circumstances soon provided the opportunity to create an inner circle of trusted lieutenants to whom he could delegate important functions.[80] Beginning with the archdeacons and rural deans, he was able to raise up new men such as S M Johnstone and R B Robinson who became his representatives and supporters throughout the Diocese.[81] A sequence of deaths in a short space of time also enabled Mowll to fill the key leadership positions with men of his own choosing. In 1935 he appointed Charles Pilcher, an old friend from Wycliffe College in Toronto and a noted Bible scholar and church musician, as Coadjutor Bishop in succession to James Kirkby.[82] The following year he was able to replace the liberal evangelical Principal of Moore College, David John Davies, with the well known Irish evangelical theologian and apologist, T C Hammond. In 1940 he chose as Assistant Bishop W G Hilliard, a Sydney man who had become the Bishop of Nelson in New Zealand and another evangelical activist, to help carry the administrative load.[83] A global evangelical, Mowll drew on the manpower of the imperial church to provide Sydney Diocese with leaders of the necessary calibre and outlook.

---

[78] Sydney Diocesan Archives [cited hereafter as SDA]. Minutes of the Standing Committee 9 (1935-1938), *passim*. *SDM*, 1 October 1934, 9-11; 1 November 1936, 206.

[79] *ACR*, 20 September 1934, 1; 8 October 1935, 6-7; 16 September 1937, 8-9; 1 September 1938, 12; 19 October 1939, 12.

[80] Sydney Synod 1934, 268.

[81] Loane, *Mark These Men*, 42-45 and 49-51.

[82] Pilcher's impeccable evangelical credentials are emphasised in Maurice Laseron, *Bishop Charles Venn Pilcher: A Biographical Study* (Sydney: n.p., 1949).

[83] Janet West, *Innings of Grace: A Life of Bishop W.G. Hilliard* (Sydney: Trinity Grammar School, 1987).

A further set of initiatives was intended to mobilise the resources of the diocese. As Mowll assessed its strengths and weaknesses, he concluded: 'we are being challenged as a Church to bring all our resources into play if we are to fulfill our obligations to the community.'[84] Critical to rising to the challenge were the clergy to whom Mowll naturally looked for the spiritual leadership of the diocese.[85] During his first six months in office, he met and interviewed all the clergy and thereafter kept in touch with them through periodic meetings of the rural deaneries.[86] This contact was the basis of a relationship which was concerned to affirm the clergy in their role, align them with his objectives, improve their working conditions and provide for their spiritual wellbeing and refreshment. As he became more familiar with the demographic condition of the diocese, Mowll recognized the near impossibility of their task.[87] The underlying problem was simply that there were not enough clergy to cope with the large numbers of people nominally in their care. By 1938 the situation was critical. Mowll set to work to attract more men into the ministry, necessarily a long-term strategy.[88] But this would not be at the expense of quality. Mowll raised the standard for ordination while also making the academic and material improvement of Moore College one of his leading priorities for the ongoing service of the diocese by a ministry with the necessary training and formation for 'faithful and effective pastoral work and spiritual witness'.[89]

No less important for the well-being and effectiveness of the Church in Mowll's strategic thinking were the lay people of the diocese. At one level he was obliged to recognise that the Church of England was, in

---

[84] Synod 1934, 282.

[85] Synod 1937, 302-3; 1939, 57. Cf. Sydney Synod 1936, 294 (on the importance of the chaplaincies). For the clergy in Mowll's time in office, see Loane, *Mark These Men*.

[86] Sydney Synod 1934, 268-9.

[87] Sydney Synod 1936, 293; Synod 1937, 286, 291-3; Synod 1938, 250-2. *SDM*, 1 June 1937, 74, 87; 1 June 1938, 87.

[88] Sydney Synod 1938, 250-2.

[89] The qualities attributed to the Rev. C.C. Dunstan, 'an example to us all', after a ministry of 60 years. Sydney Synod 1939, 38. For Mowll and Moore College, see Chapter 7 below by Mark Thompson.

principle, 'a people's church'.[90] However, their various roles in the parishes and for the diocese meant that lay people were in any case an essential component in the church's operations.[91] While he exhorted them to play a proper part in church life, Mowll went out of his way to praise the service rendered by the men and women of the church, whether prominent or little known.[92] Various arrangements were made for the theological education of those who preferred not to go into full time ministry but still wanted some training for church work.[93] Church wardens and lay readers in particular were singled out for encouragement and development. As a sign of their importance, Mowll introduced periodic commissioning services in the cathedral and around the diocese.[94] Of course getting the most out of the people of the diocese required minimizing nominal church membership. Mowll's own initiatives to this end included annual services in the cathedral for confirmees so that they might be encouraged to go on with what they had begun by working for the church,[95] and institution of the 'Archbishop's Conference on Youth Work' both as a symbol of the importance of youth in the diocese and also provision for its future.[96] Individually and collectively, the contribution of lay people were necessary for the realisation of the principle enunciated for the diocese at the outset: 'If the Church is to go forward, it depends not on the few, but on each one of us playing our part.'[97]

Formal arrangements could only take the diocese so far. As its chief pastor, Mowll aimed also to build up the quality of its spiritual life as a further condition of the church's effectiveness.[98] The power that would

---

[90] Sydney Synod 1934, 268-9; 1939, 37-8.

[91] E.g. Sydney Synod 1936, 295.

[92] E.g. the obituaries in his annual Synod address and regularly in the *SDM*.

[93] Sydney Synod 1936, 295.

[94] Sydney Synod 1934, 268-9; 1935, 305-6; 1936, 295; 1938, 259.

[95] Sydney Synod, 1935, 306.

[96] On Mowll and youthwork, see Ruth Lukabyo in chapter 9 below.

[97] *SDM*, 1 May 1934, 2.

[98] Sydney Synod 1935, 305; 1936, 286, 305-306; 1938, 247; 1939, 57. *SDM*, 1 February 1937, 3; 1 April 1938, 50; 1 June 1938, 86-87.

animate its collective life was to be found in a 'fresh vision of the Cross of Christ':

> It is only by such a vision that we shall manifest the unflinching devotion, the persistent patience, the self-denial, the courage and the optimism that mighty tasks call for, and with which they challenge the confession of our faith in Christ and our acknowledgement of Him as our Master. Then, and not till then, can we speak with any confidence of the ways and means which we must wisely adopt in order to implement for the work of human redemption the divine energy which the Spirit of God has bestowed.[99]

Thus Mowll envisaged the cross as the energising force of a spirituality geared to realising the lordship of Christ and the leading of the Holy Spirit. The priorities in its cultivation were private and corporate prayer and systematic personal Bible reading.[100] In its main elements reflecting the Keswick style that dominated interwar evangelicalism, Mowll pressed this conception of the spiritual life on the diocese.[101] While all its members were expected to take responsibility for their own spiritual condition,[102] as aids to the life of faith he taught observance of the church's seasons (especially Lent),[103] led devotional gatherings and conferences,[104] provided a platform in Sydney for Keswick speakers, and incorporated the Katoomba Convention, the

---

[99] Sydney Synod 1936, 292-3.
[100] On Prayer: *SDM*, 1 May 1934, 4; 1 July 1937, 91; 1 April 1938, 50; and Sydney Synod 1938, 247; 1939, 48. On Bible reading: *SDM*, 1 December 1934, 3; 1 August 1937, 106; 1 March 1938; 1 June 1938, 87; and Sydney Synod 1937, 290.
[101] Ian M. Randall, *Evangelical Experiences: A Study of the Spirituality of English Evangelicalism 1918-1939* (Carlisle: Paternoster Publishing, 1999), chap. 2.
[102] Sydney Synod 1934, 282-283.
[103] *SDM*, 1 February 1935, 18-19; 1 April 1935, 86; 1 January 1936, 248; 1 November 1936, 207-208; 1 February 1937, 3; 1 March 1938, 34; 1 April 1938, 50-51, 65.
[104] *SDM*, 1 July 1935, 146; Sydney Synod 1935, 305-307; 1937, 286.

local version of Keswick, into the diocesan program.[105] These measures were supplemented by endorsement of the activities of stalwart evangelical organisations such as the Evangelical Alliance and Scripture Union and by openness to new developments such as the Oxford Group Movement.[106] Establishing a consistent evangelical culture along traditional lines throughout the diocese was another side of the centralised leadership of the new archbishop.

Mowll also worked at fostering diocesan consciousness and solidarity. The primary means to this end was the use of the history of the diocese which was still not well known or appreciated in the 1930s. Mowll was aided in this important strategy by the fortuitous coincidence of several important anniversaries with his early years in Sydney. Foremost of these anniversaries was the centenary of the consecration in 1836 of William Grant Broughton as the first and only Bishop of Australia.[107] In mid-1936 the diocese staged a major public event which ran for two weeks and included special services in the historic churches of St James' and St Philip's as well as the cathedral, a Church Congress, a missionary exhibition, a 'Pilgrimage to the Broughton Churches', the opening of a church history museum, a 'Pageant of Church History' which added the 'Australian Period' to the succession of great eras in the history of the Church of England, and a broadcast address by the Archbishop of Canterbury.[108] Judged a great success, Mowll went to some lengths to define the meaning of the celebration as 'a reminder to us of our great opportunity as the Church of the British People, and, in consequence, of the extent and weight of our moral and spiritual responsibilities throughout the world'.[109] As a reminder 'of the root from which we had sprung and the amazing growth and development which the century had witnessed',[110] Broughton's Sydney-based

---

[105] SDM, 1937, 247-9. Stuart Braga, *A Century of Preaching Christ: Katoomba Christian Convention 1903-2003* (Sydney: Katoomba Christian Convention Ltd, 2003), 63-64.

[106] SDM, 1 December 1935, 272. For the Oxford Group Movement, see Randall, *Evangelical Experiences*, chap. 9.

[107] Sydney Synod 1934, 266-7; 1935, 317-18.

[108] *Bishop Broughton Centenary Celebrations. Sydney, 1936. Official Program.*

[109] Sydney Synod 1936, 281.

[110] Sydney Synod 1936, 283.

episcopate should also be a spur to further historic achievement by the continuation of his dedication and self-sacrificing service.[111] While promoting the story of the Australian church as a whole, with the disappointment of his failure to be elected Primate the previous year in the background, Mowll did it in such a way as to highlight the uniqueness of Sydney as its 'Mother Church'.

The leading symbol of what Mowll was trying to achieve for the diocese was St Andrew's Cathedral. An aspect of his Anglican consciousness, from the first he took great pride in what he called 'our beautiful Cathedral' and undertook to use it 'as the Mother Church of the Diocese' while also serving 'the needs of the great city in whose heart it stands'.[112] Its importance to Mowll was signalled when, on the death of the liberal evangelical dean of the cathedral, Edward Talbot, in July 1936, he retained this function in his own hands.[113] His twin aims of greater centralisation and spiritual impact were reflected in the hope 'that the Cathedral may become more than ever a centre of the family life of the Diocese and that it may increase in spiritual effectiveness'.[114] Its part in setting the standard for the spiritual life of the Sydney church was facilitated by making the cathedral the centre of intercession for the diocese and the introduction of an assortment of new services and functions such as the weekly Bible reading.[115] The intended contribution to the development of diocesan consciousness and shared culture was encouraged by the celebration of the cathedral's centenary, the creation of an annual cathedral festival and making St Andrew's Day a special day in the life of the diocese.[116] It was reflected too in the

---

[111] Sydney Synod 1936, 284.
[112] *SDM*, 1 April 1934, 3. Cf. Synod 1935, 296. On St Andrew's and its place in the Anglican cathedral tradition, see Edward Loane, 'Anglican Cathedrals and Sydney Anglicanism: the Shape of Cathedral Ministry and Mission,' in *Proclaiming Christ in the Heart of the City: Ministry at St Andrew's Cathedral, Sydney. Dean Cowper, Dean Talbot, and Dean Shilton*, ed. Edward Loane (Sydney: St Andrew's Cathedral, 2019), 7-48.
[113] Mowll held the position until 1947 when he appointed the brilliant young New Zealander, Stuart Barton Babbage, as the Dean.
[114] Sydney Synod 1934, 281.
[115] Eg. *SDM*, 1 June 1934, 2; 1 August 1934, 3. Sydney Synod 1935, 305-6.
[116] Sydney Synod 1937, 298.

plan for the cathedral to provide 'a happy opportunity for members of different parishes to unite in the Mother Church of the Diocese'.[117]

Reaction against Mowll

There was a downside to Mowll's focus on St Andrew's. Increased usage showed that the cathedral building was too small.[118] Mowll turned the expansion process into a significant diocesan and community event by conducting a well-publicized competition for the design.[119] The move backfired early in 1938 when the design chosen by Mowll and the other judges was roundly criticised throughout the Sydney community. A serious embarrassment for Mowll,[120] the projected cost of the cathedral extension precipitated wider questioning of his administration. The 'Million Shillings Fund' in particular was criticised as unrealistic and for pushing the diocese to its financial limits.[121] Rightly or wrongly, other criticisms held that, under Mowll, the Sydney church was socially disengaged, intellectually mediocre and inward looking.[122]

At the same time, relations with some of the clergy and people of the diocese also soured. Initially the centre of dissatisfaction was the Anglo-Catholic church of St James', King Street, already for some thirty years a thorn in the side of the evangelical Archbishops of Sydney.[123] Early in 1937, its distinguished rector, Philip Micklem, decided that it was time for him to leave Sydney. Mowll saw in the vacancy an

---

[117] *SDM*, 1 November 1935, 250-1, 252, 261; 1 November 1936, 207, 209.

[118] Sydney Synod 1937, 298.

[119] Sydney Synod 1935, 295-7; Synod 1936, 300-1. For an account of the matter, see S.M. Johnstone, *The Book of St Andrew's Cathedral Sydney* (revised and extended by J.H.L. Johnstone; Sydney: Angus & Robertson, 1968), chap. 9, which minimises the adverse response.

[120] Judd, "Defenders of Their Faith," 408-410. The design was still under consideration when war broke out in the following year. Sydney Synod 1938, 263; 1939, 65.

[121] Eg. A Group of Sydney Clergy to the Editor of "The Church Standard", 'The Million Shillings Fund,' *CS*, 10 December 1937, 13.

[122] Eg. The letter of the 'Sydney Layman' to the Editor of *The Church Standard*, *CS*, 11 February 1938, 13.

[123] Judd and Cable, *Sydney Anglicans*, 161-165.

opportunity to wind back Anglo-Catholic practices in the church by imposing on the new rector limits on ritual and clerical dress.[124] The changes introduced early in 1938 by Micklem's successor, E J Davidson (allegedly a Mowll appointee), caused deep consternation among the parishioners and led to a public controversy in which Mowll's church, in the politically charged rhetoric of the day, was accused of 'ecclesiastical totalitarianism', 'dictatorship', 'fascism' and 'diocesan autarchy'.[125] The clergy and parishioners of Christ Church St Laurence, the other centre of Anglo-Catholicism in the diocese, also felt that the historic discrimination against their church continued under Mowll, and the rector, John Hope, believed (probably incorrectly) he was forced to relinquish control of its very successful Boys' Welfare Bureau to the Home Mission Society because of churchmanship.[126] Mowll was informed (with some hyperbole) that 'there are many Anglicans in Sydney who feel that their loyalty to Christ conflicts with their desire to be loyal to the leaders of the Church in this diocese'.[127] But, convinced that he stood for 'the advancement of the truth',[128] Mowll was undeterred. Two years later, when the parish of St David's, Arncliffe, wanted to appoint as a curate the Rev G S Watts who, as editor of the

---

[124] This paragraph is based on the documents in SDA1992/26/69: 'Archbishop's Correspondence re. St James King Street (1937-1938)'. On Micklem, see John G. Beer, 'The Contribution of the Reverend Dr. Philip Arthur Micklem (1876-1965) to Anglicanism,' PhD thesis, University of Sydney, 2009.

[125] 'Crisis at S. James's,' CS, 11 February 1938, 13; 'Dictatorship in Sydney Diocese,' CS, 18 February 1938, 13 and 25 February 1938, 13. 'Autarchy' was the word used by the Nazis to describe their ideal of economic self-sufficiency.

[126] John Spooner, The Archbishops of Railway Square: A History of Christ Church, St. Laurence (Sydney: Halstead Press, 2002), 151-166. L.C. Rodd, John Hope of Christ Church. A Sydney Church Era (Sydney: Alpha Books, 1972), 86-92. Donald G. Anderson, 'The Bishop's Society, 1856 to 1958: A History of the Sydney Anglican Home Mission Society,' PhD thesis; University of Wollongong, 1990, 385. Other parishes, such as St Saviour's, Redfern, considered that they too were unappreciated.

[127] John C. Johnston to Mowll, 30 January 1938, SDA 1992/26/69: 'Archbishop's Correspondence re. St James King Street (1937-1938)'.

[128] Mowll to H.J. Bate, 28 February 1938, SDA 1992/26/69: 'Archbishop's Correspondence re. St James King Street (1937-1938)'. Judd, 'Defenders of Their Faith,' 411-415.

Church Standard, had spearheaded criticism of the diocese, Mowll refused to issue the requisite licence.[129] Although Sydney's Anglo-Catholics claimed that they were the victims of sectarian intolerance, he maintained a steadfast Protestant commitment to limiting their influence in the diocese.

More serious was the reaction to Mowll's preferment policy. Shortly after the St James' controversy began, he was confronted by a faction of up to a third of the clergy who presented a 'Memorial' in which they complained about an apparent monopoly of conservative evangelicals in diocesan appointments.[130] Led by the Warden of St Paul's College, Arthur Garnsey, the faction consisted mainly of centrist and liberal evangelicals who, having flourished under Archbishop Wright, were feeling the effect of their defeat in the election of 1933.[131] This presentation of grievances was something of an affront to Mowll: at a personal level, to his sense of himself as a leader; and administratively, as a further challenge to the homogeneous evangelical culture he was developing in the diocese. His hackles were raised further when the dispute spilled over into the public press.[132] Refusing the request to meet with them, he administered a questionnaire devised by the pugnacious T. C. Hammond to which the Memorialists in turn refused to reply.[133] An application of Mowll's own 'fellowship principle' would likely have produced a better outcome than this stalemate. Over the next few years, the Memorialists either acquiesced in Mowll's

---

[129] Parish Councillors to Mowll, 27 September 1940, with Mowll's reply, 3rd October 1940, in SDA 1991/090/010: 'Archbishop's Correspondence re. G.S. Watts and St David's Arncliffe, 1940'.

[130] The episode is examined in great detail by Robert Gordon Cooper in the soon to be published 'The Memorialists in their Ecclesiastical Context: A quest for "consent, mutual respect and fairness",' PhD thesis; Sydney College of Divinity, 2017. See also: Loane, *Archbishop Mowll*, 143-149; Judd, "Defenders of Their Faith," chap. 9; and Judd and Cable, *Sydney Anglicans*, 238-240.

[131] David Garnsey, *Arthur Garnsey: A Man for Truth and Freedom* (Sydney: Kingsdale Press, 1985), chap. 6.

[132] 'Administration of the Diocese,' *SDM*, 1 August 1938, 115-116.

[133] Geoffrey R. Treloar, 'T. C. Hammond the Controversialist,' *The Anglican Historical Society Diocese of Sydney Journal* 51.1 (June 2006), 20-35.

dominance or left the diocese.[134] This put an end to organised opposition, at least for the next twenty years, so that, although badly handled, Mowll's response had at least been 'effective'. But the episode exposed the authoritarianism that augmented centralised leadership with suppression of dissent, Mowll's professed servant leadership notwithstanding. Alarmed by the reaction against the archbishop, the Standing Committee issued a public statement in support of Mowll, but it served only to show the persistence of difference and division in the Sydney church.[135] Varying public reactions to Mowll's leadership indicated that, after almost five years, the impact of his personal style and centralised approach to diocesan administration was beginning to tell.

Church and Society

At the same time as building up the church, Mowll also attended to its relationship with the wider society. Recognising that Australia was a Christian country and that a quarter of the population of NSW was Anglican, the particular task was to make this relationship real and (as ever) effective.[136] Mowll always emphasised that the church is primarily a spiritual body with the responsibility of releasing its spiritual life into the community in order to meet 'the fundamental needs of the people'.[137] But this did not mean that the church should exclude itself from the broader affairs of the host society. Indeed, because of their moral dimension, the work of extending the kingdom of God in the world required Christian involvement in the political, economic and racial questions of the day.[138] Mowll insisted further that society should continue to have the benefits of Christian influence – its power of cultural amelioration, the 'stamina' it produced 'in the national character', the basis of moral and material welfare, and the impetus to

---

[134] On the various outcomes for the Memorialists, see Cooper, 'The Memorialists,' chap. 7.
[135] *ACR*, 29 September 1938, 8-10.
[136] Sydney Synod 1936, 290; 1937, 302-303.
[137] Sydney Synod 1934, 282. Cf. Sydney Synod 1936, 279; 1938, 243-244; 1939, 48 and 57.
[138] *SDM*, 1 February 1935, 19. Sydney Synod 1936, 286.

freedom and democracy.[139] The reciprocal benefits to the church from engagement in community life were faithfulness to its calling and an indirect means of proclaiming its message. For what it would give and receive, the new archbishop intended from the first that the church would play its legitimate part in Sydney society.

Mowll left no doubt that the principal means to this end was evangelism. In the age of 'the social gospel', when other churchmen equated the church's mission with social service, he insisted that 'The world's greatest need is evangelism'.[140] For Mowll the imperative was theological. Active evangelism was no more than obedience to the command of Christ and imitation of His example.[141] It was also an act of compassion and service, addressing the greatest need of the people of the community, freedom from the bondage of sin, moral empowerment and experience of God in Christ. Rampant materialism and rising scepticism in contemporary Sydney augmented the need 'for a vigorous evangelism that shall have for its object the reaching of the masses'.[142] Mowll pressed the responsibility on all Church members, but especially on the clergy whom he urged to 'Study evangelism; preach evangelism; live evangelism'.[143] The principal means should be 'witness', understood less as overt evangelistic campaigning than as continually drawing attention to the church and what it offered through its standard ministries. Apart from encouraging other organised effort, Mowll showed the way by himself leading such events as 'days of witness' in the parishes, the annual open-air 'services of witness' at selected beaches during the summer months and the Good Friday 'march of witness' at Easter. In line with traditional evangelical practice, his desire for effective evangelism

---

[139] See especially the important statement to the Sydney Synod in 1936, esp. 279 and 290-291. See also Sydney Synod 1937, 287-290, 292-293.
[140] Sydney Synod 1938, 247. For the wider background, Treloar, *Disruption of Evangelicalism*, chaps. 5 and 12.
[141] Sydney Synod 1938, 246-7; 1939, 46.
[142] Sydney Synod 1939, 55-57, with quotation on 55.
[143] Sydney Synod 1938, 247 (emphasis in the original).

moved Mowll to devise ways of taking the Christian message directly to the unchurched.[144]

Successful evangelism would also facilitate realisation of Mowll's second aspiration for Sydney society, its permeation with Christian influence. This would be achieved by the presence of committed, active Christian people at all levels of community life from the home to the government. From the effect of their work and witness, the benefits of Christian influence would flow continuously to society at large and 'the kingdoms of this world shall become the kingdoms of our Lord and His Christ'.[145] As a result, the Church incurred an important obligation:

> We must study to give our people a really wide outlook on life, one that includes the spiritual and acknowledges its paramount importance, one that views the world at its widest and seeks a true and just relationship to it. Only thus will they be able to see life in its right proportions.[146]

Apprehension of this need charged Mowll's education policy. Because of the benefits of inculcating 'Christian standards of life and conduct' to church and society, getting the most out of religious education in day schools, Sunday schools, and even relations with Sydney University, became one of Mowll's leading priorities.[147]

While evangelism remained the priority, Mowll also set out to develop what he called the church's 'social service'. As he observed in his first synod address: 'The Social Problem, which has very many facets, is always before our minds.'[148] On taking up office, he was impressed by what he saw already happening. Even so, although the worst of the

---

[144] Sydney Synod 1939, 54-5. Cf. Sydney Synod 1934, 265, 280-281. Mowll was gratified by the response. Sydney Synod 1935, 307; 1938, 258.
[145] Sydney Synod 1936, 286.
[146] Sydney Synod 1934, 276.
[147] *SDM*, 1 May 1934, 3-4; 1 June 1934, 3; 27 June 1934, 2-3; 1 January 1935, 2; 1 May 1937, 58-59. Sydney Synod 1934, 272-3, 274, 276, 278-279; 1935, 310-311; 1936, 288, 294-295, 297-298; 1937, 287-290; 1938, 245.
[148] Sydney Synod 1934, 278.

Depression had passed, the need was 'still very great',[149] with seemingly intractable unemployment, poverty and inadequate housing and slums still to confront.[150] Tackling social problems was also a matter of principle and calling. Mindful 'that human nature consists of body as well as soul and spirit', the church was obliged again to follow the example of Jesus and use its resources to care for people in physical and material need.[151] Working out 'the implications of Christ in the social order', Mowll asserted in his fullest pre-war statement on the subject, was also 'for the sake of developing to the greatest extent the grace of charity in our religious life and thereby increasing our effective witness'.[152] Mowll's basic task was to inform the diocese of the facts of the situation, as he did in the *Sydney Diocesan Magazine* and numerous addresses, so that it might come to appreciate and support 'the golden opportunities for advance'.[153] He also encouraged the efforts of parish clergy, particularly the innovations of R B S Hammond, and lent his support to the Social Problem Committee of the Diocese.[154] More directly, he turned his hand to building up the Home Mission Society, the church's chief instrument of social ministry.[155] In his first year in office, Mowll also inaugurated the annual winter appeal for the relief of the unemployed and needy. Critics might decry lack of social action, but under Mowll works of 'Christian love' were promoted as very much a normal part of the

---

[149] Sydney Synod 1934, 273; 1935, 305.
[150] Sydney Synod 1934, 278-9; 1935, 302-5, 309; 1936, 285-9; 1937, 286-7; 1938, 266-7; 1939, 63.
[151] Sydney Synod 1936, 285.
[152] Sydney Synod 1936, 287, 288.
[153] Sydney Synod 1934, 273.
[154] Sydney Synod 1934, 278; 1935, 303-4; 1936, 285, 286-7; 1938, 259. E. Harley-Jones, 'An Epoch-Making Synod,' *SDM*, 1 October 1934, 11 notes the encouragement Mowll gave to the Social Problems Committee to 'bring the claims of the Christian Gospel into industrial and economic life today'.
[155] Sydney Synod 1935, 308-9. On Mowll's leadership of the Home Mission Society, see Anderson, 'The Bishop's Society,' chap. 8.

Church's mission.[156] And Mowll was always troubled by how much was left undone.[157]

The other important aspect of Mowll's social outlook was overt political interest and engagement.[158] In a characteristically Anglican manner, he recognised the necessity of involvement with the state for the effectiveness of the church's work.[159] Naturally Mowll was aware that, under the Constitution of the Commonwealth of Australia, church and state were separated. Equally he understood that the line of separation had always been blurred as both entities accepted the legitimacy of the other and appreciated the social benefits each could bring. This pragmatic relationship was enacted symbolically in the civic reception accorded to Mowll on his arrival, and in the welcomes of the Premier, the Prime Minister and the Governor General.[160] For his part, the ever courteous Mowll was always assiduous in maintaining healthful relations with the officers of state at all levels of government.[161] In this framework he saw the church as a pressure group, well able to influence the public opinion by which governments were influenced.[162] His usual practice was to make known where the church stood on issues of shared concern, and to seek the assistance of the state in matters where the church had a natural interest but lacked the authority and resources to achieve its purposes.[163] In return the church under Mowll worked with the state where possible and gave public support to various public undertakings.[164] However, in three matters he was prepared to take more direct action. Mowll's opposition to state

---

[156] Sydney Synod 1936, 285.

[157] *SDM*, 27 June 1934; 1 June 1935, 122. Sydney Synod 1936, 279; 1937, 292-293, 302-303.

[158] Mowll declared his interest in politics at the outset. 'Civic Reception to Archbishop Mowll,' *ACR*, 22 March 1934, 8.

[159] With 'Education and Moral Regeneration', 'Legislation' was one of the three interrelated realms of making public life. Sydney Synod 1937, 287-8.

[160] Sydney Synod 1934, 265.

[161] Eg. Sydney Synod 1935, 292-3; 1937, 280.

[162] Sydney Synod 1935, 300-301; 1938, 266.

[163] Eg. Sydney Synod 1938, 263-267.

[164] Eg. Sydney Synod, 1935, 302-3, 304-5; 1937, 286-7. *SDM*, 1 February 1937, 3-4; 1 April 1937, 42; 1 May 1937, 59.

aid for Catholic schools strengthened a broader socio-political movement,[165] but his failure after five years of agitation to secure the closing of the Royal Easter Show on Good Friday and end the use of state lotteries to fund public hospitals showed that the church did not always possess the political influence to defeat such competing interests as the Royal Agricultural Society and the State Treasury.[166] While he did not always achieve his objectives, the new archbishop persevered in his responsibility to contend in the public domain for the moral and spiritual interests of the Anglican Church in Sydney.

Conclusion

In August 1938, as Mowll prepared to leave the diocese for the world missionary conference to be held at Tambaram in India, the Standing Committee organised a valedictory in the Sydney Town Hall. Filled to overflowing, presided over by Justice Boyce of the Supreme Court and addressed by the Premier, Bertram Stevens, church and state came together to celebrate Mowll's achievement in almost five years as Archbishop of Sydney.[167] The thunderous applause and praise for his initiative, courage, unprecedented pastoral care for the clergy and moral leadership of 'inestimable' value indicated that doubts about Mowll's appointment had been dispelled, at least among his supporters. For the certitude Mowll brought to Sydney as a traditional evangelical, an Englishman and a convinced Anglican determined to extend the kingdom of God and harvest the benefits of British civilisation had established his leadership, raised morale and set a clear direction for the diocese. In the process he had renovated its organisational and spiritual life and asserted the place of the Church of England in Sydney society in overt evangelism, acts of social service,

---

[165] *SDM*, 1 August 1937, 106-107, 110; 1 October 1937, 138; 1 November 1937, 154-155. On the state aid question, Ben Edwards, *Wasps, Tykes and Ecumaniacs: Aspects of Australian Sectarianism 1945-1981* (Brunswick East, Vic.: Acorn Press, 2008), chap. 10.

[166] On Good Friday, Sydney Synod 1934, 279-280; 1935, 307-308; 1936, 289-292. On state lotteries, Sydney Synod 1935, 300-302; 1936, 288-289, 1939, 61- 62.

[167] 'Valedictory to the Archbishop and Mrs. Mowll,' *SDM*, 1 September 1938, 137-8.

affirmation of the cultural value of the Christian presence and energetic pursuit of moral and spiritual causes. Yet there was an unmistakably defensive tone in the claim that the Town Hall meeting was 'a complete vindication of his Grace's four and a half years of dynamic effort amongst us'.[168] It was directed against those whose concerns about Mowll's appointment seemed to have been justified – the centrist and liberal evangelicals and Anglo-Catholics, and critics of some of his decisions and measures – whose resentment of his authoritarian leadership had recently surfaced. By 1938 the limits of what he could achieve socially and politically were also coming into sharp focus. Even so, by this point Mowll had stamped his character and authority on the diocese and become its dominant figure. The challenges and developments of the two ensuing decades were not so much distractions or deviations from his approach as new settings in which to work out the fundamental commitments and priorities he had established as the new Archbishop of Sydney.

---

[168] 'Valedictory to the Archbishop and Mrs. Mowll,' *SDM*, 1 September 1938, 137.

5. The Wartime Archbishop

Colin Bale

Archbishop Mowll's time in Sydney in the 1930s had not been easy. The war years saw the Archbishop move into clearer water and show his great capacity as a leader. Archbishop Marcus Loane wrote of Mowll's response to the outbreak of war in 1939 as allowing all his strength and abilities to be utilised. Such were Mowll's efforts and plans during the war period that Loane believed the period 'established his (Mowll's) position as a great diocesan bishop'.[1] The authors of *Sydney Anglicans* remarked how Mowll's 'energetic response to demanding situations was best seen during the Second World War'.[2]

Archbishop Mowll, like many people in Australia, watched with concern the events unfolding overseas, particularly in Europe, during the latter 1930s. He penned his thoughts in a pastoral letter published in the October 1939 issue of the *Sydney Diocesan Magazine* about the outbreak of war:

> Up till the last minute our hopes and prayers were that war might be averted. England laboured much and risked much for peace. When the history of the last few years is written the verdict on that point will be unequivocal. Unless this evil thing which is now threatening civilisation is stamped out, freedom and security can never be guaranteed. We have too many proofs of the light breaking of the pledged word...[3]

It is clear from this and other statements made by Archbishop Mowll that he viewed the war against the totalitarian states as justified, indeed necessary. He spoke of the 'unbelievable oppression' which these

---

[1] M. Loane, 'Mowll, Howard West Kilvinton,' *The Australian Dictionary of Evangelical Biography* (Sydney: Evangelical History Association, 1994), 274.
[2] Judd & Cable, *Sydney Anglicans*, 240.
[3] Archbishop's Letter, 26 September 1939, *Sydney Diocesan Magazine*, (cited hereafter as *SDM*), 1 October 1939, 1.

states brought to conquered countries.[4] In April 1940, the Archbishop was adamant about the rightness of the British cause:

> Our virtues are Hitler's vices, and our vices are his most prized virtues ... Kindliness, tolerance, justice, truth – those individual liberties won so hardly and so dearly prized, to him are objects of contempt and pity. His standards are set against ours ... It is a struggle between right – as God gives us to see the right – and wrong. The Christian religion makes it impossible for us on any terms to accept the Nazi conception of life.[5]

Archbishop Mowll was an Englishman and he viewed the Australian population as British and thus morally invested in the conflict occurring in Europe. This is evident in his letter of December 1940, when reflecting on the ability of Britain to win the Battle of Britain and withstand the German bombing of the Blitz he wrote: 'This last year has made us all proud to be British. The experiences of the last six months have been a triumph for the strength and resolution of British character ... our foe is immensely strong and determined and all our reserves of endurance, courage and will-power will be called upon during this coming year'.[6] Mowll's view of the Britishness of Australia was not just some wistful, imperial perspective. Australia was indeed very British and so his perspective was largely accepted. The historian W K Hancock noted in 1930 that the official *Commonwealth Year Book* recorded 98% of Australians, apart from Aboriginal and Torres Strait Islander peoples, as British subjects, either born of British stock in Australia or who were recent British migrants.[7] What is interesting, however, in the Archbishop's pastoral letters in the *Diocesan Magazine* over the war years is a growing sense and awareness of Australian identity. In 1945, he said this in a sermon: 'We have to think of our fighting men of the AIF, who gloriously upheld the traditions of Australia in the Middle East and wrote the epic of Tobruk; the Militia

---

4 Archbishop's Synod Address, reported in *SDM*, 1 November 1939, 5.
5 Archbishop's Letter, *SDM*, 1 April 1940, 2.
6 Archbishop's Letter, *SDM*, 1 January 1941, 1.
7 W. K. Hancock, *Australia* (London: Ernest Benn, 1930), 46. 'British' means the different Anglo-Celtic groups of the British Isles including Ireland.

Forces that endured the swamps and jungles of New Guinea, and held the enemy at bay...'[8]

Archbishop Mowll was also aware of the potential for conflict in the Pacific region, noting the belligerence of Japan in the 1930s, especially in China. He understood that the entry of Japan into the war on the side of Germany and Italy would be extremely difficult for the British Empire and would threaten imperial interests in both the Pacific and Indian Oceans. He addressed the Diocesan Synod about this in 1940:

> We have watched with increasing attention the struggle in the field of diplomacy, by which both parties to this titanic struggle have sought to enlist a great Eastern Power in their interests ... We trust that the wiser counsels which seem to have stayed the hands of Japan on the very eve of a further commitment to warlike enterprise may grow stronger and prevail.[9]

With the outbreak of war, Archbishop Mowll set out what the Diocese of Sydney would do in response to the declaration of war in 1939: 'As Christians we must pray for the victory of the right and the establishment of peace among the nations ... and side by side with the call to prayer is the call to work'. Prayer and supportive activity were the watchwords for him.[10]

Mowll moved quickly to ensure that there were regular times of prayer about the war throughout the diocese. For him, prayer was the primary duty of the clergy and, indeed, of all Christian people, especially at this time of national emergency. A special form of service was devised in September 1939 and distributed widely. Daily services of prayer were arranged at the Cathedral. The Archbishop of Canterbury requested that Sunday 1 October 1939 be set aside as a day of prayer throughout the Empire. Archbishop Mowll was keen to do this and requested that the special form of service that had been devised be used at all churches on that day. In April 1940 Archbishop Mowll proposed another day of

---

[8] *SDM*, October 1945, 4.
[9] Archbishop's Charge to 25th Synod, *SDM*, 1 December 1940, 6.
[10] Archbishop's Letter, *SDM*, 1 October 1939, 1.

prayer throughout the diocese: 'Our first duty is to pray. I propose that Sunday, April 21, shall be another Day of Prayer throughout the Diocese in connection with the war, and I am issuing another Form of Prayer to use on that day and on subsequent occasions'.[11]

There was another Empire-wide day of prayer on 26 May 1940. Again, the Archbishop urged active support of this proposal. He spoke in glowing terms of the response to the call to prayer in his diocesan letter of 29 June 1940: 'May 26 – the King's Day of Prayer – saw the churches crowded out. In many cases worshippers could not gain admission and participated in services while standing in the Church grounds. At the Cathedral hundreds remained standing because the entire seating accommodation was occupied'.[12]

The cathedral, as the archbishop's seat, organised regular services focused on what was called 'War Witness'. The list of services was extensive:

1. *Daily Prayer Services, 12 noon to 2 p.m., Monday to Thursday in each week.*
2. *Monday in each week (5.30 p.m.), prayer by name for the men of the fighting forces of the parishes. Special Commemoration of the men of the fighting forces at the daily services of sung Evening Prayer.*
3. *Tuesday, 3.30 p.m., 6th Division; Wednesday, 3.30 p.m., 7th Division; Thursday, 3.30 p.m., 8th Division; Friday, 3.30 p.m., 9th Division.*
4. *Friday in each week, Day of Continuous Intercession, 7.30 a.m. to 9.30 p.m.*[13]

From 1 April 1940, he requested that the cathedral bell be rung for a minute each day at noon. His reasoning was simple: 'I am asking that all who hear it will pause to pray. I suggest that this should also be done in all our parishes'.[14]

---

[11] Archbishop's Letter, *SDM*, 1 April 1940, 2.
[12] Archbishop's Letter, *SDM*, 1 July 1940, 1.
[13] *SDM*, 1 June 1941, 9.
[14] Archbishop's Letter, *SDM*, 1 April 1940, 2.

Archbishop Mowll was also keen to engage with the other denominations in times of prayer. He seems to have been a keen proponent of these ecumenical prayer meetings. In April 1940 he wrote, 'On Monday, April 22, another United Day of Prayer in connection with the war will be held in the Chapter House, with sessions at 11, 2.30, and at 8, at which I hope many will find it convenient to be present. Leaders of other Churches have promised their co-operation'.[15]

Archbishop Mowll made sure there were special services for triumphs and tragedies as the need arose. In his January 1941 letter, he noted two such services: 'The past month will stand out in Australian history for the victory of the Second AIF at Bardia. This magnificent achievement, which removed the threat to Egypt and the Suez Canal, was celebrated by a Thanksgiving Service at the Cathedral on January 10'.[16] In the same letter he later mentioned another special service: 'On the previous Monday a Memorial Service was held in the Cathedral for the victims of the (German) raiders in the Pacific, and especially for the escorts of the British evacuated children who had perished in the Rangitane'.[17]

On 1 December 1941 came the report on the loss of the HMAS Sydney in an engagement with an enemy raider off the Western Australia coast. It was soon realised that there were no survivors of the 650 officers and ratings on board. Archbishop Mowll was shocked at the news and said that his sympathy went out to those who had been bereaved.[18] A memorial service for those lost on HMAS Sydney was held on 4 December. The cathedral was overcrowded.

Once Japan entered the war in December 1941 on the side of the Axis, and Australian service personnel, notably the men of the 8th Division, became prisoners-of-war, there were regular services to pray for them. On the anniversary each year of the Fall of Singapore (15 February) there was a special service for the relatives of prisoners of war in

---

[15] Archbishop's Letter, *SDM*, 1 April 1940, 2.
[16] Archbishop's Letter, *SDM*, 1 February 1941, 1.
[17] Archbishop's Letter, *SDM*, 1 February 1941, 1.
[18] Archbishop's Letter, *SDM*, 1 January 1942, 1.

Japanese hands. The Archbishop was particularly moved by the heartache of these relatives. In 1944 he wrote, 'While many have received news there are also many who have heard nothing ... I met one mother who had lost both husband and son in the War, and who had not yet had any news of her only surviving son, who, she hoped, might be a prisoner of war in Japanese hands.'[19]

Archbishop Mowll realised that there would be a need for some of the clergy of the diocese to leave parish duties and serve as chaplains in the armed forces. He wrote: 'With the calling up of men to enlist for the duration of the war, special Chaplains must be provided, and I am inviting Clergymen between the ages of 30 and 40, who are physically fit, to offer for this service.'[20] A significant number of clergy accepted his call. As well as calling for suitable clergy to volunteer as chaplains, the Archbishop recognised the need for funds to support them. In the First World War, the Australian government only paid the stipend of chaplains once they departed on overseas service. Assuming this would again be the case, the Archbishop sought the funds needed to support the chaplains.

The Diocesan Magazine often carried accounts from the chaplains about their ministry in the armed forces. Early in April 1940 the Archbishop received letters from two chaplains, Revs F Hulme-Moir and L Swindlehurst, who went with the troops on the first transports (ships) overseas. The letters detailed the different aspects of chaplaincy ministry: 'attendances at Holy Communion, at Bible classes and other services'.[21] These chaplains referred to 'the great number of individual talks with the men' they had, and 'the various personal services' which they rendered to the men.[22]

By March 1942, the Archbishop was reporting that the number of Sydney clergy taking up chaplaincy positions was quite high: twenty-nine full-time and 12 part-time.[23] The greater number of chaplains

---

[19] Archbishop's Letter, *SDM*, 1 March 1944, 4.
[20] Archbishop's Letter, *SDM*, 1 October 1939, 2.
[21] *SDM*, 1 April 1940, 14.
[22] *SDM*, 1 April 1940, 14.
[23] *SDM*, 1 May 1942, 11.

served with either the AIF or the AMF. A number of chaplains served with the RAAF and RAN.

The large number of clergy serving as chaplains meant that there were not sufficient ministers to cover all the parochial positions in the diocese. The Archbishop recognised that this would be the case early in the war and encouraged greater lay participation in parish ministries. In October 1939, he wrote about the extra responsibilities for clergy who were having military training bases either established in their parishes, or where existing bases were increased in size: 'In view of the extra calls which must come to many of them to minister to the military units in their parishes, I hope lay members of the several congregations will be as helpful as they can by helping in the work of the parishes in whatever way possible'.[24]

In the February 1942 issue of the *Sydney Diocesan Magazine*, the Archbishop wrote that 'the greatest and most distinctive contribution' the diocese could make to the nation in this time of conflict was spiritual.[25] He listed three things in particular: 'to minister comfort and spiritual counsel; to carry on the religious education of the young and old, and particularly to encourage the spirit of prayer'.[26] As the Archbishop, he was mindful of the ongoing needs of the parishes, so he added that the war made 'spiritual ministrations in the parishes more necessary than ever. Such ministrations are great national necessities and the adequate discharge of them is a great national duty'.[27]

Evangelism remained a priority for the Archbishop throughout the war years. In his Synod address in 1939, he set this out: 'the present crisis in world affairs offers an opportunity for a vigorous presentation of the old Gospel of man's hopelessness apart from the redeeming power of Christ Jesus our Lord'.[28] The Archbishop noted that many people were ignorant of the Gospel because of increasing secularism and growing

---

[24] Archbishop's Letter, *SDM*, 1 October 1939, 2.
[25] Archbishop's Letter, *SDM*, 6 February 1942, 1.
[26] Archbishop's Letter, *SDM*, 6 February 1942, 1.
[27] Archbishop's Letter, *SDM*, 6 February 1942, 1.
[28] Archbishop's Synod Address, *SDM*, 1 November 1939, 8.

biblical illiteracy.[29] He knew the opportunities that chaplains had as they ministered to service personnel to share the gospel and was keen to see some of these ministry experiences recorded in the *Diocesan Magazine*. One chaplain thoughtfully articulated this:

> You ask me what is a chaplain's job. The day very often begins with 'Reveille' and ends long after lights out...There is tremendous work to be done in the distribution of comforts ... There is, too, the censoring of letters and overseeing of the canteens; the hundred-and-one commissions entrusted to one – little things, many of them, which take a lot of time ... There are the sick and the wounded and the dying to be visited and cheered and helped; above all, one has to remember the reason which brought one here – that men should be led to a saving knowledge of Jesus Christ.[30]

The work in the parishes also had to have an evangelistic focus. In 1944 an Evangelistic Campaign was organised in the Diocese. The Archbishop noted that a number of clergy spoke of the difficulty of getting people along to a week-night evangelistic meeting, so he instructed clergy in October 'to give a course of evangelistic sermons on Sunday evenings'.[31]

At the outbreak of the war, the Archbishop proposed to establish an emergency fund to support the Diocese's efforts in caring for service personnel. Thus, the Church of England National Emergency Fund (CENEF) was created. Its purpose was clear: 'CENEF was brought into being for the purpose of assisting chaplains in ministering to the material and spiritual needs of Servicemen in the Military and Air Force Camps of the Diocese and in catering for those on leave in Sydney'.[32]

---

[29] Archbishop's Synod Address, *SDM*, 1 November 1939, 8.
[30] Rhoda Astles, *The Story of CENEF* (Edgecliff, Sydney: Bilson-Honey Pty Ltd, 1946), 21.
[31] Archbishop's Letter, *SDM*, 1 August 1944, 3.
[32] *5 years of tireless effort for the fighting and auxiliary services: the achievement of the Church of England National Emergency Fund* (Sydney: CENEF, 1944), 1.

It was a mammoth undertaking and needed both money and significant numbers of volunteers to make it work. A women's auxiliary, the Sydney Diocesan Churchwomen's Association (SDCA), was established. Its activities were numerous:

> 1. Canteen work in the various centres. 2. Raising funds for CENEF. 3. Bedmaking in hostels. 4. Donating comforts for chaplains to distribute at home and overseas. 5. Assisting in Citizens' Appeal Days, and making comforts, from material supplied, for the Australian Comforts Fund. 6. Donating groceries for the church canteen. 7. Helping over-pressed clergy in the parishes. 8. Helping to develop the spiritual life and moral standard of the community in the atmosphere of war by the spirit of prayer and by showing friendship to those serving in the Forces and their relatives.[33]

The head of the SDCA was Mrs Mowll and she was tireless in her efforts with the Association. By war's end, SDCA had nearly 9,000 enrolled members and there were 125 parish branches.[34]

Work was quickly underway with CENEF. In August 1940, the Archbishop noted that there were 94 branches of the Sydney Diocesan Churchwomen's Association, with 2356 members. Six huts had been erected in various military camps and in the grounds of St Andrew's Cathedral. A further four huts were planned for other camps.[35] During the war years more accommodation and services were provided. The extent of the work of CENEF is best seen in the table of statistics of services offered during the war years, and some images of the work presented in the *Church of England National Emergency Fund* booklet (see page 102).

Many letters of thanks were received by CENEF from service personnel who benefitted from its ministry. Just three extracts will give an indication of how important this ministry was to many men and

---

[33] Astles, *The Story of CENEF*, 2.
[34] Astles, *The Story of CENEF*, 2.
[35] *SDM*, 1 August 1940, 10.

women in the armed forces. An undated letter from Corporal Thomas Duffield was written to the Secretary, St Andrew's Hut:

> I wish to thank you for the wonderful work you and all your committee and band of wonderful workers are doing for the troops ... I come from South Australia and have never been away before from home, and I felt rather lost until I visited the Church Hut, and it made me feel closer to home to have such beautiful meals and a nice clean bed to sleep in ... May God bless you and reward you for all your work.[36]

The second letter is from Irene Rinkin, a RAAF Aircraftswoman:

> Dear Mrs Dunstan, I am writing these few lines to thank you and your fellow workers for the hospitality and kindness shown me when I stayed at the CENEF at the weekends while in Sydney ... I have found a pal in A C W Dawes who used to stay at CENEF too ... thank you all for everything you did for me, and I only wish I could make you understand how I appreciate all those kindnesses and attention you all gave so cheerfully.[37]

Flight Lieutenant I Edwards wrote,

> On behalf of the officers of this unit I desire to express our sincere thanks and appreciation for the facilities and comfort provided by your organisation. During our short stay in Sydney prior to embarkation for our second turn of tropical service we found the hut a very comfortable convenience; also we met many Service friends, who were also passing through Sydney. Please convey our thanks to the voluntary helpers for their work.[38]

The role of Mrs Mowll in overseeing the work of CENEF, as well as the time she spent in the huts ministering to service personnel,

---

[36] *SDM*, 1 January 1944, 18.
[37] *SDM*, 1 January 1944, 19.
[38] *SDM*, 1 May 1944, 19.

demonstrated her servant leadership of the organisation. She literally impacted thousands of people in this ministry. Stuart Piggin records how at her funeral, one man standing outside the cathedral on the site of the wartime huts, said, 'There are not many in the world like her. Many a time she put her hand on my shoulder and gave encouragement during the war'.[39]

CENEF ACTIVITIES OF S.D.C.A. VOLUNTARY WORKERS.

Number of Meals and Beds Provided, to 31 January 1946.

For Men of the Forces

Meals   **Beds**

St. Andrew's Huts, opened 12/2/1940

Canteen with Recreation, Writing and Rest Rooms

Reorganised as Temporary CENEF Memorial Centre,

19/2/46

3,078,322

Men's Hostel (St. Andrew's Place)

Opened 25/8/42 – Closed 1/5/46

133,433

Reopened for Service and Ex-Servicewomen 1/6/46

Hostel (St Paul's Redfern)

Opened 22/5/43 – Closed 12/2/46

30,000

Hostel (St. John's, Glebe)

Opened 17/8/44

7,726

---

[39] Stuart Piggin, *Evangelical Christianity in Australia: Spirit, Word and World* (Melbourne: Oxford University Press, 1996), 132.

Hostel (Holy Trinity, Miller's Point)

Opened 7/7/45

5,693

For Officers

Cathedral Officers' Hut

Canteen with Recreation, Writing and Rest Rooms

Opened 1/11/45

73,730   -

Hostel (St John's Milson's Point)

3,845

Opened 15/8/44 – Closed 1/4/46

For Men and Women of the Services

CENEF Club, King's Cross

Canteen with Recreation and Writing facilities

Opened 11/6/42 – closed 31/12/45

500,000   -

For Nursing Sisters

Canteen and Hostel (St. Andrew's Place)

Opened 29/11/41 – Reorganised 1/6/46

35,295   17,184

For Women Officers

Canteen and Hostel (St. Philip's, Church Hill)

Opened 4/8/44 – Amalgamated with Nurses' Club

in St. Andrew's Place 1/6/46
15,268   3,023

For Servicewomen

Canteen and Hostel (Lower Chapter House)

Opened 1/9/42 – Sleeping accommodation moved

to Men's Hostel (St. Andrew's Place) 1/6/46
131,162   24,665

For Royal Australian Navy

Opened 28/6/43 – Closed 30/9/46 (St Peter's, Watson's Bay)
106,345   10,940

For R.N. and R.A.F.

Canteen (Mascot Aerodrome) Breakfast and cut lunches

Opened 1/6/45 – Closed 30/9/45
9,947   –

TOTAL
3,950,069   236,509[40]

---

40 Astles, *The Story of CENEF*, 29 – 30.

St. ANDREW'S HUT-CANTEEN

The original Cathedral Hut was opened on 1st February, 1940 by His Excellency Lord Wakehurst K.C.M.G.

The original Cathedral Hut.

The Cathedral Hut Kitchen.

St. Andrew's Cathedral, Sydney, showing the huts erected to provide amenities for service personnel.

Distribution of Comforts at C.E.N.E.F. Office.

St. Andrew's Hut Canteen.

41

---

[41] 5 years of tireless effort for the fighting and auxiliary services: the achievement of the Church of England National Emergency Fund, 4.

SERVICEMEN'S HOSTEL.
The first room was opened on Aug. 25, 1941
by his Excellency Lord Wakehurst, K.C.M.G.

THE NARELLAN HUT.
Opened in October, 1941.

Interior view of the Narellan Hut.

Opening Ceremony of the Narellan Hut.

THIS CLUB FOR NURSES
was opened on November 29th, 1941, by Lieut. General C. G. N. Miles, C.M.G., D.S.O.

C.E.N.E.F. Club for Naval,
Military and Air Force Nurses.

The Dormitory.

42

---

[42] 5 years, 8.

THE C.E.N.E.F. CLUB, KING'S CROSS.
Opened on June 11th, 1942.

In Woolworths Building, Darlinghurst Road.

THE HOSTEL FOR WOMEN OF THE AUXILIARY SERVICES.
Opened on September 1st, 1942, by the Lady Wakehurst.

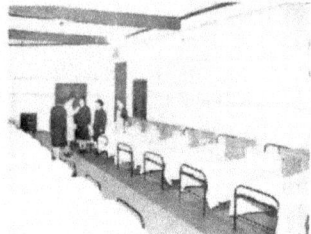

The Dining Room.

The Dormitory.

This Hostel is in the Lower Chapter House.

43

---

[43] 5 years, 12.

Post-war planning

The Archbishop was mindful that while it was right to be preoccupied with the diocese's response to the war, attention was also needed with regard to post-war planning. In his charge to the 1940 Synod, he announced that a survey had been made of the need for new churches/parishes as the city grew and new suburbs were created.[44] In 1940 he launched the Anglican Building Crusade to purchase land and erect buildings in the new suburbs. By 1944, the Archbishop was reporting that seventeen churches had been built since the Crusade began.[45]

He was also mindful that the large-scale demobilisation of service personnel would bring both problems and opportunities for gospel ministry. He wrote:

> We must vigorously prepare for the home-coming of Service men and women... (Citing an American Presbyterian leader) 'Our concern must be that they emerge from their present narrow existence into one of wider interests, sounder judgements and equipped with materials, physical and spiritual, necessary to take on mature roles in a democratic and Christian state.[46]

He continued, 'the god of this world has blinded men's minds ... Now once again we have the opportunity to be shaken out of our ruts'. Into this darkness Christians had to bring 'the sunshine of the Gospel of the glory of Christ.'[47] With more leisure time churches needed to work out how they could occupy this time with useful ministry to the people of the parishes. The Archbishop was particularly concerned that Sunday observance be maintained. Quoting Voltaire, he said, 'If you want to kill Christianity, you must first kill Sunday'.[48] For the physical and spiritual well-being of people, he argued that Sunday must be kept

---

[44] Archbishop's Charge to the 25th Synod, *SDM*, 1 December 1940, 10.
[45] *SDM*, 1 August 1944, 2.
[46] *SDM*, 1 October 1944, 2.
[47] *SDM*, 1 October 1944, 2.
[48] *SDM*, 1 October 1944, 2.

a day of rest: 'There is a real danger that Sunday, the precious heritage of our race, may be a war casualty ... If it ceases to be a day of worship it will not remain for long a day of rest'.[49]

Victory

The news of the end of the war in Europe on 8 May was greeted with great joy in Sydney. The Archbishop reported, 'a large number assembled at the Cathedral for a brief Service of Thanksgiving'.[50] The next day he participated in a United Service of Thanksgiving at the Domain, where he estimated the crowd to be larger than had attended ANZAC Day.[51]

On Victory in the Pacific Day (15 August), a thanksgiving service for the community was held in the Sydney Domain and the Archbishop was the preacher. This was a fitting way for the Archbishop to be acknowledged for his energy, creativity and spiritual leadership throughout the war years. He began his sermon by reminding those assembled that, firstly, they were to remember the goodness of Almighty God, and the two great principles of the Christian faith: 'Service to God and service to man'.[52] He continued by listing those who needed to be thanked for their service. He concluded, 'We must not forget in our thankfulness what we owe to the men and women who, by continued and devoted service, have secured for us a place among the nations and a name still in the world ... To all of these today, and particularly to those who made the Supreme Sacrifice, we tender our grateful thanks'.[53]

Archbishop Mowll's ministry during World War 2 clearly displayed his godly and energetic leadership of the Diocese of Sydney. He prioritised prayer and biblical ministry, and he organised and motivated the diocese to show forth the love of God in the extraordinary ministry to

---

[49] *SDM*, 1 October 1944, 2.
[50] *SDM*, June 1945, 1.
[51] *SDM*, June 1945, 1.
[52] Sermon Preached by Archbishop Mowll at the Sydney Domain, 15 August 1945, *SDM*, 1 October 1945, 4.
[53] Sermon Preached by Archbishop Mowll at the Sydney Domain, 15 August 1945, *SDM*, 1 October 1945, 4.

service personnel through the work of CENEF. His pastoral concern, not only for those experiencing bereavement caused by the war, but also for the many people whose lives had been so disrupted by the conflict, was evident to all. Marcus Loane's summation of Archbishop Mowll's leadership during the war years as showing him to be 'a great diocesan bishop' are more than appropriate.

6. Archbishop Mowll and the Red Book Case

Robert Tong[1]

The topic I have been given is *Archbishop Mowll and the Red Book Case.* This sounds like a title to an Agatha Christie mystery or another Enid Blyton adventure for *The Famous Five.*

There *is* a mystery about the Archbishop's direct connection and involvement with this case. In the Marcus Loane biography of Mowll[2] there is no mention of the Red Book Case. The centenary history of Moore College, by the same author, omits any mention of the case in the chapter dealing with the Principalship of T C Hammond.[3] The *Sydney Diocesan Magazine,* published monthly during Archbishop Mowll's time in office makes no mention of the case either by way of news or in the Archbishop's monthly letter. Mowll's Presidential addresses to the annual sessions of the Sydney synod from 1943 to his death in 1958 make no mention of the case. In the April 1947 number of the *Sydney Diocesan Magazine,* Mowll refers to a meeting of the Provincial Synod as 'a very happy and useful gathering'. Surely not an apt description if there was a court case about to erupt between 'Sydney' and 'Bathurst'!

Before I explore the connection between Mowll and the Red Book Case let me briefly outline the chronology of the case in the courts.

The plaintiff was the Attorney-General for the State of New South Wales, and the defendant was Arnold Lomas Wylde, Bishop of Bathurst, and the Church of England Property Trust Diocese of Bathurst. The Information commencing the case was filed in the Supreme Court on 19 April 1944. The case was heard by Roper CJ in Equity, and occupied seven hearing days in September and October

---

[1] I acknowledge with thanks the assistance of Erin Mollenhauer, Team Leader, Library and Archives, Donald Robinson Library, Moore College and Dr Louise Trott, Sydney Diocesan Archivist, in locating materials for this paper.
[2] Loane, *Archbishop Mowll.*
[3] Loane, *A Centenary History of Moore Theological College.*

1947 with judgment delivered on 17 February 1948 in favour of the plaintiff.[4] Wylde appealed to the Full Court who, by a majority, dismissed the appeal.[5] Wylde then appealed to the High Court of Australia. It took five hearing days in August 1948 and judgment was delivered on 6 December 1948.[6] For some unstated reason, only four justices sat and they were evenly divided. Accordingly, the provisions of the *Judiciary Act* came into play so that the decision of Roper CJ in Equity was affirmed.[7] Wylde agreed to abandon an appeal to the Judicial Committee of the Privy Council.[8] In return the informants accepted a payment for the defendants of nominal costs of £100 and released the defendants from substantial costs orders incurred against them in the Supreme Court and the High Court. The judgement in this case was one strand in the argument in favour of a constitution for the Church of England in Australia.

Now, what was this case about?

And why was the Attorney-General for the State of New South Wales involved? In short, the case reports disclose that the informants were some twenty-three parishioners representing eight parishes in the diocese of Bathurst who objected to the use of a service book, *The Holy Eucharist,* which carried the endorsement of the diocesan bishop. That book reprinted the 1662 Book of Common Prayer service for the administration of the Holy Communion *with additions.* The book had a red cover. The parishioners contended that the additions were not lawfully authorised and thus a breach of the charitable trusts for the use of the land on which the parish church stood. The main instigator of the proceedings was a Canowindra solicitor, Ernest Athol Sharpe.[9]

---

[4] *Attorney-General v Wylde* (1948) 48 State Reports (NSW) 366. Hearing September 23,24,25,30 and October 1,2 and 7.

[5] Sir Fredrick Jordon CJ, Sir Percival Halse Rogers and Mr Justice Nicholas.

[6] *Wylde v Attorney General (NSW)* [1948] HCA 39; 78 Commonwealth Law Reports 224. Hearing August 11 -13, 16 and 17. Latham CJ, and Williams, Rich and Dixon JJ.

[7] *Judiciary Act* 1903 section 23 (2) (a).

[8] See David Galbraith, 'Just enough religion to make us hate: an historico-legal study of the Red Book Case', PhD Thesis; UNSW, 1998, 239ff.

[9] Ruth Teale, "The 'Red Book' Case" *Journal of Religious History* 12/1 (1982): 74–89, 78.

Enforcement of charitable trusts requires the agreement of the Attorney-General and proceedings are mounted in the name of the Attorney-General.

Who were the lawyers?

The plaintiff/informants instructed H. Minton Taylor, a senior partner in the firm of Allen Allen & Hemsley. He briefed H. A. Henry and Clive Teece KC. The defendants instructed R. H. Browning of Roxburgh & Co, who briefed A. B. Kerrigan and F. W. Kitto KC.

What do we know of the events preceding the court hearings?

Ruth Teale says that the Red Book was distributed for use in Bathurst Diocese in Advent 1942.[10] Opposition to its use arose in a number of parishes. The parishioners took their complaint to Archbishop Mowll, in his capacity as Metropolitan of New South Wales.[11] '...because the Bathurst laymen were seeking advice on their ecclesiastical and legal rights (Mowll) referred them to Canon TC Hammond of Moore College.'[12]

Some six months after the introduction of the *Red Book,* a parish meeting in July 1943 at All Saint's Canowindra, considered a letter from T C Hammond critiquing in detail the *Red Book.* Bishop Wylde was not able to answer questions about the use of the *Red Book* to the satisfaction of the objectors. There was further correspondence. Just before Christmas 1943 (21 December), Allen Allen and Hemsley, the solicitors for the informants wrote to Wylde's solicitors:

> May we be permitted, for our own part, to say how much we regret the position which has arisen and how reluctant we are to have to carry out our instructions, but we feel that the position is not of our clients' making, and that they have every justification for taking such action as they deem necessary to protect their rights and the rights of other members of the Church of England in the Diocese. We

---

[10] Teale, "'Red Book Case'," 79.
[11] Teale, "'Red Book Case'," 79.
[12] Judd & Cable, *Sydney Anglicans,* 253.

think it is a tremendous pity that in a time of war a controversy such as this and having such far-reaching effects should be allowed to continue or even to have been initiated. We venture also through you to remind the Bishop that the Church in Australia, after about thirty years of patient effort, seems very near to the adoption of a constitution which makes adequate provision for Prayer Book revision. The work of framing the constitution has been carried out during the long period of time mentioned by the ablest minds of the Church, and the consensus of opinion throughout has been that the Book of Common Prayer contains the only authorised forms of service, and that the same should not be departed from except in consequence of alterations or substitutions authorised by the Church itself in constitutional manner. Everything, therefore, points to the wisdom of the manual being withdrawn throughout the Diocese, and if this is immediately done, then, of course, the Information and Statement of Claim, which is in course of preparation, will not be filed.[13] (emphasis added)

That Mowll was already aware of the Red Book is evident from his 16 June 1944 letter to Wylde:[14]

---

[13] The Rev Canon D J Knox, Rev Gordon J S King, A L Short & F L Hedges, *What is the Red Book? An account of the Bathurst case. Summary of the Proceedings from commencement to September 1945* (Anglican Church League, n.d.), 3.

[14] This letter is Exhibit 6 in the case heard by Roper CJ in Eq, T.C. Hammond *The Bathurst Ritual Case*, 79 and 180. The Sydney Diocesan Archives do not hold copies of correspondence between the Informants and Mowll or between Mowll and Wylde. It is widely thought that Archbishop Mowll left instructions to burn his papers. Archbishop Sir Marcus Loane, Mowll's Executor, states 'It is false to say that "A/b Mowll left instructions to burn his papers". They were burnt – but not on his instructions. Bishop Hilliard as commissary sent Miss Huntley, one of the Archbishops' secretaries, out to Bishopscourt to sort things out. She burnt the papers without advice or supervision.' M.L. Loane 15 August 1998, hand written note in the Diocesan Archives.

My dear Bishop,

I now have had time to read the 'Red Book' and the other papers you sent me in connection with it. if I may say so I think that you would be well advised to withdraw it from use in your Diocese.
Believe me,

Yours sincerely,

Howard Sydney.

Bishop Wylde did not withdraw. At this point Mowll is no longer a part of the printed narrative.

Teale says that Mowll 'referred the aggrieved laymen to the Principal of Moore Theological College,'[15] the redoubtable T C Hammond.[16] Now, if one is to enter the jousting lists then it is imperative to engage the best champion. In Warren Nelson's biography of Hammond there is this instructive passage:

> Such litigation had frequently taken place in England in the second half of the nineteenth century as churchmen tried to resist the intrusions of ritualists and Anglo-Catholics. The shelves of Hammond's study in Dublin had contained bound volumes of the transactions of the Church Association (an Association which Bishop [then Canon] J C Ryle had described as being as necessary to the defence of England as the Army and Navy were). ... The areas of contention were well known: crucifixes and roods, the confessional, altars, the mixed cup, wafer bread and prayers for the dead. Bewildering to even sympathetic non-Anglicans as these things may be, for embattled Anglicans they were the flags and battle markers of a huge attempt to turn back the Reformation. Hammond himself, as we

---

[15] Teale, "'Red Book Case'," 79.
[16] The Rev Canon Thomas Chatterton Hammond, (1877-1961), Principal, Moore College (1936-1953).

have seen, had been embroiled in similar cases in Ireland.[17]

The *Red Book* was literally a book with a red cover, the contents reprinted the Book of Common Prayer service for the Holy Communion with some additions of certain actions and ceremonies. The book also contained a commendation for its use over the name of the Bishop. A similar book was in use in the diocese of Riverina but that book omitted the commendation of the diocesan bishop. The Riverina book was covered in blue cloth. The additional ceremonies provided for the ringing of a sanctus bell at particular points during the service and also for making the sign of the cross at particular points in the service. The Supreme Court of New South Wales held that the additional ceremonies were illegal as they were contrary to the trusts on which the property was held.

Hammond's involvement as the driving force in the litigation is clear. After the case concluded, he published *The Bathurst Ritual Case*,[18] two hundred and sixty-one pages of key documents and transcripts of evidence of some of the witnesses cross-examined before Justice Roper. Hammond wrote the preface and there is no suggestion in that preface that he was conducting this whole exercise on behalf of Archbishop Mowll. However, McIntosh's chapter on Hammond credits Hammond for 'his prosecuting (for Mowll) of the long court case against the Bishop of Bathurst's *Red Book*.'[19] In the time available to me, I have not been able to locate documentary evidence that Hammond was directed by Mowll.

The most comprehensive study of the Red Book Case is Galbraith's PhD thesis[20] followed by Teale's journal article referred to earlier. Both are sound starting points for further examination of the case. However,

---

[17] Warren Nelson, *T. C. Hammond: Irish Christian* (Edinburgh: Banner of Truth, 1994), 114.

[18] *The Bathurst Ritual Case,* with preface by T. C. Hammond (Sydney: George Dash, n.d.).

[19] John A. McIntosh, *Anglican Evangelicalism in Sydney 1897 to 1953* (Eugene: Wipf & Stock, 2018), 267.

[20] Galbraith, 'Just enough religion to make us hate'

both are written from a firmly held Anglo-Catholic perspective. Subsequent authors draw on the Teale account.[21]

The wider context

It would be remiss not to place this five-year episode of the Red Book Case in its wider context. The Allens letter of December 1943 places this controversy 'in a time of war'. By December 1943 in Europe, the 'Dam Busters' had conducted their raid (May 1943), the Allies had retaken North Africa and the famous Australian Ninth Division was on its way home to defend us from the Japanese. Closer to home, Pearl Harbour (December 1941), the fall of Hong Kong (December 1941), the sinking of the Royal Navy capital ships *Repulse* and *Prince of Wales* (December 1941), the fall of Singapore (February 1942), had all happened. The light cruiser HMAS Perth was lost in the battle of Sunda Strait (1 March 1942) where the casualties included the ship's chaplain, the Rev Ronald Bevington, an Englishman who was a licenced clergy man in the diocese of Sydney.[22] Now in January 1943, Army Intelligence Officer Donald Robinson was able to attend a church service with Padre Marcus Loane in Port Moresby.[23] By May, Loane's unit was assigned to Wau to join with the Americans in repelling the Japanese. Loane ministered to the wounded and buried the dead, as he trudged over the Bulldog Track a dozen times or more. So much for 1943.

You will recall that Roper CJ heard the case in September and October 1947. Before judgement was delivered in February 1948, Mowll had left Sydney on 16 December 1947, for the five-week Lambeth

---

[21] Judd and Cable, *Sydney Anglicans*, 253-255; Geoffrey Treloar, 'T. C. Hammond the controversialist', *Anglican Historical Society Journal* 51/1 (2006): 20-35.

[22] On Bevington, see Stuart Piggin & Robert Linder *Attending to the National Soul, Evangelical Christians in Australian History 1914-2014* (Clayton: Monash University Publishing, 2020), 196. Bevington's fiancée was Sheila Nicholson who later married Dr John Knox the brother of Broughton Knox. Dr Catherine Hamlin AC was one of Sheila's sisters. For the Diocese of Sydney World War 2 Military Chaplains, see the list in the 1947 Year Book for the Diocese, 136 - 7.

[23] Allan M Blanch, *From Strength to Strength, A life of Marcus Loane* (North Melbourne: Australian Scholarly Publishing, 2015), 75.

Conference to be held in London starting in July 1948. The Archbishop and Mrs Mowll journeyed first to East Africa where he preached and visited missionaries. The journey continued through the Congo to West Africa and then onto England. Lambeth was followed by the first Assembly of the World Council of Churches in Amsterdam. The Mowlls returned to Sydney by flying boat on 26 October 1948. They had missed a coal strike and bitter winter in June.

In this context why should a court skirmish over churchmanship occupy front of mind for the Archbishop of Sydney?

Post script

Teale suggests two reasons for the antagonism between Sydney and the country dioceses of the province of New South Wales. First, when the original diocese of Australia was divided:

> The country dioceses justly felt that they had been inadequately endowed (in buildings and clergy retaining state stipends) at the time of their separation from Sydney; they bemoaned the way in which the Sydney Diocese had appropriated the Moore Estate, left originally to the Diocese of Australia but used as the foundation endowment of the College that bears that name.[24]

Secondly, differences in churchmanship became embedded in the various dioceses in the first half of the 20th century. Relationships varied between 'strained' and animosity. However, when Sir Marcus Loane became Archbishop of Sydney (1966) and later Primate (1978), he was determined to rebuild relationships throughout Australia and particularly with the other New South Wales bishops. As part of this he initiated grants of $25,000 to Riverina and Bathurst:

> The money would be a gift from the funds of the Endowment of the See to the endowment funds of those two dioceses. When the Endowment was established in 1855, the Diocese of Sydney had within its boundaries the areas that became the dioceses of Riverina and Bathurst.

---

[24] Teale, "'Red Book Case'," 85.

Loane saw it as a matter of principle that a proportion of the Sydney funds should be shared in the way he proposed. He saw it as right and fair. So did the synod. Not only did it pass the proposed ordinance but amended it to provide gifts of $25,000 each to the endowment funds of two additional dioceses, Armidale and Grafton.[25]

Loane initiated two further gifts for the same amount to the four dioceses in 1980 and 1981.[26] Archbishop Robinson in 1990 initiated grants of $100,000 to the four dioceses.[27]

By February 2018 the dire financial position of the diocese of Bathurst led the godly gospel-minded Bishop Ian Palmer to meet with Archbishop Davies to talk frankly about the situation, knowing that the Diocese of Bathurst would be unable to fund his successor. A plan was developed. The overriding concern was not to see the demise of Anglican ministry in western NSW. Bishop Barker's vision was to see the gospel expand and grow, with churches committed to Christ and proclaiming Christ in fellowship with their bishop. It was suggested and agreed that if the Diocese of Bathurst were willing to elect a new bishop, with the approval of the Metropolitan, then this would be a tangible expression of partnership between the two dioceses. Both Diocesan Synods endorsed a plan where the Diocese of Sydney will provide $250,000pa to fund the episcopal and registry functions of the Bathurst Diocese for a period of 6 years. Originally, when Bathurst was separated from Sydney in 1870, Bishop Barker was able to secure the nomination of Samuel Edward Marsden, the grandson of the great Samuel Marsden who was 'resolutely' evangelical.[28] With the election of the Rev Mark Calder as Bishop of Bathurst in 2019, 'resolutely evangelical', episcopal leadership has returned.

---

[25] Blanch, *From Strength to Strength*, 303-4. Sydney Synod Ordinance 50 of 1978.
[26] Ordinance 38 of 1980 and Ordinance 19 of 1981
[27] Ordinance 41 of 1990. Robinson by Ordinance 35 of 1988 made grants of $25,000 to the dioceses of North West Australia, Northern Territory, and Carpentaria.
[28] Judd & Cable, *Sydney Anglicans*, 85.

7. Archbishop Mowll and Moore College

Mark D Thompson

When Howard West Kilvinton Mowll arrived in Sydney on 1 March 1934, the principal of Moore Theological College, David John Davies, was recovering from surgery. Davies' health was in serious decline. A month later he would take six months recuperative leave in the UK and in a little over a year he would be dead. The health of its principal was, however, not the most serious challenge the college was experiencing as the new Archbishop arrived. Opposition to the liberal-evangelical tenor of Davies' theology had grown in recent years. Enrolments were weak. In March 1934, there were eighteen resident students and fourteen non-resident. The college library was also close to disarray, an impediment to study which further exacerbated the growing disquiet. The college buildings were in need of significant renovation. To cap it all, the college was once again in debt and its overdraft was growing. To some, the future of Moore College was beginning to look uncertain.

Janet West's library lecture on Davies is subtitled 'A principal embattled'. She portrays him as a godly and principled man who was opposed by powerful laymen on the Moore College Committee.[1] No doubt he was a godly man and his pastoral concern for his students is clear from the testimonial plaque affixed to the student residence shortly after his death. However, uneasiness about Davies and his theology was evident much wider than simply among a small cabal within the Committee. Concern was voiced both in the diocese and in the college itself. Marcus Loane later wrote that 'the Diocese was split from top to bottom over questions of Modernism' so that there was 'a dreadfully low state of things by the end of the twenties'.[2] Davies was opposed by some of his own students. One was Stephen Bradley, later

---

[1] J. West, 'David John Davies—A Principal Embattled' (Unpublished Moore College Library Lecture, 1988, held in the Moore College library).

[2] M.L. Loane, letter to the Rev. John A. McIntosh, March 1994. Cited in Blanch, *From Strength to Strength*, 18.

to become Presiding Bishop in the Church of England in South Africa. He wrote of how the bishop coadjutor of Sydney, Sydney Kirkby, asked him to go to Moore College since 'its principal and staff were definitely liberal and not at all in tune with the Sydney Diocese and he wanted someone to resist from inside'. Another of those students, arriving at Moore a little later than Bradley, was Marcus Loane. They and a few others gathered to pray that 'either [the principal] should change his attitude towards the "faith once committed to the saints", or he should resign'.[3] Other students rallied around Davies in support, resulting in a palpable and unpleasant divide in the student body.

Mowll's plan to transform the college

Howard Mowll knew that his theological college was in trouble even before RMS Orford steamed through the heads of Sydney Harbour. News had already reached him about the fragility of the college and correspondence with him in the months prior to his arrival had raised significant questions about its leadership and direction. He attended his first meeting of the college committee later that month (March 1934). Only two months later, he was able to inform the committee that he had lunched at the college twice, was thoroughly dissatisfied with the food, but more importantly was 'anxious to raise the whole tone and standard of the College and its training'.[4] In his first Presidential Address to a Sydney synod, delivered on 10 September 1934, while Davies was still on his way back from the UK, he made clear his intention: 'With respect to Moore College itself, I trust that before long we may be able to rebuild the College, transforming it into what it should be, in view of the great purpose it is designed to serve'.[5] The report of the Moore College committee to the synod that year commented that '[s]ince the arrival of His Grace the Archbishop he has shown great interest in the College, which he has visited on several occasions and has presided at every meeting of the Committee'.[6] But

---

[3] S. Bradley, *The Great Adventure* (Clareinch, South Africa: Church of England in South Africa, 2016), 33. West, 'Davies', 16–18.
[4] Loane, *A Centenary History of Moore College*, 136.
[5] *Year Book of the Diocese of Sydney 1935*, 274.
[6] *Year Book of the Diocese of Sydney 1935*, 375.

when he spoke to the synod about 'transformation', was Mowll simply talking about the plant and the finances?

After all, the new Archbishop was no stranger to theological education. Immediately after completing his own theological study, he had served for the best part of ten years as a member of the faculty of Wycliffe College in Toronto, Canada from October 1913 until May 1922 (with a few months leave in which he served as a chaplain on the western front in 1918). He had tutored in patristic theology, served as Professor of History, developed and taught a course of training in evangelism, ran missions and was tireless in taking up opportunities to teach in various parts of Canada on behalf of the college, and served as Dean of Residence. He had been mentored in the early days at Wycliffe by Professor W H Griffith Thomas, who had been Principal of Wycliffe Hall in Oxford for five years before moving to Toronto in 1910 (he had also been a nominee for Archbishop of Sydney in 1909). Mowll would characteristically downplay his own intellectual ability, but he was a graduate of King's College and Ridley Hall, Cambridge and had been awarded honorary doctorates from Cambridge (1922), Wycliffe College (1923), and Emmanuel College, Saskatoon (1931). He had a clear view of theological education which was uncompromisingly orthodox and evangelical, and embraced the highest academic standards without surrendering a focus on pastoral ministry, evangelism and global mission.

The more significant concerns Mowll had for Moore College in those early years made it into the daily papers. In December that year *The Sun* reported on 'A New Policy for Moore College':

> Soon after his arrival in Sydney, Archbishop Mowll made it clear that he realised the urgent need that the ministers of the Church should be well equipped intellectually and educationally. In order to secure a high level of ability in clergy of the Diocese, says 'Church Times', the Archbishop is introducing the principle that a matriculation pass will be required of all students entering Moore College and a

University degree for all seeking ordination. The policy of the college will be shaped accordingly from now on.[7]

It is sometimes suggested that it was T C Hammond, Davies' successor, who spearheaded the raising of academic standards at Moore College. There is a great deal of truth in this. However, the evidence suggests that Mowll himself was more involved than is often realised. Even before Hammond was appointed, while Davies was still recovering in England, Mowll had set about his plan. His first presidential address outlined the strategy: 'We must never rest content until the general standard for our men is a theological course following upon a University degree. As a first step towards reaching this goal the rule should be enforced that no man is to be admitted to Moore College until he has passed the University Matriculation Examination.'[8] Undoubtedly it was under his direction that throughout 1934 the college committee rejected a number of applicants who had not attained matriculation.

In the short term, this new policy put further pressure on enrolment numbers. There were only five new students when the academic year began on 8 March 1935, with a total of twelve resident on the campus and fifteen others who were not in residence. The resultant financial constraints meant the vice-principalship was left vacant, following the resignation of George Corrie Glanville in mid-1934 (he had been passed over twice as acting principal during the principal's illness – first for Arthur Wade, Rector of St James' Croydon, and then, when Wade was injured, for William Hilliard, the Headmaster of Trinity Grammar School – he understandably took this as a vote of no confidence). The old house was closed down. The principal took a reduced stipend and had to supplement his income by marking leaving certificate examination papers.[9] A man who was seriously ill was being further worn down by the situation in which he served.

---

[7] The Sun (Sunday 2 December 1934), 26.
[8] *Year Book of the Diocese of Sydney 1935*, 274.
[9] Loane, *Centenary History*, 137–8.

Meanwhile the Archbishop appointed the newly ordained Marcus Loane as resident tutor and chaplain at the College. On a number of counts this was a strange appointment. It is difficult to imagine that Mowll was unaware of Loane's experience of the College under Davies. Indeed, Loane himself knew that Davies would not welcome his appointment to the staff.[10] Furthermore, Loane had not served in a parish and the Archbishop was concerned the College prepare men for parish ministry. However, the Archbishop was determined and, despite objections from Loane himself along these lines, made the appointment. The writing was on the wall. Mowll was going to ensure the transformation he desired.

Archdeacon Davies attended the College Committee meeting on 21 June 1935, suffered a heart attack the next day, and died in Royal Prince Alfred Hospital on 29 June. It was a tragedy which drew a large outpouring of sympathy, even from those who had voiced their concerns about Davies' principalship. In his letter for the *Sydney Diocesan Magazine* dated 1 August 1935, Archbishop Mowll spoke of how Davies had 'given himself unstintingly to the work of the Diocese, the Christian Church in Sydney, and the Masonic fraternity'.[11] A very large number of friends and fellow students attended his funeral in the cathedral. Tragic though Davies' death obviously was, it did give Mowll an opportunity to realise further his plans for transforming the college. He once again appointed Arthur Wade as Acting Principal.

The concentrated attention given to the college at this moment meant that its dire condition became more widely known. In his presidential address to the Synod on 23 September 1935 Mowll remarked,

> The death of Archdeacon Davies and the desire to find the best possible man as his successor has made the financial position of Moore College a matter of specially [sic] anxious concern. There is an overdraft of £5,000 and the building needs to be rebuilt, or extensively repaired. A new

---

[10] Blanch, *Strength*, 55.
[11] *Sydney Diocesan Magazine* (cited hereafter as *SDM*), 1 August 1935, 170.

Chapel is needed and more adequate financial provision for the staff.[12]

The Archbishop's plan to secure the college's future involved the amalgamation of Moore College with the parish of St Philip's Sydney (York Street). The property in Newtown would be sold, the new principal would become simultaneously the rector of St Philip's church, and plans would be drawn up to rebuild the college on the block of land surrounding the church. This would provide better facilities and a more stable flow of income. It might even make it easier to secure the services of the right person to be the next principal.

The amalgamation ordinance and the sale ordinance were both introduced in the first week of the 1935 synod. The amalgamation ordinance was passed in the second week but the sale ordinance was not. Apparently, an impassioned speech by Herbert Langley Tress, one of the trustees, scuttled the idea. Mowll himself spoke in the debate, a tactic which somewhat backfired. As a result, the responsibilities for the parish of St Philip's and those of the principal of Moore College would be combined, but their properties would not. In the years to follow the wisdom of that decision would become clear.

Appointing his first principal

Mowll's plan for the transformation of the college also involved the appointment of a scholar with unambiguously clear evangelical convictions as its principal. He was in perfect agreement with the committee, which reported to the synod in September 1935 that 'the future of the College largely depends on the man selected as Principal'.[13] The Rev Thomas Chatterton Hammond was suggested to him. There is no evidence that Mowll and Hammond had met previously (at least none that I have been able to access), but Hammond had visited Sydney in 1926 in the midst of the Prayer Book controversy. During that visit, he had impressed leading evangelicals in the city with his ability to defend the Protestant character of the Church of England. No doubt he appealed to the same people who had been vitally

---

[12] *Year Book of the Diocese of Sydney 1936*, 311.
[13] *Year Book of the Diocese of Sydney 1936*, 450.

concerned about the theological direction of the college only a year before. Hammond was the General Secretary of the Irish Church Missions, and though at 58 years of age he would be the oldest man appointed to the office of principal (then or since), he had an international reputation as a fiercely intelligent evangelist, apologist and theologian. The standing committee of the diocese was informed at its October meeting that a nomination for the principalship had been made (just three months after Davies' death), but the appointment was not announced until 20 November. The *Sydney Morning Herald* reported the appointment on 26 November with the comment, 'Mr Hammond has the reputation of being a brilliant philosophical and theological scholar, and is a good preacher'.[14] The paper reported that Hammond accepted the appointment by cablegram on 5 December.[15] He took up his responsibilities as principal and rector in Sydney on 14 April 1936, arriving onboard the very same ship which had carried the Archbishop two years before. (In another delightful convergence, Hammond had been farewelled at Portsmouth by Arthur Lukyn Williams, who had been principal of Moore College from 1878 until 1884, when it was located on what had been Thomas Moore's property at Liverpool, prior to its relocation in Newtown.)

The appointment of T. C. Hammond as principal of Moore College was not without controversy. He was not everybody's first choice. He had a reputation as a strident Protestant, an effective controversialist and a bit of a 'street fighter', but what experience did he have as a theological educator? More concerning to some, would he introduce a more aggressive form of conservative evangelicalism, in stark contrast to the moderation and tolerance of a variety of views that had characterised the tenure of his predecessor? Contributors to *The Outlook,* 'a small paper with a private circulation among some of the Sydney clergy', voiced just this concern: '[U]nless he is less intractable than on his former visit, his success will come only through the withdrawal of many liberal minded men from all matters outside their own

---

[14] *Sydney Morning Herald* (Tuesday 26 November 1935), 10.
[15] *Sydney Morning Herald* (Friday 6 December 1935), 12.

parishes'.[16] Yet, as the Archbishop pointed out, Hammond was also a man of undeniable intellectual ability. Mowll introduced the new principal at the 1936 synod as 'the first Gold Medallist of the University of Dublin' and 'an outstanding teacher'.[17] Earlier in the year, at his official welcome on 14 April, Hammond himself had been more circumspect: 'There is no more important duty in the world than the training of men for the sacred ministry of the Gospel. There is no field of study so extensive, with so many ramifications, as the field of theology, and, in a humble way, I trust I may be able to bring some contribution to the great cause we have at heart'.[18]

Pursuing the highest academic standards

Mowll himself might have watched carefully during those early months, aware of the concerns raised by Hammond's reputation as a polemicist. However, he remained undeterred from his plan to transform the college 'into what it should be'. He soon discovered that Hammond was equally determined to move things in the same direction. The Archbishop presided over the Moore College committee meeting in August 1936 when it was agreed to extend the college course from two to three years, two years studying towards the ThL and a third year of special studies. It is clear that Hammond was enthusiastic about this development, and may indeed have been the initiator of it – he was certainly the one who brought the proposal before the committee – but given he was at that time only four months into the role, it seems reasonable that Mowll was also heavily involved.

This consistent push towards a higher academic standard faced an early test with a proposal from one of Mowll's own strong supporters, the rector of Gladesville, the Rev D J Knox. In the same month in which Mowll began his ministry as Archbishop, Mariam Annette Grant executed a trust deed by means of which she transferred to the Church of England Property Trust of the Diocese of Sydney her property at 106

---

[16] *The Outlook,* March 1936. Cited in W. Nelson, *T. C. Hammond: His Life and Legacy in Ireland and Australia* (Edinburgh: Banner of Truth, 1994), 101.
[17] *Year Book of the Diocese of Sydney 1937,* 297.
[18] *Sydney Morning Herald* (Wednesday 15 April 1936), 12.

Georges River Road, Croydon Park. In that trust deed she renamed the property But-Har-Gra after her parents and both of her husbands.[19] The property was to be held 'solely for charitable purposes for and in connection with the Church of England in the Diocese of Sydney as shall from time to time be determined by the Archbishop of Sydney for the time being and by the Standing Committee for the time being of the Synod of the Diocese of Sydney'. In November 1937 Mowll wrote to Knox to suggest the latter's dream of a Bible school, which would provide an alternative route to Moore College for those who had not the opportunity to matriculate, might be realised through this property. A month later the Moore College committee resolved to establish such a school. Plans were made to open on 12 March 1938, but at the eleventh hour T. C. Hammond insisted that those who completed the Bible school course would still need to matriculate. He was supported, and perhaps much more than supported in this, by Archbishop Mowll, who, after all, only four years earlier had introduced the matriculation requirement. Mowll wrote to the Diocese on 1 March that 'the Moore College Committee has reaffirmed the decision that matriculation is the normal standard for entrance to the College' and that only in exceptional circumstances might the course at But-Har-Gra Bible School serve as alternative to matriculation.[20] He was not going to allow the Bible School to become a way of watering down the advances made in the academic standards at Moore College. In the end, Knox backed away from the honorary principalship, which was taken up by Archdeacon Wade, and the School opened with five students as planned. The Archbishop explained to the diocese that the Bible school was designed for educating church workers rather than the clergy.[21] It was closed in 1943 when the property was repurposed as a hostel for women students during the war.[22]

---

[19] John and Mary Button, Captain Frank Hart, and Captain C. Hamilton Grant.

[20] *SDM* 1 March 1938, 35.

[21] *SDM* 1 March 1938, 35.

[22] The aftermath of the But-Har-Gra affair was ongoing distrust of T. C. Hammond on the part D. J. Knox, who felt Hammond had gone back on his word. This also affected Marcus Loane, who regarded himself as protégé of

A fascinating brief footnote to this continuing concern to maintain a high academic standard alongside a gospel ministry focus, can be found in Archbishop Mowll's address ten years later to the Anglican Church Congress in Melbourne, which he attended as a representative of CMS. In it he reported on the previous day's discussion at the Australian College of Theology.

> Yesterday, for instance, at the meeting of the Australian College of Theology, we were discussing a resolution that Greek should be no longer a compulsory subject for Th.L. I thought of a request which I received from the Principal of a Javanese Theological College, after the outbreak of war, that I would send him half a dozen Hebrew grammars from Sydney, because he could no longer obtain them in Holland.[23]

The juxtaposition of those two discussions, one with an Australian institution seeking to make theological studies more accessible by lowering academic standards and the other with a college struggling in much more adverse conditions that remained resolute in their determination to teach the biblical languages, spoke for itself. 'We must have a world outlook or perish', Mowll continued. The evangelisation of the world — 'evangelise or perish' — went hand in hand with rigorous and rich biblical training.

Knox's, and Knox's son D. B. Knox (later Principal of Moore), who had applied to enter Moore College in 1938 but withdrew in the wake of this incident and would subsequently study theology in St John's Highbury, London. M. L. Loane, 'Memories' (unpublished memoir, 2004), 76–8 cited in Blanch, *Strength,* 68. M. Cameron, *An Enigmatic Life: David Broughton Knox, Father of Contemporary Sydney Anglicanism* (Brunswick East, Vic: Acorn, 2006), 48–9. The letters between D. J. Knox and Archbishop Mowll from this time (held in the Samuel Marsden Archives at Moore College) testify to a strained but unbroken relationship between the two in the wake of this incident.
[23] H. W. K. Mowll, 'Address, Anglican Church Congress, Melbourne, November 19, 1947', reprinted in *Seeing All the World: A Study of Christian Missions Today. The Moorhouse Lectures, 1947* (Melbourne: Ruskin Press, 1947), 109.

Mowll now had in place the first of the three principals he would have the opportunity to appoint. He had secured the matriculation standard for entry into the college and overseen a general uplift in its academic standards. In May 1939, the college reported to the diocese that there were 22 students studying for the ThL, 6 more studying divinity in the university, and 8 accepted for entrance in the following year. 'This affords gratifying evidence that the decision to raise educational standards is meeting with success'. Yet the author of that report, writing in the Archbishop's magazine, could also remark: 'A great deal remains to be done in order to make the premier theological college in Australia worthy of its position and of the Diocese of Sydney'.[24]

The physical renovation of the college

Next, an appeal was launched for the renovation of the college buildings. The lecture hall had been extended at the end of Hammond's first year in office (1936).[25] In his presidential address to the 1937 synod, the archbishop declared 'I shall not rest content until we have a new block of students' rooms and sufficient bursaries to enable all the men in the College to be free from Catechists duties so that they may be able to concentrate wholly on their studies'.[26] At the beginning of the next year (1938), he announced that the college committee was now engaged in modernizing the existing bedrooms. He invited parishes to contribute the cost of a room and to have a brass tablet commemorating that fact affixed to its door.[27] By the end of the year the fabric of the college had been transformed and the Archbishop could report to the synod that 'the whole standard of the College work has been raised' and 'the time is more than ripe for us to set our hands seriously to the task of erecting additional buildings'.[28]

In July 1937, the Archbishop and the college committee had appointed Rev Sid Stewart, rector of St Andrews Roseville, as Honorary

---

[24] *SDM*, 1 May 1939, 10.
[25] Loane, *Centenary History*, 141.
[26] *Year Book of the Diocese of Sydney 1938*, 296.
[27] *SDM*, 1 January 1938, 5.
[28] *Year Book of the Diocese of Sydney 1939*, 253.

Organising Secretary and he began the task of raising the necessary funds. He spearheaded the appeals which enabled the renovation of the existing buildings. He advertised an appeal targeting £3000 to build a new chapel to replace the original Broughton Chapel, then crumbling due to faulty foundations. However, in August 1942 the college committee received news of an extraordinary gift for the entire sum. The Rev Frank Cash, rector of Christ Church Lavender Bay and Assistant Registrar of the Australian College of Theology, provided the money to build a new chapel in memory of his son John Francis, who had died in an air battle over the Mediterranean a year before. Over the next few years more money would be added by the Cash family and others who had lost loved ones in the war and the design evolved into a grand small-scale replica of the chapel at King's College, Cambridge. Before it was completed, work began on constructing several new wings of student accommodation. The first, with room for 14 extra students, was opened in June 1944 and a second, accommodating a further 15 students, in April 1948.[29] The Governor-General opened the John Francis Cash Memorial Chapel on 20 November 1950 and the third and final wing, accommodating a further 21 students was opened in March 1953. This new wing incorporated elements of the old and now redundant Broughton Chapel.[30] This was the same month that T C Hammond informed the Archbishop of his intention to retire from the principalship.

Financial provision

Resetting the theological direction, raising the academic standards, and renovating the plant – each of these was accomplished or well underway within the first five years of Mowll's time as Archbishop. The remaining task was running down the college debt and establishing the financial provision for needy students. The Archbishop kept drawing these needs to the attention of the diocese in his monthly newsletter, which listed those who had contributed to the Moore College Appeal. An annual Embertide Appeal was instituted for the

---

[29] *Sydney Morning Herald,* Saturday 17 June 1944, 5; Saturday 10 April 1948, 10.
[30] *Sydney Morning Herald,* Saturday 29 March 1952, 5.

training of men for the ministry at Moore College. By the end of the Second World War, what had been a £5000 debt when Hammond arrived had been whittled down to £207. However, the cost of building would soon turn the figures red again. In 1952 Mowll would tell the synod that 'the financial situation of the College is one of growing concern to Church people'. He mooted the idea of an annual parochial assessment to provide for the training of students.[31]

In retrospect, Mowll's appointment of Hammond was a masterstroke. It marked a turning point in the college's history and set a trajectory upon which successive principals would build. More widely, Mowll came to rely particularly heavily upon Hammond, especially in controversial matters. The Principal acted as his chief theological advisor at the time of the Memorialist controversy (1938), the Red Book Case (1947), and the dispute over clerical vestments (1949). No doubt partially in recognition of this contribution, Hammond was made an Archdeacon without territorial jurisdiction in 1949. However, Mowll continued a lively interest in the college, which he saw as integral to his larger strategy of strengthening and growing evangelical Christian ministry within and beyond the diocese. The student body had trebled in size over the period of Hammond's principalship: from 27 (of whom only 12 were resident in the college) in the year prior to his appointment (1935) to 80 (all resident) in the year of his retirement (1953).[32]

Appointing his second principal: M L Loane

By the end of Hammond's time as principal, the Archbishop's vision for the College had been largely realised. The question now became how to build on that strong foundation for the future. The retirement of T. C. Hammond as principal in 1953, though the 76-year-old continued to serve as rector of St Philip's, provided an opportunity to move the College forward into the next stage of its life. The ordinance which combined the principalship with the ministry at St Philip's was repealed and Hammond's successor would be freed to devote his time

---

[31] *Year Book of the Diocese of Sydney 1953*, 48.
[32] *Sydney Morning Herald*, Saturday 20 September 1952, 6.

exclusively to the leadership of the college, at least in theory. However, the question of just who this should be remained. Mowll took his time. Marcus Loane, the vice-principal, seemed an obvious choice. Yet the Archbishop, now 63 years old himself, was at the same time considering what to do about the need for an additional assistant bishop for the diocese. He approached Loane with a choice. He could become a bishop and continue as vice-principal, or he could be appointed principal. Loane thought the first proposal was in practice unworkable and was keenly aware of the need for continuity in the College staff. After all, the staff would be seriously depleted in the next year, since not only was Hammond retiring, but Alan Cole had indicated he would leave in the new year to serve in South-East Asia, Herbert Minn had gone overseas to study for a doctorate, and Broughton Knox had not yet returned from Oxford after completing his.[33] He opted for the second proposal, to take up the principalship, but still the Archbishop seemed to linger. At last, in October, he announced that Canon Marcus Loane would become principal of Moore College at the beginning of 1954.[34] Sadly, with the loss of all the Archbishop's private papers, we may never know 'the full story of the appointment', something Loane alluded to in a letter to his friend Bishop Alf Stanway, then serving in Central Tanganyika, on 6 December.[35] What is clear is that Loane was a widely popular choice for the role.

Just as intriguing at this point was the appointment of the vice-principal to replace Loane. Once again, the details would seem lost to us. However, it does not seem that the new principal was the one who was responsible for the appointment. He told Stanway in January of the next year that his preferred choice would have been Harry Bates.[36] In the end the Archbishop appointed Broughton Knox. Knox's appointment created a level of anxiety for a number of people. Alan

[33] Loane, 'Memories', 41, cited in Blanch, *Strength,* 120.
[34] *Sydney Morning Herald,* Monday 26 February 1953, 5.
[35] Blanch, *Strength,* 122.
[36] M. L. Loane, 'Letter to Bishop A. Stanway, 17 January 1954', cited in Blanch, *Strength,* 124.

Blanch has suggested that Hammond's unhappiness at the transition may well have been in large part because of Knox's appointment. He had had experience of Knox as a member of the faculty from February 1947 until he had left for doctoral studies in November 1949. Even as a junior member of the Faculty, he peppered the principal and the college committee with suggestions for improvement. The minutes of the committee record a seemingly never-ending series of letters from Mr Knox with his proposals. These proposals ranged over academic matters, the state of the library, administrative procedures, student finances, and the process for selecting appropriate candidates for ordination. Knox was energetic, full of ideas, confident and determined. He had a vision of the college that he seemed to be pursuing even at this early stage. Marcus Loane had been acting principal during T C Hammond's leave in the second half of 1947 and 1948 and so had been the direct recipient of much of this. Perhaps this lies behind his comment to Stanway as he took up his new responsibilities: 'What I am afraid of is that he [Knox] will try to push his policies in ways which will be very much for my discomfort'.[37] And then there was the other factor: Broughton Knox was, after all, Marcus' brother-in-law.

There is no evidence that Mowll's interest in the college abated during the principalship of Marcus Loane, despite being increasingly occupied with national and international matters as Primate (he had been elected Primate in 1948). There seemed to be an almost endless round of meetings and reports relating to a proposed new constitution for the Church of England in Australia and quite a few overseas trips. Yet the archbishop still chaired every meeting of the college committee and its executive when he was in Sydney. He sponsored the various appeals for funds for the college. In his presidential address to the 1955 synod, he expressed his desire for the further expansion of the college: 'We must press forward in providing adequate endowments for the salaries [sic] of lecturers and for research scholarships, so that the ablest students may continue at the College, after the completion of their

---

[37] M. L. Loane, 'Letter to Bishop A. Stanway, 17 January 1954', cited in Blanch, *Strength*, 124.

ordinand's course, in order to read for higher degrees'.[38] He supported the move to establish an annual assessment on the parishes of the diocese to provide for the training of men for the ministry in 1957. A year earlier, he had been heavily involved in the college's centenary celebrations and led the procession from St Luke's church to Thomas Moore's grave progressing to the original site of the College.[39]

However, it soon became clear that Archbishop Mowll had not given up on his plan to appoint Marcus Loane as a bishop-coadjutor. In the end, Loane's tenure as principal would be one of the shortest, four years from the beginning of 1954 until the end of 1958.[40] Mowll had come to rely on Loane more and more as the decade wore on, even though his workload was already heavy enough as principal of the college. But the Archbishop's own workload was massive and he was increasingly occupied with caring for Mrs Mowll, who had first fallen ill in 1954, but whose condition had rapidly deteriorated in 1957. She died on 23 December that year. In the midst of this great loss, Mowll approached Loane once again on the subject of taking up the office of bishop-coadjutor alongside Bishops Hilliard and Kerle. Amid the Archbishop's profound grief, it would have been near impossible to deny him. The plan was that in the short term Loane would continue as principal of the college while beginning to exercise responsibility as a bishop. He would continue to live at Newtown and the bulk of his teaching load would be taken up by Alan Cole, who had recently returned from the UK and who had preached the synod sermon in 1957 (he would also preach at Loane's consecration). Loane wrote to Stanway

---

[38] *Year Book of the Diocese of Sydney 1956*, 45.

[39] *Year Book of the Diocese of Sydney 1957*, 50.

[40] Only one previous principal had a shorter time in office, Thomas Hill who was removed by the Trustees after only just over three years as Principal (September 1883 – November 1888). Loane, *Centenary History*, 61–71; N. Hubbard, 'Thomas Ernest Hill: Principal of Moore College 1885–8' (Unpublished paper read before the Church of England Historical Society, 3 July 1980).

in January 1958 that 'the Archbishop would like to appoint Alan to succeed me'.[41]

Appointing his third principal: D B Knox

Much, perhaps too much, has been made of Mowll's original intention of appointing Alan Cole. Certainly Cole had a very great deal to commend him. He was an outstanding scholar, an engaging preacher, thoroughly committed to a godly personal ministry and the importance of a theological college's priority of preparing pastors. What is more, he, like Mowll, had served as a missionary in Asia. But Cole was determined to return to the mission field and declined Mowll's suggestion. The next obvious choice was the vice-principal, Broughton Knox. However, Knox had been somewhat of a thorn in the Archbishop's side during the constitutional debates (as had his fellow faculty member Donald Robinson) and he had made powerful enemies.[42] He had recently been the subject of a vicious and somewhat scurrilous attack by the Central Churchman's Movement prior to the 1957 synod, which described him as 'one of the hereditary High Priests of the Central Executive of the Party' (the Anglican Church League).[43] His determined reformed and evangelical theology was viewed with horror by some. Dean Eric Pitt would later write to the Archbishop of Canterbury suggesting that 'the appointment of Dr Broughton Knox to the Principalship of Moore was the most tragic mistake Archbp. Mowll made'.[44] So it might have been obvious, but it was also seen as a

---

[41] M. L. Loane, 'Letter to Bishop A. Stanway' (20 January 1958) cited in Blanch, *Strength*, 155.

[42] In the 1957 Sydney Synod Knox had made two attempts to have the *Book of Common Prayer* and the *Thirty-nine Articles* included in the Fundamental Declarations of the Constitution in order the reinforce the Protestant character of the denomination. Cameron, *Knox*, 165–6.

[43] The Four Just Men, *The Background to Synod. A confidential guide to candidates for election, their party allegiance and qualifications, for the private information of members of the Synod of the Diocese of Sydney* (Sydney: Hermitage Press, 1957), 17. Cited in Cameron, *Knox*, 154.

[44] E. Pitt to G. Fisher, 14 November 1960, *Correspondence and Papers of Archbishop Fisher* (London: Lambeth Palace Archives), vol. 235, p. 168. Cited in Cameron, *Knox*, 162. In the next month, Pitt would write to Fisher again

controversial choice. Yet precisely because this was the case, Mowll's decision to appoint him needs to be understood as considered and deliberate. He knew what he was doing. He made the appointment in the face of strong arguments to the contrary from significant people. What is more, when the time came for the decision, the trustees were unanimous and they received a 'hearty concurrence in its choice' from the college committee (and even Dean Pitt, himself a member of the Committee did not oppose the appointment).[45] There was enthusiasm for the appointment as well as reserve. As it happened, this was the last appointment Archbishop Mowll was to make before his death on 24 October. His death, less than two weeks before the 1958 synod (which opened on 3 November) meant his largely finished presidential address, was read to the Synod by Bishop Hilliard. In it he reported,

> The appointment of the Vice-Principal, Dr D. Broughton Knox, to succeed Bishop Loane as Principal of Moore College will take effect at the end of the year. Dr Knox has served on the staff of the College since 1946. More recently, as Vice-Principal, his lectures on Theology have greatly impressed those who have heard them, and show the fruit of his preparation at Cambridge and at Oxford, and in Sydney. At a time when the College is showing great expansion, it is fortunate to have a man who knows the College and its needs well, and whose theological learning has already made a deep impression. He is popular with both staff and students.[46]

These are hardly the remarks of a man who felt compelled to make the appointment against his better judgment or as a last resort.

---

insisting 'I am sure we must get rid of Dr Knox and Robinson from Moore College, which is the key to our problem'. E. Pitt to G. Fisher, 2 December 1960 cited in Cameron, *Knox*, 167. But then in the same letter he describes T. C. Hammond as 'the former principal and a great trial to any Liberal thought'.
[45] 'Minutes of Special Meeting of the Committee of Moore College, 9 October 1958 (held in the Samuel Marsden Archives at Moore College, among the Knox papers). Cited in Cameron, *Knox*, 163.
[46] *Year Book of the Diocese of Sydney 1959*, 226.

The Knox appointment was Mowll's last great gift to Moore College. Of course, he could hardly have known how long or significant Knox's term as principal would be. In what would be two tumultuous decades of rapid social change, Knox would be responsible for building the college into a place with an international reputation for a thoroughly biblical and richly theological training for Christian ministry, and for a persistent, even dogged, determination to assess all thought and practice in line with the teaching of the Bible. He refused to play intellectual rigour, pastoral effectiveness and even personal piety off against each other, and, as students of those days continue to testify, 'we were taught how to think biblically not just what to think in order to conform to systems or institutions'.[47] He shaped the modern Moore College and, in very large part, the Diocese of Sydney.

Mowll's lasting legacy

When Howard Mowll arrived in Sydney the situation at Moore College was precarious. Some wondered whether it would survive. It had lost the confidence of many of the clergy of the diocese and even its own students. At the end of his time as Archbishop the college had healthy enrolments, a strong young faculty, and strong academic standards. The college had been transformed: physically, theologically, and even spiritually. It was playing a crucial role deepening and strengthening Christian witness in the city. Mowll did not achieve this alone, of course. Yet it could not have been done without his continuous support and his wisdom in a number of critical appointments. In Marcus Loane's assessment, few institutions in the diocese 'could have owed more to [Archbishop Mowll's] energy and his enterprise than Moore College'.[48] Almost a century after his arrival, it is fitting that we remind ourselves of the contribution which, under God, he was able to make.

---

[47] This comment comes from conversations with a number of alumni from the year of 1960 during a gathering at Moore College in February 2020.
[48] Loane, *Archbishop Mowll*, 216.

8. Howard Mowll and the Church of England in South Africa[1]

Mark Earngey

Introduction

The story of South African Anglicanism has been told many times by ecclesiastical historians. The central elements of the narrative include the controversial modernism of Bishop John Colenso of Natal that led to the first Lambeth Conference in 1867, the controversial determination of Bishop Robert Gray of Cape Town that led to the independently constituted Church of the Province of South Africa (CPSA) in 1870, and the controversial dedication of a small group of evangelical Anglican churches which refused to join Bishop Gray's Church and remained loyal to the Church of England. This group of churches became known as the Church of England in South Africa (CESA) and according to the standard historiography its champion in the mid-twentieth century was the Archbishop of Sydney, Howard W K Mowll (1890-1958).[2] The best accounts of the relationship between Archbishop Mowll and the then struggling denomination come from the pens of Anthony Ive and Rev Peter Spartalis, both active members of their respective CESA and Sydney Anglican churches.[3] Their works

---

[1] I am indebted to Andrew Atherstone, Mark Thompson, Stephen Judd, and Jake Griesel, for their proofreading and commentary on this essay.

[2] The CESA was renamed REACH-SA in 2013 but due to the historical period under consideration this essay will refer to the denomination as the CESA.

[3] Anthony Ive, *A Candle Burns: The Story of the Church of England in South Africa* (Natal: Kohler Carton & Print, 1992), 101-102. Peter J. Spartalis, "From Silvertrees to Lambeth: the Australian Connection and the Church of England in South Africa, 1933-1948" (MTh. Thesis, Australian College of Theology, 1990). See also: Cameron, *Phenomenal Sydney,* 41; Stuart Piggin, 'Australian Anglicanism in a Worldwide Context', in Bruce Kaye (ed.), *Anglicanism in Australia: A History* (Carlton South: Melbourne University Publishing, 2002), 213–16; Colin Buchanan, *Historical Dictionary of Anglicanism* (Maryland: Rowman & Lichfield, 2015), 423 and *The A to Z of Anglicanism* (Plymouth: Scarecrow Press, 2009), 433. It is intriguing to note the relative silence

articulate the major contours of Mowll's efforts to support the CESA, and Spartalis provides an excellent account of the many challenges facing the Archbishop who was torn between his ecclesiastical responsibilities within Australia and his evangelical sympathies abroad. Indeed, both of these works underscore the importance of Howard Mowll to the story of South African Anglicanism.

Yet significant sources containing the correspondence related to Mowll and the South African story have been hitherto unexamined. This has resulted in an historical record which cannot adequately account for statements such as CESA Registrar D G Mills to Principal Marcus Loane of Moore College on 2 February 1959, that 'Mowll became our active enemy.'[4] Similarly, the current consensus cannot be easily squared with Marcus Loane's comment to CESA's Stephen Bradley on 17 February 1959 that 'I cannot be a party to anyone who insists on describing our late Archbishop as an 'enemy''.[5] These unexamined and strong statements do not map easily onto the received history of Mowll and the CESA. But nor should they be treated only in isolation and mislead us into a wholesale inversion of the narrative. Rather, they suggest that there are surprising elements of the story about the relationship between Howard Mowll and the CESA which need to be told. Thus, this essay attempts to revise moderately the received account of Mowll's relationship with the CESA, thereby shedding new light on his support of the church and illuminating his significance in the context of twentieth-century global Anglicanism.

Cambridge, Canada, China, and the Cause of CESA

'I came in contact by correspondence with several of the Church of England congregations in South Africa through their generous

---

concerning the CESA in Loane, *Archbishop Mowll,* and the absence of mention of the CESA in Marcus Loane's entry for Howard Mowll in Brian Dickey (ed.), *The Australian Dictionary of Evangelical Biography* (Sydney: Evangelical History Association, 1994).

[4] Mills to Loane, 2 February 1959. "Archbishop's Office, Correspondence Overseas, CESA", 1990/43/9, Sydney Diocesan Archives (referred to hereafter as SDA).

[5] Loane to Bradley, 17 February 1959. "Archbishop's Office, Correspondence Overseas, CESA", 1990/43/9, SDA.

contributions, through CMS, to the work in western China.' So wrote Archbishop Mowll to Bishop Francis Batty of Newcastle, New South Wales, on 10 December 1942. This comment came within a tense interchange between the two Australian bishops related to the chief concern of the CESA, which was to secure a bishop for their church. Without episcopal oversight, the CESA was unable to ordain clergy, confirm candidates, provide effective oversight for their geographically and ethnically diverse churches, and most critically, be recognised as a legitimate Anglican church within an Anglican Communion increasingly tethered to the Lambeth Conference. In the same letter to Bishop Batty, Mowll declared, 'I have always felt, from my knowledge of the facts, that this ostracism of these Church of England congregations has been one of the most regrettable episodes in our Church history of recent years, and apparently a lamentable exhibition of bigotry on the part of the Church in South Africa.'[6]

Though his first contact with the embattled CESA occurred in Western China, Howard Mowll's 'knowledge of the facts' most likely began many years before in England. His familiarity with fighting for the evangelical cause began in Cambridge with his association with the Cambridge Inter-Collegiate Christian Union (CICCU) and its watershed controversy on the authority of the Bible and the desired breadth of evangelicalism. Fred Morris was the President during the controversy and Howard Mowll succeeded him in taking up the cudgels for conservative evangelicalism. Morris would later liken the CICCU struggle to that facing the CESA: 'The Archbishop of Sydney is an old friend of mine from Cambridge days when we were associated in a somewhat similar struggle to prevent the CICCU from being suppressed by the Student Movement. The glorious result of that struggle and of Howard Mowll's presidency of the CICCU, was the gradual emergence of the IVF which is doing such fine work in the world to-day.'[7] Mowll served as President of the CICCU for a record five terms between 1911-12. During this time he may have formed a

[6] Mowll to Batty, 10 December 1942. "Archbishop's Office, Correspondence Overseas, CESA", 1990/43/9, SDA.
[7] Morris to Robinson, 18 June 1955. Peter Spartalis Papers, 096/1/1-1, Moore Theological College.

friendship with William 'Cairo' Bradley, whose beach missions and evangelistic events he would later encourage in Sydney, and whose son Stephen he would later encourage in ministry.[8] But the most important connection Mowll made at the time was with the Church of England's leading evangelical churchman who would soon play a pivotal role in his support of the CESA.

Edmund Arbuthnott Knox (1847-1939), Bishop of Manchester, was according to Sir Marcus Loane, 'undoubtedly the most influential leader of the Evangelical party in the Church of England for a generation after the death of John Charles Ryle.'[9] Knox ordained Howard Mowll to the diaconate in Manchester on 21 September 1913 and remained a constant source of affection and advice to the future Archbishop, such that Spartalis described him as Mowll's 'mentor'.[10] On 1 October 1913, Mowll sailed for Canada to serve as a tutor on the faculty of Wycliffe College in Toronto. Here he developed friendships with Anglican clergyman and scholar W H Griffith Thomas, influential evangelical rector of St. Paul's on Bloor Street, H J Cody, and Ellen Knox who was sister to Bishop Edmund. On 7 June 1914 Mowll was ordained to the priesthood in Canterbury in England, and over the course of the next tumultuous decade served as an Army Chaplain in Abbeville in France between 1918-1919 in addition to his increasing responsibilities at Wycliffe College. In the middle of June 1922 Howard Mowll was nominated as suffragan bishop for Western China, and on 24 June that year he was consecrated at Westminster Abbey by Archbishop Davidson, with his recently retired friend Bishop Knox joining in the laying on of hands.

---

[8] As recounted by Stephen Bradley to Hugh Gough, 10 October 1961. "Archbishop's Office, Correspondence Overseas, CESA", 1992/26/74, SDA.
[8] Morris to Robinson, 18 June 1955. Peter Spartalis Papers, 096/1/1-1, Moore Theological College.
[9] Loane, *Makers of Our Heritage*, 140.
[10] Spartalis, "From Silvertrees", 174. Knox also assisted in Mowll's consecration in Westminster Abbey on 24 June 1922.

Edmund Knox was also a determined supporter of the CESA, and his retirement in 1920 meant he was more able to support its cause.[11] On 16 November 1928, he wrote to his friend and CESA clergyman, Rev Norman Bennett: 'I believe it to have been and still to be grievously wronged. If by any act of mine I could restore it to communion with our Church, I would perform that act'.[12] In addition to correspondence with colleagues in support of the CESA, Knox wrote regularly in defence of the CESA in the *Church Record* and the *Argus*. Spartalis observes that he became the president of a small organisation known as the Church of England in South Africa Aid Society, and that despite being in his eighties, 'undertook during the remainder of his life to advise the CESA as to how they could secure their own bishop'.[13] Among the various other members of the CESA Aid Society, two are of particular relevance: the Irish evangelist and theologian, Thomas Chatterton Hammond and Howard Mowll.[14] The latter is especially important, for in 1936, Knox advised Bennett to play the 'Australian card' and appeal to the recently enthroned Archbishop of Sydney for advice on a suitable bishop and the possibility of pursuing a publicity campaign for the CESA.[15] This advice was evidently appreciated, for fifteen years later Bennett sent Mowll a copy of his book *In Search of the Truth: A History of the Church of England in South Africa,* with the personally handwritten note on the inside of the cover: 'To the Archbishop of Sydney in grateful acknowledgement of all the help he

---

[11] It is an intriguing coincidence that the first CESA synod, held on 10 February 1938, was organised by one Mrs. Arbuthnot, whose surname bears a striking coincidence to the unusual middle name of Edmund Knox.

[12] Quoted in Spartalis, "From Silvertrees", 30.

[13] Spartalis, "From Silvertrees", 30. The CESA Aid Society is sometimes referred to as the "CESA Defence Committee". It is uncertain whether the "Church of England Defence Association" which was formed in Natal in the nineteenth century is associated with this group. However, the CESA Aid Society is not to be confused with the "Church of England Defence Association" groups in Canada and Australia, nor the Birmingham Church of England Defence Association, nor the very significant Church Association based in England.

[14] Spartalis, "From Silvertrees", 89

[15] Spartalis, "From Silvertrees", 84, 86.

has given in guiding the destiny of the Church of England in South Africa.'[16]

Enthronement, Early Support, and Ensuing Struggle

On 13 March 1934, Howard Mowll was enthroned before a crowded congregation in the Cathedral of St. Andrew in Sydney. Shortly thereafter, in November 1935, T C Hammond was appointed Principal of Moore Theological College, Sydney and also rector of the nearby parish of St Phillip in York Street. In the same year, Mowll received a letter from Norman Bennett asking for a young clergyman to assist the CESA Zulu missions in Natal. Stephen Bradley, son of the celebrated evangelist William 'Cairo' Bradley, became aware of this missionary opportunity, and spent several months working under Hammond at St Phillip's before sailing for Durban in 1936. Bradley would later remember this missionary endeavour as being 'invited' or 'sent' by Mowll to South Africa.[17] Some caution is required here, for historians have sometimes been overly hasty in describing Bradley's missionary move in similar terms.[18] As Marcus Loane wrote to Stuart Barton Babbage when commenting on Peter Spartalis' thesis in 1990, 'This is an exaggeration; there was no 'request', though Stephen Bradley always liked to say that Archbishop Mowll had 'sent' him. The Archbishop suggested his name and encouraged him to accept, but that was all. Bradley was never responsible to the Archbishop nor answerable to the Diocese of Sydney. But he and others always liked to think and talk as though he had the official Diocesan backing.'[19] Confirmation of the substance of this defensive comment can be found in Howard Mowll's own hand. In a letter to him on 9 August 1952,

[16] Norman Bennett, *In Search of Truth: A History of the Church of England in South Africa* (Salisbury, Rhodesia: Norman Bennett, n.d. [1951]). The presentation copy of this book is located at "Documents Relating to the Church of England in South Africa", AU-MTC-334-1, Moore Theological College.

[17] Stephen Bradley, "Cameos: Memories concerning the CESA". Peter Spartalis Papers, 096/1/1-1, Moore Theological College.

[18] Spartalis, "From Silvertrees", 174; Ive, *Candle,* 102; Judd and Cable, *Sydney Anglicans,* 221.

[19] Loane to Babbage, 20 October 1990. Peter Spartalis Papers, 096/1/1-15, Moore Theological College.

Mills wrote, 'That man, having been sent by Your Grace.' Archbishop Mowll penned firmly in the margin, 'No His [sic] own suggestion'.[20] None of this detracts from Bradley's extraordinarily successful ministry in South Africa, nor does it discount Mowll's agency in bringing the CESA opportunity before him. But it does indicate that Bradley's missionary move ought to be attributed more to his own efforts rather than flowing from diocesan deputation or the archiepiscopal authority of Howard Mowll.

The most significant act of support for the CESA from Mowll came the following year. On 24 August 1937 Archbishop Mowll penned a letter containing detailed advice on establishing a legal constitution for the CESA churches. It was addressed to Rev Norman Bennett of the CESA and was also forwarded to Canadian Bishop of Saskatchewan George Lloyd.[21] 'I have taken the advice of some able legal friends', wrote Mowll, 'and the following solution seems to them and to me the best in all the circumstances.' In general, the solution advised the calling of a convention for the congregations to frame a constitution, the securing of an enabling Act of Parliament to give the CESA congregation a solid basis as a corporate body, and an appeal to the Archbishop of Canterbury to secure a bishop. In particular, the solution advised that certain details ought to be articulated in the constitution: that the members of the convention have always been members of the 'Mother Church', that they adhere to the doctrine of the *Thirty-nine Articles of Religion* and worship according to the *Book of Common Prayer*, a declaration of their lack of episcopal oversight and its corollaries concerning confirmation and ordination, and mention of the importance of a training school for future clergy. Mowll also noted that the appeal to Canterbury should point out that the supply of another bishop need not imply 'schism'. Rather, he suggested that the Greek Uniate church and the dual episcopal economies in Antioch should serve as their example. Towards the end of the letter, and probably to the disapproval of the CESA, Mowll suggested that a

---

[20] Mills to Mowll, 9 August 1952. "Archbishop's Office, Correspondence Overseas, CESA", 1990/43/7, SDA.
[21] Mowll to Bennett, 24 August 1937, cited in Peter Spartalis, "From Silvertrees", 95-96.

financial compromise with the CPSA over the Cape Town church property might facilitate the granting of the appeal. Finally, Mowll mentioned that should the appeal not be successful, this constitution would, nevertheless, put the CESA in a stronger position for future efforts to secure a bishop.

As with the Bradley historiography, so too does the CESA constitutional history require some untangling. Spartalis correctly observes that Ive mistakenly believed that Mowll himself prepared the draft constitution that the CESA afterwards studied, approved, and adopted in 1938.[22] In fact, Mowll sent detailed advice *for* a constitution, which detailed advice came from 'some able legal friends'. This advice was then studied by the CESA leadership before they drafted their constitution and afterwards approved and adopted it in 1938. However, Spartalis is on shakier ground with his assertion (following Judd and Cable) that the 'committee's leading members' included renowned Sydney canon lawyer H Minton Taylor and T C Hammond. The aforementioned letter from Loane to Babbage explains the matter: 'Archbishop Mowll did not 'arrange for a committee in Sydney to draft a constitution' for the C.E.S.A. [p. 97]; what he did was done in a private capacity – he enlisted the help of Mr H.R. Minton Taylor and T.C. Hammond to prepare a draft.'[23] In other words, the language of 'committee' tends to overemphasise the number of those who advised Mowll. The two 'able legal friends' to which Mowll referred were simply the lawyer Taylor and theologian Hammond.

Nevertheless, Loane's emphasis on Mowll's activity as being in his 'private capacity' needs some clarification. Loane intended to ensure that Mowll's procurement of legal advice was not misunderstood as an official act on behalf of the diocese of Sydney. However, the provision of this procured advice within the letter to Bennett needs to be understood in line with the formal signature Mowll used in his correspondence: 'Howard Sydney'. Furthermore, it ought to be understood in line with the plural pronoun used by Archdeacon

---

[22] Spartalis, "From Silvertrees", 97; Ive, *Candle,* 102.
[23] Loane to Babbage, 096/1/1-15, Peter Spartalis Papers, Moore Theological College.

142

Samuel Johnstone in his capacity as Registrar for the Diocese of Sydney in a letter to Bishop Lloyd of Saskatchewan: '... we have been trying to give the South African people every possible help over the training of Ordination candidates, etc. advising over a constitution...'[24] Thus, whereas Loane correctly states that the procurement of advice was done in Mowll's 'private capacity', it is also correct that the provision of the advice to the CESA issued from the efforts and public offices of some of the leading churchmen of the diocese.

This historiographical nuancing of Mowll's role reflects the delicate church politics in which he found himself embroiled shortly after sending off his letter of advice. On 11 February 1938, three leading members of the CESA (Rev E. W. Lasbrey, Rev Alan Ewbank, and D. G. Mills) sent a letter to the Archbishop of Canterbury, Cosmo Lang, which included their newly minted constitution and requested that he consecrate a bishop for the oversight of their churches. Within a month later, Archbishop Lang replied to Lasbrey and firmly declined their request: 'This in my judgment would be simply to recognise and perpetuate a state of schism between the Church of the Province and 'The Church of England in South Africa'. I thus, cannot consecrate, consent to a consecration, or even recognise the CESA as coming under my metropolitical jurisdiction.'[25] On 11 May Mills forwarded the rejection letter to Mowll, who on 20 May replied, 'I am very sorry indeed to note its contents.' Perhaps with a sense of the great challenges ahead, Mowll added: 'The issues are so far-reaching that I must take time to weigh them up and will let you hear further as soon as I am able to do so.'[26]

---

[24] Johnstone to Lloyd, 20 December 1940. "Archbishop's Office, Correspondence Overseas, CESA", 1992/26/73, SDA. Johnstone speaks in the third person about Mowll in the following sentence so in this instance he is not writing as Mowll's personal secretary. I am grateful to Robert Tong for his discussion about the work of the Registrar in relation to the Archbishop.
[25] Lang to Lasbrey, 9 March 1938. "Archbishop's Correspondence, Church of England in South Africa", 90/43/10, SDA.
[26] Mowll to Mills, 20 June 1938. "Archbishop's Correspondence, Church of England in South Africa", 90/43/10, SDA.

The Search for a Bishop Begins

Three days later, an urgent letter from Ewbank arrived on the desk of Mowll. Hearing that Mowll's upcoming overseas travel plans included a short visit to Canada, and conscious of the supportive stance of the Canadian evangelicals, Ewbank suggested that 'Australia, Canada, and South Africa meet and help the last named by consecrating me, South Africa's chosen representative.'[27] Mowll replied on 22 July with great caution, noting that any decision 'may have serious repercussions around the Anglican communion' and that he was not prepared for any consecrations while in Canada, but was looking forward to their opportunity for consultation.[28] After some further thought, Mowll wrote to his old friend from Toronto, Dr Cody and briefed him on the situation. This letter, dated 25 July, reflects an important nuance in Mowll's stance towards the CESA. He was cautious about the proposal to consecrate a new bishop but wondered whether Bishop John Renison of Athabasca might be willing to 'go out to South Africa to be in charge of one of these Churches and able to ordain and consecrate.' On the one hand, Mowll felt that consecrating a new bishop would have 'very big repercussions' and yet on the other hand that 'we cannot leave these congregations to their fate.'[29]

Mowll sailed for Canada on 1 September 1938 and spent three days among his old friends in Toronto. A conference was held at Wycliffe College and, in addition to Alan Ewbank, consisted of Howard Mowll, Dr Cody, Prebendary Hinde of London (Principal of Oak Hill College), and Archdeacon Johnstone of Sydney. While the group was supportive of the CESA cause, they were resolute in their opinion not to consecrate Ewbank, nevertheless providing some advice for how to encourage the CESA in their circumstances. Leaving his old stomping ground, Mowll travelled onwards to England, Edinburgh, and then to the Tambaram Conference in Colombo, before returning to Australian shores on 23

---

[27] Ewbank to Mowll, 23 June 1938. "Archbishop's Correspondence, Church of England in South Africa", 90/43/10, SDA.
[28] Mowll to Ewbank, 22 July 1938. "Archbishop's Correspondence, Church of England in South Africa", 90/43/10, SDA.
[29] Mowll to Cody, 25 July 1938. "Archbishop's Correspondence, Church of England in South Africa", 90/43/10, SDA.

February 1939. Upon arrival, he opened a confidential letter from Archbishop Cosmo Lang dated 21 January. In what might be termed a rather 'passive-aggressive' tone, the Archbishop of Canterbury shared his awareness of a rumour that Mowll was considering the consecration of Ewbank, 'one of the clergy attached to the dissident Congregations in South Africa'. 'I cannot suppose for a moment', Lang continued, 'that you would entertain any such suggestion as of course it would involve a most serious breach of order within the Anglican Communion.' Superciliously stating that Mowll's being 'far away in Sydney' may mean he lacked the facts of the matter, the Archbishop concluded: 'I do not use the word 'guidance' because I am quite certain that even if there is any substance in the rumour concerning Mr Ewbank there can be no possibility of your acceding to his suggestion about a separate bishop for these Congregations.'[30]

The rumour which sparked this letter from Cosmo Lang was passed on to him by the General Secretary of the CMS, Prebendary W William Cash. Though a definite evangelical, Cash evidently opposed the idea of consecrating a bishop for the CESA. Thus he informed Canterbury with the promise that he could verify 'that the matter is indubitably in the mind of the Archbishop of Sydney' and other bishops too.[31] In addition to the letter to Mowll, Archbishop Lang calculated that correspondence with the Primate of Australia, Archbishop Henry Le Fanu of Perth would be illuminating. He suggested to Le Fanu that 'if the necessity arose … you might be able to prevent the Bishops of Australia committing an act of real hostility to the CPSA and creating a definite schism within the Anglican Communion.'[32] Le Fanu replied on 17 April with a denigration of Mowll's churchmanship ("Mowll is not so much a low churchman but not a churchman at all") and a promise to write to all the bishops in Australia who he believed would unanimously protest against such a consecration.[33]

---

[30] Lang to Mowll, 21 January 1939. "Archbishop's Correspondence, Church of England in South Africa", 90/43/10, SDA.
[31] Cited in Spartalis, "From Silvertrees", 109.
[32] Cited in Spartalis, "From Silvertrees", 109.
[33] Cited in Spartalis, "From Silvertrees", 109.

Mowll, though unaware of this primatial backchannelling, did not roll over for the Archbishop of Canterbury. He replied on 14 April and relayed his concurrence concerning an amicable arrangement for the CPSA and CESA. 'Now that you have so kindly directed my attention afresh to the problem', wrote Mowll, perhaps with barbed intention, 'I am making the most careful enquiries into the whole situation'.[34] In fact, Mowll had been already doing much more than that. Writing to Mills on 22 April, Mowll reiterated his cautiousness about the proposal of consecrating a bishop for the CESA (Mills had actually asked for two). However, Mowll also revealed to Mills what he had advised Ewbank while in Canada:

> ... to take every means of uniting the members of the Church of England congregations together, by means of visits and a magazine enabling them to know more about each other; to have a regular form of service for recognising those who are fully prepared and are ready and desirous of being confirmed so that they are admitted to Holy Communion in an orderly way, and thirdly if need be to send candidates to Moore College where they can be trained for the ministry. If you can only afford to pay their passage money they would have to serve in the Diocese of Sydney for the number of years which their training covered as in the case of candidates from New Zealand and elsewhere. By this means your immediate needs as members of the Church would be met and the chairman of your conference would really exercise all episcopal functions save ordination and confirmation.

> Archdeacon Johnstone has cabled you about an invitation coming from you to send two of our leading Clergy to hold Missions and to strengthen by fellowship the ties between us. I hope that this may be possible. I have also asked the Archdeacon as a result of information which you have sent him and which he collected on my behalf in Canada and

---

[34] Mowll to Lang, 14 April 1939. "Archbishop's Correspondence, Church of England in South Africa", 90/43/10, SDA.

England to draw up a statement which will convince the lay mind of the need of your congregations to have a Bishop.[35]

Clearly, Mowll cared deeply for the situation of the CESA and sought to see them flourish as much as possible in the absence of episcopal oversight. He also knew how sensitive such support was, and asked Mills not to publish the letter; it was fine to discuss its contents, 'but only as possible lines of action without direct reference to the fact that any proposals have emanated from me.'

On the same day as he sent his letter to Mills, Mowll also wrote to Sir Thomas W K Inskip, a leading evangelical churchman and politician recently promoted to Secretary of State for Dominions.[36] Mowll had met with Inskip at the House of Commons during his overseas trip the year before and had raised the situation with the CESA. In this letter, however, Mowll forwarded a copy of the Archbishop of Canterbury's letter and asked for Inskip's advice on whether it would involve a breach of order for Mowll or other Australian bishops to consecrate a bishop for the CESA. In addition to that fundamental question, Mowll also sought advice on three related matters: firstly, whether any statute or regulation would hinder him from joining other bishops in such a consecration; secondly, whether there was any ordinance of the Church of England akin to the Nicaean canon concerning multiple bishops in one town; thirdly, whether it is not possible for the Church of England to be 'as elastic as the Roman Communion' in this matter (with reference to the dual episcopal economies in Antioch).[37] The significance of this letter cannot be overstated. On the same day that

---

[35] Mowll to Mills, 22 April 1939: "Archbishop's Correspondence, Church of England in South Africa", 90/43/10, SDA.

[36] Thomas Inskip was as prominent an evangelical as Bishop Knox or Bishop Chavasse. He fought against Prayer Book revision in the 1920s, belonged to the committee which drew up the Brentford Concordat in 1931, and served on the National Church League in various capacities (Chair of Council, Vice-President, President) during the same time. In September 1939 he became Lord Chancellor and was raised to the peerage as Viscount Caldecote.

[37] Mowll to Inskip, 22 April 1939. "Archbishop's Correspondence, Church of England in South Africa", 90/43/10, SDA.

Mowll supplied the CESA with calm advice in the absence of a bishop, he sought legal advice for the presence of a bishop. The Archbishop of Canterbury may have been somewhat surprised that this was what Mowll meant by 'making the most careful enquiries into the whole situation.'

Indeed, the Archbishop of Canterbury was nervous. Especially so, since Mowll's reply did not reach him for some time later. Lang sent an urgent telegram ('WROTE YOU IMPORTANT LETTER JANUARY 21 I AM STILL AWAITING REPLY') and an additional letter on 3 May 1939, which letter mentioned that the rumour of Ewbank's consecrating still persisted, and that such a consecration would involve a very serious breach of order within the Anglican Communion.[38] Mowll wrote to Cosmo Lang once more to reassure him that no break of church order was being considered, to which the Archbishop of Canterbury replied on 2 June 1939 with cordial thanks and warmth. 'No one realises more than I do the difficulties created by the situation in South Africa and the concerns of many who sympathise in some respects with the Church of England Congregations there but who perhaps do not know as I do the whole history of that situation and all its complications.'[39] With Canterbury's fears somewhat allayed, Mowll then chaired a committee meeting in Sydney on 29 August specifically focused upon the South African situation. The ten-man committee resolved to appoint a commissioner to report the facts of the South African situation to Mowll and also to communicate the arrangement of the commissioner to the Archbishops of Canterbury and Cape Town.[40] The committee also agreed not to take these steps until their next meeting, which meeting never eventuated due to the outbreak of war in Europe that was declared four days later.

---

[38] Lang to Mowll, 3 May 1939. "Archbishop's Correspondence, Church of England in South Africa", 90/43/10, SDA.
[39] Lang to Mowll, 2 June 1939. "Archbishop's Correspondence, Church of England in South Africa", 90/43/10, SDA.
[40] Those in attendance were Mowll, Prebendary Hinde, Archdeacons Begbie, Johnstone, and Wade, Canon Langford-Smith, Principal T.C. Hammond, and Messers A.L. Blythe, W.J.G. Mann, and H. Minton Taylor.

The War Years and the Growing Battle to Support the CESA

Over the course of the next seven years, Mowll's activity was largely focused upon local ministry in the midst of the war effort. Nevertheless, he continued to take up the cause of the CESA. Frustrated that the Archbishop of Canterbury would not consecrate them a bishop, and that the Canadian and Australian doorway to consecrate Ewbank seemed shut, the CESA began pursuing the possibility of episcopal consecration by presbyters. Mowll was evidently alarmed that such an extremely irregular path was being envisaged. On 19 April 1940, he wrote letters to Mills and Ewbank, both of which strongly warned that presbyterian consecration would estrange their sympathetic evangelical friends abroad and also give greater opportunity for their opponents to disavow them as breaking away from the Mother Church.[41] However, once again, Mowll supplied practical advice. In his letter to Ewbank, Mowll encouraged an *in extremis* permission of non-presbyteral administration of Holy Communion:

> I think that an alternative suggestions [sic], which seems to be indicated in your letter, might meet the present distress, namely, that a certain number of catechists, carefully instructed, should be permitted to minister Communion in those districts where the Church at present is unable to supply a regular Ministry. Such catechists should be required to sign a declaration, as you suggest, acknowledging that the powers which they possess have been given in view of an urgent necessity to provide the ministrations of the Sacraments to those who would otherwise be deprived of this blessing, or be forced to sever their connection with the Church of England, and that such provision must immediately terminate on the restoration of the full order of the Church of England. Precedence for this action can be found in the fact that

---

[41] Mowll to Mills, 19 April 1940; Mowll to Ewbank, 19 April 1940. "Archbishop's Correspondence, Church of England in South Africa", 1992/26/73, SDA.

similar privileges were conferred on Deacons in the early days of the Church of England, and that even as late as the time of Archbishop Usher [sic] Deacons were in charge of parishes in Ireland, as that Bishop's survey of the diocese of Meath abundantly witnesses. Instances of the same sort can be found in the history of the Church in Australia within the last century.

In his letter to Mills, he also outlined how Sydney could assist with the training and ordination of clergy:

> There are difficulties in the way of ordaining men for service in South Africa directly. I have no jurisdiction in that part of the world, and it would invite collision with the Bishops in the matter of letters dimissory, which would probably be referred to the Archbishop of Canterbury, and raise the whole issue as to the authority resident in the Vicar General. It is quite possible, however, for young men in South Africa to apply for admission to Moore College, and if war conditions prevent them coming here to undertake a course of study in the Australian College of Theology prescribed course. When they are ready to sit for examination the Principal of Moore College could write to the Registrar and ask for permission for them to sit for examination under proper supervision, as prospective Moore College candidates hindered from coming by war conditions. In that way young men could obtain their Th.L. or part of it. If war conditions continued so long it would occupy a period of at least two years before they got full Th.L. They could then, if they so desired, apply for ordination in the Diocese of Sydney, and after serving here for a period it would be possible for them to return to South Africa when positions there were offered to them.

Notwithstanding Mowll's warning about presbyteral consecration, the CESA still continued to pursue this desperate path into 1941. Mowll too was desperate. However, his desperation was chastened by the importance he placed upon church order. 'The situation there has become most acute', he wrote to Canon Frank Bate, Secretary of the Colonial and Continental Church Society, 'and unless something is done speedily I fear the cause will be lost.' The purpose of his letter was to stir Canon Bate, Bishop Christopher Chavasse, Prebendary Hinde, and Albert Mitchell of the National Church League, into action over this 'grave emergency' that they might 'save the situation.' Indeed, given Bate's connections with the Archbishop of Canterbury, Mowll wondered whether he was prepared to go to South Africa as Bishop of the CESA.[42] Things ground to a halt. Bate was talked down by Bishops Chavasse and Cash (formerly CMS General Secretary) and did not go to South Africa. By 1942, the CESA had ceased seriously pursuing presbyteral consecration.

The enthronement of Archbishop William Temple on 17 April 1942 did not effect any immediate changes to the precarious politics surrounding the CESA. The Second World War raged on, and the ecclesiastical battles did so too. Australian Primate Le Fanu reminded Temple of his plans to monitor Mowll and his hope that consecration would not occur ("I do wish the good Archbishop of Sydney would give up his efforts to keep the South African 'C of E' congregations going.").[43] Bishop Francis Batty of Newcastle informed Mowll that he had published an article 'on the history of the schism' in the *Church Standard* during December 1943, and warned the Archbishop of Sydney about the disturbing rumour of his efforts to consecrate a CESA bishop.[44] Mowll wrote back and defended the CESA against the 'lamentable exhibition of bigotry on the part of the Church in South Africa'. Never afraid of a fight, Mowll went as far as to say to Batty that 'I have often felt badly that I have not done more in my present position to befriend and help those who have been so generous to the missionary work of our Church.' He revealed that he refrained, largely,

---

[42] Mowll to Bate, 7 May 1941. "Archbishop's Correspondence with the Church of England in South Africa", 1992/26/73, SDA.

[43] Cited in Spartalis, "From Silvertrees", 140.

[44] Batty to Mowll, 8 December 1942. "Archbishop's Correspondence with the Church of England in South Africa", 1992/26/73, SDA.

because of his other friendships and prayerful hope that things would be put right without further friction.[45]

Mowll's Ministry Training Strategy

In the meantime, Mowll's plan to supply clergymen to the CESA was underway. The hope was that a modest supply of ministers would assist the expansion of the CESA. Initially the scheme seemed to be successful. In April 1940, Warron Brown came across from South Africa on the 'Nestor' and arrived at Moore College. After completing his studies Brown was ordained and became rector of St. Stephen's Willoughby in Sydney. In June 1944, Mills and Ewbank urgently pressed Mowll to return the recently made rector for service in South Africa. Even though Brown had not completed his obligation to serve in Sydney for two years after ordination, Mowll approved his release from Sydney, and he returned home in August 1944. The next year Mills reported to Mowll that Brown presided, with 'encouraging remarks' at the vestry meeting of Holy Trinity Church in Cape Town. Mills considered the Moore College-trained CESA clergyman to be a success story for Mowll's clergy supply scheme. 'It is obvious that Mr. Brown has had the type of training in Sydney that is required in this sister dominion,' wrote Mills, 'and although he has only been at the Cape a few weeks, we feel sure that he will prove as time goes on, a great strength to our churches here.'[46] However Brown decided to return to Sydney and became Rector of St Peter's Cooks River in May 1952.

Indeed, the clergy supply scheme yielded mixed results. In November 1942, Gordon King, Rector of St Peter's in East Sydney, heard about the desperate ministry needs in the CESA through Bradley, and corresponded with Mills about potential opportunities. King, a Moore College-trained Australian man ordained by Mowll in 1937, initially perceived his desire to serve in South Africa as a call from God but ended up backing out as he could not bind himself to the terms and

---

[45] Mowll to Batty, 10 December 1942. "Archbishop's Correspondence with the Church of England in South Africa", 1992/26/73, SDA.

[46] Mills to Mowll, 12 June 1945. "Archbishop's Correspondence with the Church of England in South Africa", 1992/26/73, SDA.

conditions placed upon his ministry position by Mills (e.g. sending weekly returns about visitations made to the Church Council). King was acutely conscious of the power of the Church Council and its potential to unseat the incumbent clergyman, something to which Mowll had drawn attention as he advised Warron Brown in 1944.[47]

This became a particular issue in the case of Tom Butler. A member of Holy Trinity in Cape Town, Butler moved to Sydney to train at Moore College around May in 1947. Because his wife and young family remained behind in South Africa, Mowll made an exception to the two-year curacy obligation such that Butler could return after one year at St Mark's Harbord in Sydney. He returned to South Africa in the first half of 1952 and replaced Warron Brown as curate to Stephen Bradley who was greatly encouraged by his assistance. However, in the same letter in which Bradley spoke warmly of Butler, he also shared about being 'just a little perturbed' that his new curate had suggested that the CESA had departed somewhat from Church of England standards and practices, and that this was the opinion widely held in the Sydney Diocese.[48] By 1954, Butler's ministry at Holy Trinity was in ruins. Vicar-General Hooker Rowden informed Mowll that Butler had been 'most disgracefully treated' though Registrar Mills informed Mowll that Butler was 'consistently rude' to him and other members of the Church Council.[49] Writing in June 1954 to Mowll, Butler indicated that the exertion of authority by Mills (who was Senior Warden of Holy Trinity) lay behind the tension. Eventually Butler was asked to resign and offered nearly £400 to sail back to Australia with his family. However, in July 1954 he took up a position at St. John's Wynberg in

[47] Brown to Mowll, 10 June 1944; Mowll to Brown, 23 June 1944. "Archbishop's Correspondence with the Church of England in South Africa", 1992/26/73, SDA.
[48] These concerned the use of individual communion cups, the irregularity of some presbyteral ordinations, and the practice of admitting unconfirmed persons to the Lord's Table. Bradley to Mowll, 15 May 1952. "Archbishop's Correspondence with the Church of England in South Africa", 1990/43/7, SDA.
[49] Rowden to Mowll, 11 March 1954; Mills to Mowll, 20 May 1954. "Archbishop's Correspondence with the Church of England in South Africa", 1990/43/8, SDA.

Cape Town which had recently aligned with the CPSA. Butler described it to Mowll as a wonderful provision, and Mowll was glad for Butler also. Yet, like Warron Brown, Butler returned to Sydney, becoming the curate-in-charge of Helensburgh in 1958.[50]

While his clergy supply scheme was less successful than desired, Mowll did have one outstanding contribution to the CESA during this time: a surprise visit to Cape Town. On 16 December 1947, the Archbishop and Mrs. Mowll left Sydney to visit the diocese of Central Tanganyika on their way to the Lambeth Conference in England. They arrived in Cape Town on the 'Corinthic' on New Year's Day 1948 with Mowll neither informing CESA nor CPSA clergy of his visit (a shrewd decision to avoid the accusation of partisan politics). Mowll was not only entertained by Archbishop Darbyshire of Cape Town but was given the Archbishop's concurrence to confirm CESA candidates: 'It is more important that people should receive confirmation, if it be possible, than that I should insist upon strict regularity as to request you refuse such an invitation if it were offered.'[51] With this, the Archbishop of Sydney confirmed 38 candidates for the CESA at Holy Trinity in Cape Town, assisted by Canon Pearce and Warron Brown (Bradley was ill with mumps). News of Mowll's confirmation service was published in various leading South African newspapers and was met with great celebration among the CESA ranks. The following year's CESA synod unanimously passed a resolution, with acclamation, stating 'that this indeed was an epoch-making event'. In addition to this public ministry Mowll also took the opportunity to spend one and a half hours privately with Registrar Mills, outlining how they ought to develop their church and supplying some hope about the prospect of representing the CESA cause at Lambeth.

Lambeth 1948: Triumph and Tragedy

Howard Mowll's last great effort on behalf of the CESA began during the Lambeth Conference at Canterbury in 1948. One of the concerns

---

[50] Butler to Mowll, 14 June 1954. "Archbishop's Correspondence with the Church of England in South Africa", 1990/43/8, SDA.
[51] Darbyshire to Mowll, 31 December 1947. "Archbishop's Correspondence with the Church of England in South Africa", 1992/26/73, SDA.

of the conference was the effort required to unite the Nandyal Anglicans to the new Church of South India, and Mowll hoped that this consideration might extend to the CESA. An informal meeting to discuss the South African question took place between Archbishop Fisher of Canterbury, Archbishop Clayton of Johannesburg, Bishop Fisher of Natal (brother to the Archbishop of Canterbury), Bishop Parker of Pretoria, Bishop Chavasse of Rochester, Bishop Cash of Worcester, and Archbishop Mowll of Sydney. At this pivotal meeting, and in their correspondence and meetings in England subsequent to Lambeth, this powerful group of bishops proposed a set of processes which would eventuate in an appropriate concordat between the CESA and CPSA, and in a CESA bishop who supplied evangelical episcopal supervision and who served as suffragan to the Archbishop of Cape Town. Sometime around this meeting Mowll had also met his old Cambridge CICCU friend, now Bishop Fred Morris of North Africa. Morris later recollected the advice given by the Archbishop of Sydney:

> He said, as he was leaving, "I think, Fred, if you went to S. Africa and took one of the C.E.S.A. Churches, without ministering as a bishop for a time but showing yourself as loving them [the CPSA] (not their practices), they would agree to your exercising your ministry as a bishop." These were not the exact words but the gist of it ... It seems like a rather long term policy![52]

Mowll's Lambeth proposal was not only a long-term policy, but a delicate one. Bishop Leonard Fisher of Natal in his capacity as Dean of the Province communicated to the Archbishop of Canterbury that the CPSA bishops were extremely nervous about the legal implications of recognising that CESA churches had never left the Church of England.[53] Fisher already had a fractious relationship with the CESA (being locked out of a Natal church in 1934) and his opinions would not have helped his brother to take a favourable view of their cause.

---

[52] Morris to Mills, n.d. [1953]. Peter Spartalis Papers, 096/1/1-1, Moore Theological College.

[53] Spartalis provides a detailed account of Mowll's interactions in London in "From Silvertrees", 155-167. Morris to Fisher, 4 December 1954, cited in Spartalis, "From Silvertrees", 160 n34.

Nevertheless, these conversations, and those which probably took place during the trips made to Australia by the Archbishop of Canterbury in 1950 and the Archbishop of York in 1951, were constructive. In 1953, Archbishop Fisher appointed Rev J P Hickinbotham to visit South Africa with a view to producing a suitable basis for negotiation between the CESA and CPSA. However, the resulting proposal, known as 'The Thirteen Points', caused consternation within the CESA. The anti-Hickinbotham party considered them as betraying the costly stand that previous generations had taken to secure the CESA and the pro-Hickinbotham party considered them a viable proposal that did not warrant obstinacy. Heated debates took place in the CESA synod of 1953 and the 'Thirteen Points' were eventually rejected in the synod of 1954. Its leading most vocal opponents were, among others, Mills, Bradley, and Bennett.[54] Indeed, support for the 'Thirteen Points' was a contributing factor behind the departure from CESA of Vicar-General Rowden, Deputy Vicar-General Molyneux, and the Moore College-trained curate from Holy Trinity Cape Town, Tom Butler.

It was within this context that Mowll's relationship with Mills disintegrated to the point of no return. The Archbishop of Sydney had communicated with Vicar-General Rowden and others after the Lambeth Conference, but the absence of contact with Mills had left the Registrar frustrated and suspicious. On 9 August 1952 he penned an extraordinarily frank letter to Mowll which, across nearly six pages, relayed a damning report he had received of Mowll's meeting in Lambeth, and claimed that the Archbishop of Sydney now opposed the church that he had once championed:

> The subtle picture, of course, is in a word, that you completely capitulated to the amazing attack against us by the Bishops of England, who should have been our friends, and that as a result, not only was the committee a complete failure, and your advocacy of our cause a failure, but a terrible handle was given to the Anglo-Catholics, to be able to say in this country that the Evangelical Bishops, (again so-called), in England themselves, not only thought

---

[54] Ives, *Candle*, 116-123, where a full list of the 'Thirteen Points' may be found.

nothing of us, but were active in preventing us receiving any assistance.

Unfortunately, Mills had not only misinterpreted Mowll's silence as guilt, but he had received an erroneous report about the Lambeth meeting. In Mowll's personal copy of Mills' letter he scribbled various marginal notes which pointed out the factual errors. Mills' report claimed that Lambeth appointed the meeting, to which Mowll wrote: "No The [sic] A of C privately at my suggestion". The report claimed there were six evangelical English bishops and one CPSA representative, to which Mowll wrote: 'No 1 or 2 [English evangelical bishops] 3 [CPSA persons]'. Similarly, it claimed the English evangelical bishops attacked CESA, to which Mowll wrote: "The Bp of Natal". Lastly, the report claimed that Mowll did not mention the Silvertrees Agreement of 1933, to which he wrote: 'was referred to by Rochester'. In one place, Mowll bracketed out a whole paragraph in which Mills explained how his 'collapse' at Lambeth allowed the Archbishops of Canterbury and York to see his 'weakness' of which they could take 'full advantage.' After years of support for the cause of the CESA Mowll was not willing to be unreasonably berated. So, on 16 September 1952 he cut all diplomatic connection with Mills. Mowll replied with only two short sentences: 'I am sorry and amazed to receive your letters of 9th August. They make it impossible for me to discuss further with you the matters to which you refer.'[55]

Mills was flattened by the Archbishop of Sydney's sudden snub. Without the knowledge of her husband, Mrs Mary Mills wrote a moving handwritten letter to Howard Mowll on 5 December. She recounted the many ways in which Mowll had helped the CESA and the enormous evangelical efforts that her husband had put in to strengthen the witness of their church. However, Mowll's lack of communication after Lambeth had apparently put a heavy strain on her husband, and his cessation of communication now dealt him an even heavier blow: 'I very much fear for my husband's health now, as a result of your Grace's refusal to have any more correspondence with

---

[55] Mowll to Mills, 16 September 1952. "Archbishop's Correspondence with the Church of England in South Africa", 1990/43/7, SDA.

him.' 'This is a woman's plea', she concluded, 'for one who has staked everything he holds dear, to keep the evangelical witness right, in a country which is fast falling in the habit of ignoring the worship and service of our Lord.'[56] Another petition on behalf of Mills came from Bradley on 11 December. The almost four pages rehearsed the great efforts of the CESA Registrar over the course of his life, and Bradley stated that he knew of no other man whose Christian witness had been more effective during his time in South Africa. He acknowledged that Mills had endured many heavy blows of disappointment during the CESA's prolonged search for a bishop, and that they perhaps had placed too much hope on Mowll and what he could have achieved at Lambeth. Nevertheless, he earnestly prayed that the Archbishop could see a way to re-open correspondence with Mr. Mills.[57] Six months later, Bradley got a reply: 'It was a painful surprise and disappointing for me', wrote Mowll, 'to receive letters in which I was accused of 'sinister' activities and to be threatened with the publication of my letters without regard to my personal wishes.' Notwithstanding Mowll's hope for the CESA, he could not accede to Bradley's request to reopen communications with Mills.[58]

While it is important to notice the increasing internal division within the CESA concerning a compromise with the CPSA, it is also important to observe the evolution of Mowll's opinion over a solution to the impasse. In a confidential letter to Rev Stanley Wakeling, Rector of St. John's in Wynberg (CPSA), dated 3 December 1952, Mowll shared his opinion that 'as time has gone on I feel more convinced that the only solution to the problem of the C.E.S.A. lies in some kind of rapprochement with the Church of the Province.' He knew that the long heritage of grievances made many in the CESA feel that rapprochement with the CPSA would be a betrayal, yet on the other hand, he felt that if the present isolation continued then it would be

---

[56] Mrs Mills to Mowll, 5 December 1952. "Archbishop's Correspondence with the Church of England in South Africa", 1990/43/7, SDA.
[57] Bradley to Mowll, 11 December 1952. "Archbishop's Correspondence with the Church of England in South Africa", 1990/43/7, SDA.
[58] Mowll to Bradley, 18 May 1953. "Archbishop's Correspondence with the Church of England in South Africa", 1990/43/7, SDA.

increasingly difficult for the CESA to maintain their conformity to Church of England worship and polity.[59] He put the point more strongly to Vicar-General Rowden shortly before the defeat of the 'Thirteen Points' in the CESA synod of 1954: 'One cannot help feeling sad to think that the C.E.S.A. seems to be drifting onto rocks which may destroy it.'[60] Rowden agreed with this sentiment, replying that 'It appears the C.E.S.A. will be liquidated from within.'[61]

Fred Morris: The First CESA Bishop

There was, however, a silver lining to these storm clouds. It came in the form of an intriguing handwritten note added by Rowden to his letter: 'Dear old bishop Fred Morris is being pressed to come here, thinking it could put things right.' Though Rowden thought such a move might break Morris' heart and hoped that Mowll could dissuade him from coming, this approach would eventually prove to be the long-awaited solution for CESA's desperate search for a bishop. Rowden was evidently not privy to the fact that Mowll had himself encouraged Morris to explore episcopal ministry in the CESA when they met in England back in 1948. Thus, though Mowll's hope for rapprochement between the CESA and CPSA seemed stalled, the friendship with his old CICCU collaborator for the gospel began to bear fruit. In 1953, Bradley and Mills requested the ageing Bishop of North Africa to come to the aid of the CESA. Mills, lamenting to Morris that 'Sydney abandoned us', was even open to the idea that Morris might visit South Africa sporadically every two years and exercise episcopal ministries for the CESA.[62] In January of 1955, Bishop Morris accepted the invitation to South Africa and became the Rector of Christ Church,

---

59 Mowll to Wakeling, 3 December 1952. "Archbishop's Correspondence with the Church of England in South Africa", 1990/43/7, SDA.
60 Mowll to Rowden, 2 March 1954. "Archbishop's Correspondence with the Church of England in South Africa", 1990/43/8, SDA.
61 Rowden to Mowll, 11 March 1954. "Archbishop's Correspondence with the Church of England in South Africa", 1990/43/8, SDA.
62 Mills to Morris, 24 June 1953. Peter Spartalis Papers, 096/1/1-1, Moore Theological College.

Hillbrow in Johannesburg. It was, in the words of the CESA historian Tony Ive, a 'turning point' in the history of the denomination.[63]

Mowll would have been privately delighted about the arrival of Bishop Morris in South Africa. Throughout the previous two decades he had unsuccessfully sounded out several bishops to relocate and serve the CESA but the seed he planted with Morris in 1948 was the only attempt which bore real fruit. However, Mowll remained publicly circumspect, and for good reason. Since the death of Archbishop Le Fanu of Perth in 1947 the Australian Primacy returned to Sydney, and since the visit of the Archbishop of Canterbury in 1950, the need for constitutional reform was impressed upon the Australian church. These two facts alone go a long way to explain Mowll's *festina lente* approach to the rapprochement of the CESA and CPSA after Lambeth.[64] However, they also explain his reticence to be seen to be too aligned with the CESA around the time of Fred Morris' arrival in South Africa. In November 1954, Mowll wrote to Broughton Knox, then editor of the *Australian Church Record*, about a letter submitted for publication by Mills. Mowll was grateful that Knox sent him a copy of the letter and asked that a précis of the letter be published instead. 'The precis could', advised Mowll, 'avoid emphasis of the help which it is claimed has been received from the Diocese of Sydney as well as personal references.'[65] In June the following year, Marcus Loane vetted another article for Mowll, this time one written by Bishop Morris. Loane considered the article to be a very discreet and balanced statement which made two references to Mowll over the CESA constitution and the confirmation of candidates at Holy Trinity Cape Town. 'There is nothing otherwise', wrote Loane, 'which could commit you in any way at all.'[66] Mowll

---

[63] Ive, *Candle,* 126.

[64] The 'Red Book' case also contributed to the complex ecclesiastical politics of the time.

[65] Mowll to Knox, 3 November 1954. "Archbishop's Correspondence with the Church of England in South Africa", 1990/43/8, SDA.

[66] Loane to Mowll, 21 June 1954. "Archbishop's Correspondence with the Church of England in South Africa", 1990/43/8, SDA.

replied with a short note to Loane: 'Concerning article submitted by Bishop Morris please delete reference to me re constitution page 6'.[67]

Mowll's position was made even more complicated by events which occurred in the first half of 1955. The Archbishop of Canterbury visited South Africa in April 1955, and upon Howard Mowll's suggestion that this presented a golden opportunity to find an amicable settlement, Bishop Morris, Bradley, and the church wardens from Christ Church Hillbrow met with Archbishop Fisher at Johannesburg airport shortly before his return to England. Despite the CESA delegation suggesting alternative arrangements, Fisher insisted that if Bishop Morris was to become a co-adjutor bishop to the Archbishop of Cape Town, then he would need to subscribe to the canons and constitution of the CPSA (which included the wearing of a mitre and cope). This, and the Archbishop of Canterbury's insistence upon the 'Thirteen Points' was too much for the CESA delegation, and the meeting ended unhappily.[68] At the CESA synod held six months later, Fred Morris was elected as the Bishop of the Church of England in South Africa, and an international media frenzy ensued with the news that the Archbishop of Canterbury had declared that this action would put Bishop Morris outside of the Anglican Communion.[69]

Later that year Bishop Morris requested Archbishop Mowll to consecrate an assistant bishop for the CESA. Mowll's reply was short and was, regretfully, a negative answer. However, the lengthy unsent draft of Mowll's reply reveals the rationale for his reservation:

> If I could act simply as a private individual I would long to be able to come to your help. I find it impossible to avoid the fact that in my present position any action which I may take must be interpreted in the light of my office as Archbishop of Sydney and Primate of Australia. I have been elected by the Diocesan Synod to the one position

[67] Mowll to Loane, undated. "Archbishop's Correspondence with the Church of England in South Africa", 1990/43/8, SDA.
[68] Fred Morris' undated memorandum. Peter Spartalis Papers, 096/1/1-1, Moore Theological College.
[69] Ive, *Candle,* 132-139.

and by the Bishops of Australia to the other position, and I do not feel that I can take a course of action which would seriously implicate those whom I have been called to serve.

It seems to me that there is the gravest difficulty in trying to secure the Consecration of a Bishop anywhere but on South African soil. I clearly see your problem and know how much you and others must feel the need for continuity. It is with great reluctance that I have to say that I do not see how I at present can come to your help. I feel sure that you will recognise that this is a decision which is determined solely by my obligations to the Church in Australia. For you personally I can only feel the warmest affection and admiration for the courageous stand which you have taken.[70]

The Question of Episcopal Succession

As time marched onwards, Bishop Morris grew more anxious to secure episcopal continuity. Throughout 1956-1957, he wrote four letters to Mowll requesting the consecration of Stephen Bradley, often reminiscing about their partnership in the CICCU battles of old and reminding Mowll of his prayerful appreciation for his old Cambridge friend. To Morris' distress, none of the letters received a reply, although privately Mowll continued to take an interest in the CESA situation. On 17 April 1956, he had Marcus Loane prepare a memorandum about the legality of consecrating a bishop in Sydney.[71] On the same day he wrote to Leslie Wilkinson (Principal of Oak Hill College, London) and explained his dilemma: 'at the present time I do not want Sydney to become a storm centre in the controversy between Fred Morris and the Archbishop of Canterbury ... Sydney cannot afford to increase its opponents with our situation over the constitution still

---

[70] Mowll to Morris, 16 December 1955. "Archbishop's Correspondence with the Church of England in South Africa", 1990/43/8, SDA.
[71] Loane to Mowll, 17 April 1956. "Archbishop's Correspondence with the Church of England in South Africa", 1990/43/8, SDA.

undecided.'[72] Morris understandably felt isolated, and ventilated to Mills that 'I must admit that Mowll has been a dis-appointment [sic] to me, I think he could have done more for us ... We must realise that Mowll has had difficulties; there is another side and until we can hear both sides, it is difficult for us to judge correctly.'[73]

Fred Morris may not ever have heard Mowll's side in its entirety, for shortly before midnight on 24 October 1958 the Archbishop of Sydney suddenly, but peacefully, died. Upon hearing the tragic news, Bradley urgently cabled Marcus Loane in the name of Bishop Morris (who was sick) and the CESA to communicate their deepest sympathy. Loane replied on behalf of the church in the diocese of Sydney: 'It is so great a loss that we cannot possibly foresee what it will mean in the life of the Diocese. The Archbishop always felt a special affection for Bishop Morris, as a friend from his C.I.C.C.U. days and the one whom he succeeded as President of the C.I.C.C.U.'[74] A week later, Bradley updated Loane on Morris' situation: 'Indeed we have been quite alarmed about Bishop Morris' health. He took the news of Archbishop Mowll's passing very hardly as they had been lifelong friends ever since their C.I.C.C.U days.'[75] Morris retired from the CESA in Easter the following year and passed away in June 1965. Before his death, Morris privately remarked to the new CESA Registrar, Herbert Hammond:

> Archbp. Howard Mowll, bound me to confidence in his correspondence. He was an old and valued friend; he was full of sympathy in my coming to S.A. but he always refused to support me officially for fear of damaging his influence in Australia ... H.M. valued the work of the

---

[72] Mowll to Wilkinson, 17 April 1956. "Archbishop's Correspondence, Church of England in South Africa", 90/43/10, SDA.

[73] Morris to Mills, 3 May 1957. Peter Spartalis Papers, 096/1/1-1, Moore Theological College.

[74] Loane to Bradley, 30 October 1958. Peter Spartalis Papers, 096/1/1-1, Moore Theological College.

[75] Bradley to Loane, 6 November 1958. Peter Spartalis Papers, 096/1/1-1, Moore Theological College.

C.E.S.A. and my connection with S.A. and he urged us to avoid litigation and bitterness.[76]

There remains an important lingering question in the wake of Howard Mowll's death, namely, whether the Archbishop of Sydney approved of the irregular consecration of Stephen Bradley by Bishop Morris consecrating alone at Holy Trinity Cape Town on 8 March 1959. This became a thorny issue later that year when Morris Riddell, who was ordained by Bradley, joined the CPSA and was re-ordained the following year by the Archbishop of Cape Town who had apparently consulted the Archbishop of Canterbury in the matter. The implication was, of course, that Morris' consecration of Bradley was invalid or somehow defective.

CESA historian Tony Ive asserts, without citation or quotation but with some degree of specificity, that some time before his death Mowll sent Morris a personal letter with express approval of the election of Bradley and advised him to consecrate alone in the absence of assistance.[77] This is quite an extraordinary claim, especially in light of Mowll's desire to see rapprochement between the CPSA and CESA and his history of alarm over the CESA's previous pursuits to irregularly consecrate a bishop. In his correspondence, Mowll had ignored four of Morris' letters about consecration by 10 October 1957. Moreover, not only did Bradley avoid informing Mowll about his election as bishop on 5 April 1957 but Mowll avoided any reference to Bradley's bishop-elect status in his cordial but short letters to the "Ven. Bradley" on 22 January and 11 March in 1958. It was just over three months after his death that Mills attacked 'the recent compromise by Mowll' and lambasted the former Archbishop of Sydney as 'our active enemy.' And it was a week after this that Loane wrote to Bradley and declined assisting in his consecration and stated that 'I cannot be a party to anyone who insists on describing our late Archbishop as an 'enemy'.'[78] However, it is evidence from Archbishop Hugh Gough that runs most contrary to

[76] Morris to Hammond, 17 January 1961. Peter Spartalis Papers, 096/1/1-1, Moore Theological College.

[77] Ive, *Candle,* 143.

[78] Loane to Bradley, 17 February 1959. "Archbishop's Correspondence with the Church of England in South Africa", 1990/43/9, SDA.

Ive's claim. Writing to Archbishop Joost de Blank of Cape Town on 24 November 1959, Gough claimed:

> I know that Archbishop Mowll, when I saw him in 1957, was very much against the proposal which was then being suggested, that Bishop Morris should consecrate Mr. Bradley as Bishop. I know that he would have been very upset indeed to have learnt that this Consecration took place.[79]

Six months earlier, Gough had made similar remarks to Archbishop Frank Woods of Melbourne:

> Fortunately I had the opportunity, when I was here two years ago of talking to Archbishop Mowll on this matter and know that he would have most strongly disapproved of this consecration. Moreover, I privately know that he was very upset by various things that had been said and done, and by the way in which his name was often used in an unjustifiable manner to support questionable action. Unfortunately, however, this private knowledge that I have is not generally shared in this Diocese. Sooner or later a situation will arise when I shall have to take some official action. But at present I feel it wise to refrain from saying anything public.[80]

Although the 'private knowledge' referred to by Gough was not generally shared public knowledge in the Sydney diocese, there were some who were privy to the intricacies of Howard Mowll's relationship with the CESA. On 16 Feburary 1959, Marcus Loane, Clive Kerle, R B Robinson, D Broughton Knox, and D W B Robinson met at Church House to discuss the possible results of Bradley's upcoming consecration (T C Hammond was away from Sydney at the time). This group communicated, with meticulously careful wording, three main

---

[79] Gough to de Blank, 24 November 1959, "Archbishop's Correspondence with the Church of England in South Africa", 1990/43/9, SDA.
[80] Gough to Woods, 27 July 1959. "Archbishop's Correspondence with the Church of England in South Africa", 1990/43/9, SDA.

points to Bradley: firstly, that Mowll acted privately and unofficially in his support of the CESA and the same support could not be guaranteed in future; secondly, that the irregular nature of Morris consecrating alone would make it difficult for the CESA to be recognised any further as part of the Church of England; and thirdly, that there was no guarantee that a future Archbishop of Sydney would recognise Bradley as a bishop or recognise the orders of men ordained by Bradley. The concluding paragraph was especially important, for in addition to reiterating their qualified personal support, these five Sydney clergymen admitted that the CESA "appears to have exhausted all avenues of obtaining a Bishop by regular means" and as such 'we do not see that it has any other course open to it but the one it is contemplating.'[81] This was especially valuable advice, since the five Sydney clergymen most likely knew that Mowll's successor, Hugh Gough, was not favourable to the CESA. Indeed, in the aforementioned letter to Archbishop Woods of Melbourne in July 1959, Gough made his position clear: 'I myself do not support the Church of England in South Africa, particularly after the entirely wrong action of Bishop Morris in consecrating Bradley.'

In the absence of Howard Mowll's letter to Fred Morris, the best evidence in support of Ive's significant claim comes from a letter to Donald Robinson from Stephen Bradley on 13 January 1960. 'Archbishop Mowll definitely suggested to Bishop Morris', wrote Bradley, 'as to myself that the consecration by one bishop was valid even if irregular.' After citing a 1937 letter from Mowll to Norman Bennett, and with strikingly similar wording to that used later by Ive, Bradley continued: 'While, shortly before his death he wrote to Bishop Morris not only reiterating the above statement, but supplying precedents for the same.'[82] It is, therefore, curious that Peter Spartalis bracketed out this whole section of his own photocopy of Bradley's letter and wrote 'NO' in capitals within the margin, and it is also intriguing that Ive's description of Mowll's express support of Morris

---

[81] Robinson to Bradley, 25 February 1959. Peter Spartalis Papers, 096/1/1-1, Moore Theological College.
[82] Bradley to Robinson, 13 January 1960. Peter Spartalis Papers, 096/1/1-1, Moore Theological College.

is framed in such similar words to that of Bradley. Indeed, in 1958 Ive himself wrote to Morris in strong support of his consecrating Bradley alone: 'it is a matter of proceeding with the consecration now, without the assistance of other bishops, or not at all.'[83] It is possible that both Bradley and Ivey based their claims upon Mowll's 1937 advice when, in fact, the Archbishop of Sydney had changed his mind in the decade prior to his death. Nevertheless, it is also still possible that Mowll wrote the remarkable letter to which Ive refers in support of Bradley being consecrated alone. To whom else would he have entrusted such explosive but encouraging advice, but his old Cambridge stalwart for the evangelical cause, Fred Morris? However, in the absence of the letter to which Ive refers, we need to treat his uncited claim with some degree of caution.

Conclusion

Uncertainties aside, we may be sure that Archbishop Howard Mowll went to great lengths – largely in a private and unofficial capacity – to support the CESA. He sent advice for a constitution, he encouraged Stephen Bradley to consider ministry in Natal, he asked various friends to serve as bishop for the CESA, he sent detailed advice concerning the furthering of fellowship between CESA churches, he advised about temporary forms of confirmation, he encouraged lay administration of Holy Communion in extraordinary circumstances, he established an informal scheme for training and ordination of clergy in Sydney, and he leveraged an extraordinary array of ecclesiastical relationships in the service of securing episcopal oversight for the CESA. However, as he increasingly sought rapprochement between the CESA and CPSA, both the CESA and the CPSA increasingly hardened their stances towards each other. Mowll was therefore delighted that his old Cambridge friend Fred Morris took up his advice and fought for the evangelical cause in South Africa, and he may well have supported his old Cambridge friend in standing alone to consecrate Bradley. Whereas the previous historiography has smoothed over much of the relational turbulence between Mowll and the CESA, it is now clear that during

---

[83] Ive to Morris, 12 December 1958. Peter Spartalis Papers, 096/1/1-1, Moore Theological College.

his time as Archbishop and Primate Howard Mowll was tremendously torn between his ecclesiastical responsibilities within Australia and his evangelical sympathies abroad. One can only imagine what joy it would have brought him to witness the consecration of Dudley Tucker Foord as Bishop of CESA on 12 February 1984 at St Andrew's Cathedral in Sydney which took place with the approval of the Archbishops of Canterbury, Cape Town, and Sydney, the CESA Bishops and Registrar, the Anglican Consultative Council, the Primate of Australia, and with his friend and fellow former Archbishop of Sydney Sir Marcus Loane in the pulpit, opening his address with the words:

> A service for the consecration of a Bishop, in the Church of God, is always solemn and significant. This particular service has an historic interest and strategic importance of the greatest moment. Here, in the oldest Cathedral of the Church in Australia, we are to set apart a Bishop for the Church of England in South Africa.[84]

---

[84] "Foord Consecration Looks to Heal Rift", *The Australian Church Record* 1795 (20 February 1984).

9. Archbishop Mowll and His Ground-Breaking Vision for Youth Ministry in the Diocese of Sydney

Ruth Lukabyo

Archbishop Howard Mowll was an evangelical activist whose goal was to galvanize the diocese for mission both at home and abroad. One of Mowll's key missional strategies was to establish structures for evangelising and training youth. He had a ground-breaking vision for youth ministry that was to transform the diocese and ensure the gospel was passed down to the next generation. He was an Archbishop for the young. Mowll led the way in this strategic focus on youth, often pulling others along with him. Don Robertson, who worked at the Youth Department in the 1950s, claims that his strategy in the Diocese 'was revolutionary at the time, the rest of the Church had to catch up with it'.[1]

Mowll appointed key leaders and created new organisations that were ground-breaking. He appointed a missioner to youth, then later a chaplain to youth. He was a central figure in establishing the Youth Department, the Church of England National Emergency Fund (CENEF) leadership training centre, the Port Hacking campsites, Camp Howard, and the 'Youth to Youth' missions of the 1950s. This chapter will argue that there were two reasons for his strategic focus. First, it was shaped by his early ministry experiences in the CSSM (Childrens' Special Service Mission) and IVF (InterVarsity Fellowship). Second, he was responding to the social context of the 1930s and 1940s. After war and depression, in Australian society there was a real sense of guilt and responsibility to youth and a hope that they would build a new future for the young nation.

---

[1] Rex Harris and Don Robertson, interviewed by Ruth Lukabyo, 5 June 2021. Rex Harris also worked with the Youth Department in the 1950s.

The influence of Mowll's background

Mowll's student experiences formed him and shaped his priorities as Archbishop of Sydney. He had been formed as a Christian leader in the fledgling evangelical student ministries. He was appointed president of the Cambridge Inter-Collegiate Christian Union (CICCU) in 1910, not long after the group broke away from the more liberal Student Christian Movement.[2] As president he affirmed an evangelical approach to the Scriptures and encouraged the group to 'win others for Christ'.[3] As a young man, Mowll was also involved in Scripture Union (SU) beach missions in the summer holidays.[4] The InterVarsity Fellowship (the wider organisation to which the CICCU belonged) and Scripture Union (SU) strategically sought to convert young people at beach mission or at camp, then train them in university ministry. These young people would become future evangelical leaders in church and society that would transform the nation with the gospel. This same strategy came to shape the goals of the youth organisations in Sydney and shaped Mowll's thinking in the diocese too.[5]

As the Archbishop of Sydney, Mowll remained involved with the work of the para-church youth organisations despite his heavy workload. This indicates both his focus on young people and the fact that these organisations had formed him. He was a patron to the Evangelical

---

[2] The CICUU leaders were later prominent in forming the InterVarsity Fellowship of Evangelical Unions seeking to establish a 'truly Evangelical witness' throughout the world. Howard Guinness, *Journey among Students* (Sydney: Anglican Information Office, 1978), 42.

[3] Loane, *Archbishop Mowll*, 45.

[4] Loane, *Archbishop Mowll*, 57, 58.

[5] This strategy was articulated best in Sydney by Howard Guinness and later by Paul White and Charles Troutman. Troutman and White spoke about the "unbreakable circle" between the work of SU and the IVF. When Charles Troutman came to Sydney in 1953 to work with the IVF, he believed that this strategy was already shaping the work and "had a hunch" that Mowll brought it from the UK. "Charles Troutman 3," 30 June 1990, *Oral History*, The Ark Repository, Moore College,
https://moorecollege.access.preservica.com/index.php?name=SO_6e20903a
-f659-49c0-a9fc-418519da3cf1

Union at Sydney University,[6] president of the Crusader Union of NSW,[7] and world-wide president of Scripture Union.[8] He supported organisations that nurtured vigorous, personal faith in young people 'as the result of effective evangelism and training in leadership'.[9]

The historical context

Mowll was not the only evangelical with a focus on young people in his time; many conservative evangelicals turned their attention to ministry to young people. The Australian historian, Geoff Treloar, argues that amongst evangelicals internationally in the 1930s, there was a change in focus from evangelising working men to evangelising youth.[10] David Bebbington argues that in the UK many evangelical leaders believed that the way to respond to the challenge of liberal theology was to evangelise youth, to 'win the next generation to the truth'.[11]

Australian evangelicals had a similar concern for youth. Many felt a great sense of responsibility for young people who were living through depression and facing another war. For example, Canon W G Hilliard in the synod of 1934 preached that evangelism was needed more than ever, especially amongst the young.

> I believe that we have a special responsibility to our youth, both because on them has fallen the heaviest burden of the tragic failures of our civilisation, and because into their hands we must needs commit the task of the years that lie ahead. Born in the fevered years of warfare, brought up in

---

[6] Meredith Lake, 'Faith in Crisis: Christian University Students in Peace and War,' *Australian Journal of Politics and History* 56, no. 3 (2010): 449; Ruth Lukabyo, *From a Ministry for Youth to a Ministry of Youth: Aspects of Protestant Youth Ministry in Sydney 1930-1959* (Eugene: Wipf & Stock, 2020), 91.

[7] The Crusader Union of NSW was formed in 1934, the same year as his arrival.

[8] Paul White interviewed by Margaret Lamb, 3 April 1986.

[9] Crusader Union of NSW 29th Annual Report, 1958. Archives of Crusader Union NSW, Eastwood, Sydney.

[10] Geoffrey R. Treloar, *The Disruption of Evangelicalism: the Age of Torrey, Mott, McPherson and Hammond* (London: Inter-Varsity Press, 2016), 238 - 242.

[11] David W. Bebbington, *Evangelicalism in Modern Britain: A History from the 1730s to the 1980s* (London: Routledge, 1989), 226.

the debilitating atmosphere of its tragic aftermath, growing into manhood and womanhood during the greatest economic Depression in history, and amid a welter of conflicting thought: economic, social and theological, we need to be patient with them and to realise our heavy responsibility towards them ...[12]

He called on the synod to support the Board of Education, Sunday Schools and church schools in their ministries and to invest significant resources: '... For the sake of the Kingdom of God in the years that lie ahead, the Church must be prepared to work and to spend in the cause of youth of today and of the future'.[13] Hilliard and others believed that there was a 'crisis of civilisation' and that young people would need to rebuild the nation on a Christian foundation.[14] This historic context as well as Mowll's formation in student Christian organisations make sense of his strategic concern for youth.

Appointments

The challenge for Mowll was how to put his strategy to work in the diocese. One of the key things he did was to make excellent appointments. Part of his genius was his ability to appoint gifted men and find money to fund their ministry.

Mowll's first appointment as an Archbishop was Alan Begbie in April 1934 as 'Missioner to Young People'.[15] This was a new position, supported by individuals and Sunday Schools. Begbie was a 26-year-old curate and the leader of one of the first fellowship groups in

---

[12] Canon W. G. Hilliard "Synod Sermon," *Year Book of the Diocese of Sydney*, 1935, 258.

[13] Hilliard "Synod Sermon," 258.

[14] This concern was shared by the Prime Minister at the time. Robert Menzies, "The Challenge of This Hour," *Sydney Diocesan Magazine* (cited hereafter as *SDM*), 1 June 1940.

[15] "Youth and Age, Problems for Missioner," *Sydney Morning Herald*, Friday 6 April 1934, 15. *SDM*, March 1, 1934, Vol. 25, No. 3, 7. This position was supported by an appeal to individuals and Sunday Schools for two years.

Australia, at St Paul's Chatswood.[16] This group began in 1929 on Sunday mornings at 10am for worship and discussion. In September 1930, a subcommittee of the Sydney Church of England Board of Education set up a new organisation, the Church of England Fellowship (CEF), to encourage further fellowship groups.[17] For two and a half years, Begbie went to parishes and conducted missions with children after school and young people in the evenings. Begbie conducted 56 missions and afterwards, he encouraged churches to establish a fellowship group to help the young converts grow in their faith. Reports show that by the end of 1935, there were 27 registered groups in Sydney.[18] The spread of youth fellowship groups in the diocese was the outcome of Mowll's first appointment.

The next excellent appointment was Graham Delbridge as chaplain to youth in 1942. Delbridge was a young curate who went to Mowll after the war had begun, wanting permission to go as a chaplain with the armed forces. Mowll emphatically replied:

> You cannot do that, you must leave your present work as the curate at Summer Hill and come in and take over youth work and you must get the youth ready for when the war is over.[19]

---

[16] Lesley Hicks, *A City on a Hill: A History of St Paul's Anglican Church, Chatswood, 1901-1991* (Sydney: St Paul's Chatswood Parish Council, 1991), 124. There is some debate about which fellowship group was first: at St Paul's Chatswood with Begbie or at Corrimal Anglican Church under Rev. W.G. Coughlan. Stuart Piggin, *Harry Goodhew, Archbishop, Godly Radical, Dynamic Anglican* (Sydney: Morning Star, 2021), 48.

[17] These are the fore runners of contemporary Friday night youth groups. A. J. Mason, "A History of the Board of Education 1919-1949", Master of Education thesis; Sydney University, 1973, 56. The 3 members of this subcommittee were F.A. Walton, the head of the Board of Education, W.G. Coughlan, and A.G. Frazer.

[18] C. K. Hammond, "The History of the Church of England Fellowship," in Histories of Youthworks / Port Hacking Sites: opening and celebrations [2019/011], Sydney Diocesan Archives (cited hereafter as SDA).

[19] Letter from Graham Delbridge to Mark Rogers, 3 October 1977, in Histories of Youthworks / Port Hacking Sites: opening and celebrations [2019/011], SDA.

When Delbridge turned up at Church House for work Mowll said to him: 'I don't know what you are going to do or where you are going to do it, and I don't know how we are going to pay for you, but you must begin'.[20] Delbridge began work in the basement with a table, a couple of chairs and a phone. Mowll accessed funds to support Delbridge financially from the Home Mission Society (HMS) though many were critical of this decision in wartime when resources and funding for ministry was stretched.[21]

In the first few years, the key things that Delbridge did were to look after the Church of England Boy's Society (CEBS) and create a service bureau, to find young people jobs when they returned from the war, placing over 500 in the first few years.[22] He also spoke at fellowship teas and evangelistic events. He organised a launch picnic in the national park, a quarterly tea at the Chapter House, and a fellowship magazine called *The Venturer*.[23] In 1946 an ordinance was passed by the synod to provide for the salary, rent and travel expenses of the chaplain, recognising this role as separate from other diocesan organisations.[24] He gathered teams of young leaders around him and was dearly loved. He was charismatic and brought energy and unity to the existing youth ministry in churches.

Diocesan structures and committees

As well as appointments, Mowll ensured that diocesan structures and committees would energise youth ministry. The chaplain for youth had been under the care of the Board of Education, but in 1949, Mowll and

---

[20] Letter from Graham Delbridge to Mark Rogers in Histories of Youthworks / Port Hacking Sites: opening and celebrations [2019/011], SDA.
[21] Loane, *Archbishop Mowll*, 217.
[22] Letter from Graham Delbridge to Mark Rogers, 3 October 1977 in Histories of Youthworks / Port Hacking Sites: opening and celebrations [2019/011], SDA.
[23] Board of Education, minutes meeting 22 May 1943, Board of Education Minutes 1940-1948, [2019/011], SDA.
[24] "The History of the Youth Department" (1952), in Histories of Youthworks / Port Hacking Sites: opening and celebrations [2019/011], SDA.

the synod created a Youth Department that was independent. Its goals were:

- Assisting the development of Youth Work in the Parishes.
- Providing facilities for the general guidance and help of youth.
- Training of youth in leadership.
- Encouraging cooperative activities amongst youth.
- All things incidental to the matters aforesaid.[25]

At the first meeting, with Mowll in the chair, Delbridge was appointed as the Youth Director of the diocese. The Home Mission Society continued to pay for the salary of the chaplain, but the rest of the work of the department was supplied by fundraising. In a couple of years, the department included office staff as well as a field-worker. In 1946 there were 50 active branches of the Church of England Fellowship Diocese of Sydney (CEFDOS) and 1,700 active members, most aged between 14 to 18 years.[26] By the end of the decade, there was a fellowship group in almost every parish.[27] In 1950, CEFDOS was transferred to the care of the Youth Department.

Training and the CENEF Leadership Centre

Along with developing and resourcing key leaders and diocesan structures, central to Mowll's strategy was *training* young people. He understood training as giving young people opportunities to lead ministries, to grow in Christian understanding and in their ability to teach others. Each year, Mowll held services at the cathedral for the confirmees of the last two years, 'A rallying point for the youth of the diocese'.[28] In 1937 there were 1,159 males and 2,739 females confirmed.[29] He wanted to remind these adolescents of their

---

[25] "Youth Department," *Year Book of the Diocese of Sydney,* 1955, 105.

[26] "Annual Report, 1945/46" in Board of Education Minutes 1940-1948, [2019/011], SDA.

[27] Archbishop Mowll, "Presidential Address," *Year Book of the Diocese of Sydney,* 1951, 48.

[28] "The Cathedral and Youth," *Sydney Diocesan Magazine,* April 1, 1937, Vol. 28, No. 3, 48.

[29] "The Cathedral and Youth."

'confirmation promises' and inspire them to be active members and leaders in the church.

In 1946 Mowll personally directed Delbridge to establish a leadership course to train young people, especially those involved in the camping and fellowship ministries.[30] Delbridge organised evening lectures in the city two nights a week for five months of the year, and 30 young people enrolled. By 1953, there were 40 people doing this course, and another 40 doing it by correspondence.[31] The course covered theology, evangelism, the Prayer Book, and an introduction to the psychology of adolescents.[32] Mowll hoped that by the early 1950s there would be full time youth workers in parishes, and the Board of Education and Youth Department began to plan a basic course for fulltime workers.[33] Mowll still felt that this was inadequate, and encouraged the Youth Department to plan a course to train youth workers. As the diocese grew, 'He felt he would like to see in every parish, a Rector, Curate, and full-time youth worker'.[34]

Archbishop Mowll and his wife Dorothy also had a vision for training young people at a centre in the city, and they were willing to invest enormous diocesan resources into it. During the war years, the Archbishop and his wife had established the Church of England National Emergency Fund (CENEF) to raise money for the war effort at home. This was for chaplains, church huts, canteens and hostels for service men and women on leave. When the war was over, they used

---

[30] "Report of CEFDOS," in Board of Education, minutes meeting 31 May 1946, in Board of Education Minutes 1940-1948, [2019/011], SDA.

[31] Youth Department, minutes meeting 13 August 1953, in Board of Education Minutes 1940-1948, [2019/011], SDA.

[32] Board of Education, minutes meeting 13 August 1953, in Board of Education Minutes 1940-1948, [2019/011], SDA.

[33] Board of Education, minutes meeting 10 September 1953 in Board of Education Minutes 1940-1948, [2019/011], SDA.

[34] Mowll spoke about this plan at the welcome of the 2nd chaplain, Arthur Deane. Youth Department, minutes meeting September 1952.

this same fund to assist returned servicemen and to create a centre for the training of youth.[35] A fundraising brochure explained this goal:

> It is designed that the CENEF Centre shall be, as it were, a bridge over which men and women of the Services will pass over the complex period of returning to civil life.

> ... (It will) provide opportunities for recreation and for training in Leadership, in co-operation with the youth organisations of the Church, and with facilities for study.[36]

A large office building on Castlereagh St in the central business district was purchased and opened in October 1946 by the Duke of Gloucester as the 'CENEF Memorial Centre for the Training of Christian Youth Leaders'.[37] It was a costly venture, purchase and renovations cost 82,000 pounds.[38] By 1953, Mowll was still fundraising, calling the debt: 'our Everest to climb'.[39]

The CENEF Memorial Centre was an office building with four floors. On the first floor, there was an auditorium where large meetings, concerts or film screenings could take place. On the second floor, there was hostel-type accommodation for returned servicemen and country boys. On the third floor, there was office space for the different youth organisations: the Youth Department, CEBS (Church of England Boys' Society), GFS (Girl's Friendly Society), the Board of Education, CEFDOS, IVF, TCF (Teacher's Christian Fellowship) and the Crusader Union. This led to a sharing of ideas and energy across the organisations. There was also a library and prayer room. Finally, on the fourth floor there was a restaurant which was a place for young people to gather, particularly young workers in the city. In the basement, there

---

[35] Archbishop H. Mowll, "Presidential Address to Synod, 1946," *Year Book of the Diocese of Sydney 1947,* 52.

[36] Rhoda Astles "The Story of CENEF," (1946), 28, in Canons Boxes – CENEF History: Financial Statements; Hostel, CH Box 1075, SDA.

[37] CENEF Board of Management, minutes meeting 12 July 1955 in Canons Boxes – CENEF History: Financial Statements; Hostel, CH BOX 1075, SDA.

[38] Today, this would be equivalent to almost 6 million dollars.

[39] Dorothy Mowll was an enthusiastic mountain climber, no doubt this metaphor was of her creation, or inspired by her.

was a photographic laboratory for making and keeping filmstrips to show movies.[40] The CENEF building was to become an open house that facilitated both leadership training as well as a network of Christians involved in youth ministry inspiring a sense of belonging and being part of something bigger, an energy that was taken back into the parishes.[41]

The Archbishop and his wife continued to take a key interest in the centre. Dorothy herself ran the restaurant committee and often popped in to see what was happening and to connect with ministry leaders. According to Arthur Deane (Chaplain for Youth 1952-1955) it was her vision that a college for youth workers might develop at the CENEF centre on the roof, with a cyclone fence so that games could be played there.[42]

The CENEF centre was an open house that facilitated both leadership training as well as a creating a network of young Christian leaders. The majority were Sydney Anglicans, but there were many others. Rex Harris, who worked for the department at the time, claims: 'They were all milling around the Youth Department: Baptist, Methodist, Presbyterian, they all came, there was a network.'[43] He claims that the Youth Department was the largest in the world, there was nothing else like it. Harris also claimed that: 'People were coming from all around the world saying: "let's see what you're doing", because it was working.'[44] Mowll's ground-breaking vision was an example to evangelicals all over the world.

[40] Rex Harris, Ossie Emery, Alan Patrick & Helen Patrick, *The Delbridge Years: Youth Work in the Anglican Diocese of Sydney from 1942-54* (Sydney South: Anglican Press Australia, 2012), 24.
[41] Harris, *The Delbridge Years,* 51-52.
[42] Arthur Deane, interviewed by Ruth Lukabyo, 23 April 2012.
[43] Rex Harris and Don Robertson interviewed by Ruth Lukabyo, 15 May 2012.
[44] Rex Harris and Don Robertson interviewed by Ruth Lukabyo, 15 May 2012.

Campsites and Camp Howard

The next part of Mowll's strategy to evangelise and train youth, was to establish a camping ministry.[45] In 1944, he heard that a property in the Royal National Park facing the Port Hacking River was for sale and travelled down to look at the spacious house and 11.5 acres of land.[46] He persuaded the Home Mission Society to again pay the cost[47] and it was named Chaldercot after his family home back in Dover.[48] Camps began that year with very basic facilities and the personal service of Delbridge who rowed supplies across the river. Weekend camps were held by different organisations including: Inter Schools Christian Fellowship (ISCF), Fellowship groups, CEBS, Church Missionary Society League of Youth, GFS, Teachers' College and the Evangelical Union.[49]

The campsite was so popular that more space was needed. A property next door called Rathane had been bought by CENEF as a rest home for returned servicemen. Delbridge successfully persuaded Dorothy and the CENEF council to hand it over to HMS for youth work: 'we persuaded the then Archbishop's wife to let us have (it) for youth work so that we could use it when the war was over'.[50] The Department used Rathane for training, running week-long camps four times a year. In October 1947, Mowll dedicated the new hall at Chaldercot and Rathane

---

45 He was perhaps inspired by his youthful experiences of ministry with the CSSM and later when he served in Canada, he would have been aware of the IVF Pioneer Camps established by Howard Guinness (IVF missioner who helped establish the Evangelical Union at Sydney University as well as the Crusader Union) and directed by the Australian Vincent Craven.
46 Harris, *The Delbridge Years*, 17.
47 Letter from Norman Fox to Rex Harris, 1984 in Histories of Youthworks / Port Hacking Sites: opening and celebrations, [2019/011], SDA.
48 Harris, *The Delbridge Years*, 18.
49 Port Hacking Management Committee, meeting minutes 1945, in Histories of Youthworks / Port Hacking Sites: opening and celebrations, [2019/011], SDA.
50 Letter from Graham Delbridge to Mark Rogers, 3 October 1977, in Histories of Youthworks / Port Hacking Sites: opening and celebrations, [2019/011], SDA.

with 500 people who gathered at Port Hacking.[51] A few years later, Shuna, a house at Leura was purchased by CEFDOS for house-parties and hosted camps too.[52] Mowll and Dorothy remained actively involved in the camping ministry, often visiting Port Hacking and staying short breaks. There was a small cottage at Rathane where they stayed that became known as 'The Archbishop's Cottage'.[53]

Mowll's vision for training and evangelising young people would be further developed through the Camp Howard camping ministry. This was the outworking of a dream of Neville Bathgate, who became the chaplain to youth in 1956. Bathgate was passionate about youth ministry and after he finished studying theology at Moore College, he spent a year in Canada with Pioneer Camps.[54] He studied their organisation, program and use of outdoor education.[55] When he returned, he went to the archbishop to convince him that a similar ministry could be run at Port Hacking. Mowll was impressed by him and appointed him chaplain, head of CEBS and the Youth Department.

Bathgate's plan was to run holiday camps at Rathane and Chaldercot that would evangelise young people. They were to experience 'the holiday of a lifetime with Christ at the centre' (the Camp Howard motto).[56] The Youth Department ran week-long camps every school holiday for students in fourth class to the end of high school. Bathgate was committed to calling the ministry *Camp Howard* '... so named in recognition of the services to youth work of the Archbishop of Sydney, Dr Howard Mowll.'[57] At the camps, students took part in archery, canoeing and sailing, but also heard Christian talks and discussions. 'The central theme of the camp is the study of the Bible and the

---

[51] Mission Society HMS, meeting 16 September 1946, Port Hacking Management Committee, [2019/011], SDA.

[52] Harris, *The Delbridge Years*, 20.

[53] Harris, *The Delbridge Years*, 20.

[54] "600 Children Go to Camp," *Australian Church Record*, March 14, 1957, 8.

[55] Rex Harris, *The Vision Splendid* (Woodbine, NSW: Harris, 2016), 30.

[56] Harris, *The Vision Splendid*, 30.

[57] "Thousand Children at Sydney Camps," *Australian Church Record*, 6 December 1956, 9.

presentation of the Christian life.'[58] One counsellor recounted a song they had sung at the early camps, to the tune of 'Waltzing Matilda'.

> 'On the shores of the beautiful Port Hacking
> Stands the Camp that I adore,
> Where the sparkling waters always glisten
> Round National Park that we explore.'[59]

The camps were immediately very popular and in the first year there were over 1,000 young people who came to Camp Howard.

It is hard to evaluate the impact these camps had. Anecdotally there are many stories of young people claiming they were converted. Counsellors on the camp reported the 'many lads who accepted their Lord and Saviour.'[60] Camp Howard camps were run for the next 30 years and many other organisations such as Crusaders and Scripture Union were influenced by this model. When Deer Park, a new Youth Centre, was opened in June 1959, Arthur Deane spoke about the importance of 'evangelism among our youth' and claimed that the centre was 'unequalled in the Anglican world.'[61]

Missions

Mowll's final strategy to evangelise and train youth was to boost organised missions. Mowll was committed to evangelism, and mission at home and abroad. Nothing was more important. This commitment to evangelism was stirringly expressed in his presidential address to synod in 1938:

> We must give our whole-hearted attention to the great commission our Lord laid upon us – the work of evangelism at home and abroad. Nothing can compensate

---

[58] "Thousand Children at Sydney Camps," *Australian Church Record*, 6 December 1956, 9.
[59] "600 Children Go to Camp," *Australian Church Record*, 14 March 1957, 8.
[60] "600 Children Go to Camp." *Australian Church Record*, 14 March 1957, 8. Some who were converted went on to be involved in camping ministry for many years, for example, Rex Harris. Harris, *The Vision Splendid* 58.
[61] "Archbishop Opens New Youth Centre," *Australian Church Record*, Vol. 23, No.12. 9 July 1959.

for any neglect of this. It is the radical, the fundamental thing which inspires, energises, and gives real and permanent value to all else ... **Study** evangelism; **preach** evangelism; **live** evangelism.[62]

Mowll's focus on evangelism to youth can be seen in his early backing of beach missions in Sydney. He encouraged clergy to support the beach services in December and January at Coogee, Manly and Cronulla which were attended by thousands of children and young people.[63] In 1934, Mowll gave an evangelistic talk at the Manly mission, on a summer Sunday afternoon, facing the swimming pool.[64]

In the 1950s, there was an appetite for mission amongst the Australian churches in NSW. All the Protestant denominations launched missions in the local parishes, motivated by a desire for revival, but it was only the Church of England that focused on youth, due to the influence of Mowll.[65] A report in the *Sydney Morning Herald* in 1950 claimed that:

> ... with a rediscovered sense of mission, and new methods, bold attempts are being made to confront the Australian people with the claims of the Christian Gospel. No one who watches trends in our society will deny the presence of a revived spirit amongst Christians. Crusades for Christ, missions to the nation, new life campaigns are the order of the day.[66]

There was an energy in the churches to expand in the spreading suburbs and an optimism about outreach.

---

[62] "Our Archbishop's Address to Synod," *SDM*, September 1938, Vol. 29, No. 9, 128, 129.

[63] *SDM*, 1 January 1935, Vol. 26, No.1, 2.

[64] "Archbishop Mowll at Manly Pool," *Daily Telegraph*, Monday 10 December 1934, 5.

[65] The Methodists began the "Commonwealth Crusade for Christ," the Presbyterians launched a "New Life Movement" and the Congregationalists organised a "Forward Movement." Lukabyo, *Ministry for Youth*, 185.

[66] "Evangelism has New Vigour," *Sydney Morning Herald*, 9 October 1950.

This optimism was taken up by Mowll and the Youth Department in the Youth to Youth missions of the 1950s. Historian Bill Lawton claims that Mowll's missional strategy can be seen best in the Youth to Youth missions: 'evangelism was the key to progress, with the under 25s as the main target group'.[67] Mowll instructed the department to organise missions around the diocese that were led by youth and sought to evangelise other youth, particularly those with a Church of England background. The evangelism of youth was to be done at the same time as family missions in new suburbs such as: Balgowlah, Auburn, Chester Hill, Sefton, Campsie, Parramatta, St Mary's and Penrith.[68] In the first year, 15 missions were planned with the aim:

> ... to reach all of Church of England children in school years and all young people who have been confirmed in the last 10 years, and through them to reach their parents, with a view of winning them for Jesus Christ.[69]

Mowll wrote a letter to every young person confirmed in the previous year, to invite them to give money and to pray for the mission,[70] and the Youth Department printed 3,000 bookmarks to encourage people to pray.[71]

The department and the diocesan missioner George Rees[72] organised the missions but teams of young people came with them to do evangelism *youth to youth*. Teams of young people joined the rector and missioner to visit every Church of England family in the area, inviting them to church and giving them literature supplied by the Youth

---

[67] William James Lawton, "The Winter of Our Days: The Anglican Diocese of Sydney, 1950-1960," *Lucas: An Evangelical History Review* 9 (April 1990): 14.
[68] Youth Department Minutes, meeting October 1950, in Histories of Youthworks/Port Hacking Sites: opening and celebrations, [2019/011], SDA.
[69] Youth Department Minutes, meeting 17 August 1950, in Histories of Youthworks/Port Hacking Sites: opening and celebrations, [2019/011], SDA.
[70] Archbishop Mowll, "Presidential Address," *Year Book of the Diocese of Sydney, 1951,* 54.
[71] Youth Department Minutes, of meeting held 17 August 1950.
[72] Rees worked for the Board of Diocesan Missions (BDM) for nine years, 1946-1954.

Department.[73] Rees claimed that it was in harmony with Mowll's interests that his emphasis as a missioner was upon 'youth, youth, youth.'[74]

The missions continued throughout the 1950s. For example, in 1954 at Guildford, the department organised a Youth to Youth mission. The main evangelistic talks were given by Arthur Deane, who had just taken over from Delbridge as chaplain, and he spoke 'with quiet, direct persuasiveness.'[75] Teams of young people from the fellowships of Chatswood, Hurstville, Campsie and Northbridge organized concerts, social nights, quizzes, and film nights. On Saturday night, they watched the film 'What's your excuse?' starring Billy Graham, the Youth for Christ star from the US.[76] The mission gave young people leadership training while they evangelised other youth.

The Youth to Youth missions were a brilliant success. They brought young people into the churches and advocated for ministry to the whole family. After the missions, new properties were often purchased in the new areas, and mobile churches met the temporary needs of the church.[77] Youth evangelism facilitated church planting in the expanding suburban belt of Sydney. With the success of the missions, the Youth Department began to dream of evangelising every young person in Sydney and training and appointing a youth worker for every local church.[78]

Evaluation

An evaluation of the legacy of Mowll in the Diocese of Sydney, must recognise his ground-breaking vision for youth ministry.

---

[73] Lawton, "The Winter of Our Days," 14.
[74] From an interview with Rees cited by John Gray, "Evangelism in the Anglican Diocese of Sydney 1959-1989", University of New South Wales, 1994, 95.
[75] "Youth Campaign," *The Broadcaster,* 20 October 1954, 1.
[76] "Youth Campaign," *The Broadcaster,* 20 October 1954, 1.
[77] Lawton, "The Winter of Our Days," 14.
[78] *SDM,* Vol. 5, No. 9, 20 March 1955, 49.

In 1954, Mowll himself reflected in the Sydney Morning Herald on what had been achieved in the 20 years that he had been Archbishop. He particularly mentioned the growth in numbers at the theological colleges and the significance of youth work. Other achievements he mentioned were the CENEF centre, 'the youth centre for training youth leaders' and the Port Hacking campsites that ran camps and weekends that 'are an effective method of making personal contacts'.[79] He believed that these innovations in evangelism and training of youth had led to vibrant parish youth work and 'a genuine spiritual recovery among a large number of the younger generation'.[80]

After his death in 1958, Sydney Anglicans looked back on his legacy and many believed that youth work was the most significant feature. For example, the rector of Fairfield commented that in 1933 in parishes fellowships were 'very few in their infancy ... Today there is scarcely a church in the 230 odd parishes which has no Youth Fellowship'.[81] This expansion in youth work led to larger numbers at the theological colleges:

> The quickening of the gospel ministry among young people has had its effect in recruitment for full-time service. For example, when the Archbishop arrived, there were 13 full-time students at Moore College; at present there are 105. Deaconess House has had a similar expansion.[82]

---

79 He also mentioned 32 new churches built, Gilbulla the conference centre, a few welfare organisations, and the expansion of the missionary organisations, Church Missionary Society and the Board of Mission. Arch. Mowll "Primate Looks Back – and Forward," Sydney Morning Herald, Saturday 17 April 1954.
80 Mowll, "Primate Looks Back – and Forward", *Sydney Morning Herald,* Saturday 17 April 1954.
81 The Rector of St Barnabas Fairfield, "Death of an Archbishop," *The Biz,* Wednesday 29 October. 1959.
82 The Rector, "Death of an Archbishop," *The Biz,* Wednesday 29 October 1959.

Because of the healthy youth work, there was an exponential growth in the supply of clergy and missionaries to facilitate gospel work at home and abroad.

In evaluating Mowll's legacy, there is agreement amongst historians that along with overseas mission, youth ministry was a key priority in Mowll's evangelistic vision, though there is little description of what that looked like in the diocese. Piggin and Linder argue: 'The key was Moore College to send out the missionaries and the Youth Department to reach the youth'.[83] Cameron comments on Mowll's 'missionary vision and evangelistic enthusiasm',[84] that he led Sydney Anglicans in more active evangelism and understood the importance of youth work.[85] Judd and Cable claim that Mowll's 'main goal was to stimulate his diocese into a visible evangelistic witness'[86] and argue that this witness before the war was focused on Sunday School and Scripture, but after shifted to youth work.[87] This change was largely because of the influence of Mowll, and it seems his wife Dorothy shared the same vision.

Mowll reorganised the finances and structures of the diocese to achieve his vision. He was particularly concerned with evangelising and training youth, inspired by his own experiences as a young man in the para-church student movement. He established the Youth Department, built the CENEF centre, and directed the purchase of the Port Hacking properties. The youth ministry created was ground-breaking and recognised by many around the evangelical world as such. Mowll also instigated the Youth to Youth missions. Lawton argues that because of these factors there was:

---

[83] Stuart Piggin and Robert Linder, *Attending to the National Soul: Evangelical Christians in Australian History, 1914-2014* (Monash University Publishing, 2019), 274.
[84] Cameron, *Phenomenal Sydney*, 37.
[85] Cameron, *Phenomenal Sydney*, 75.
[86] Stephen Judd and Ken Cable, *Sydney Anglicans: A History of the Diocese* (Sydney: Anglican Information Office, 1987), 245.
[87] Judd & Cable, *Sydney Anglicans*, 244

... evangelistic fervour, not experienced since the days of the great tent missions in the early years of the century. It was in no small measure due to the enthusiasm and imagination of Howard Mowll who had placed energetic men into positions of leadership. They were fired with the possibility of evangelising Australia in their generation.[88]

Lawton correctly identifies that part of Mowll's genius was the appointment of gifted men such as Delbridge and Bathgate.

Mowll's legacy remains today in the Youth Department, now known as Youthworks. Youthworks has inherited the resources and campsites that Mowll and the diocese invested in the 1930s-1950s. There are campsites at Port Hacking, Nowra and the Blue Mountains, and evangelistic camping ministries that are the envy of other dioceses. Youthworks has 150 permanent employees, while most other Anglican diocese are struggling to employ one youth director. Sydney also has a theological college to train youth ministers, Youthworks College, that is unique because of its specialised focus. The college keeps Dorothy's vision alive of training full time youth workers and placing a youth worker in every parish. This legacy remains because of the ground-breaking vision of Archbishop Mowll.

---

[88] Lawton, "The Winter of Our Days," 16, 17.

10. Mowll as Primate

Geoffrey R. Treloar[1]

On 22 November 1947, in the fourteenth year of his episcopate, Howard Mowll was elected as the sixth Primate of the Church of England in Australia and Tasmania. The election came as a welcome relief to Mowll. Having come to Sydney with the expectation of becoming the leader of the Australian church, he had been deeply disappointed to miss out in 1935 when the choice of the Archbishop of Perth, Henry Le Fanu, made him the first Archbishop of Sydney *not* also to be Primate of the Church of England in Australia and Tasmania. Now the church's arrangements had been restored to what, in his mind, they should have been all along, Mowll eagerly embraced the new demands on his time and energy as he folded the additional role of Primate into his existing duties. For the last eleven years of his life, he was the Archbishop of Sydney *and* the Primate of the Australian church. For Mowll they were two sides of the one office.

Despite the importance of the office, historians of Australian Anglicanism have paid scant attention to Mowll as Primate, preferring to concentrate on more 'progressive' figures such as Bishops John Moyes of Armidale and Francis de Witt Batty of Newcastle.[2] Even the

[1] I would like to thank Sarah Mayhew of the General Synod Office, Louise Trott of the Sydney Diocesan Archives and Erin Mollenhauer of Moore Theological College for their assistance in collecting the materials on which this chapter is based. I am also grateful for comments on an earlier draft of the chapter by Brian Dickey and David Hilliard, both of Adelaide.
[2] Tom Frame, 'Local Differences, Social and National Identity 1930-1966,' in *Anglicanism in Australia: A History*, ed. B.N. Kaye et. al. (Carlton South: Melbourne University Press, 2002), 100-23. Brian H. Fletcher, *The Place of Anglicanism in Australia: Church, Society and Nation* (Mulgrave, Vic.: Broughton Publishing, 2008), chap. 7 and *An English Church in Australian Soil: Anglicanism, Australian Society and the English Connection Since 1788* (Canberra: Barton Books, 2015), chap. 8. Loane, *Archbishop Mowll*, chap. 9 provides an account of Mowll as Primate. Loane's concentration on Mowll's travels implies there was little else of importance to recount. The Primacy

obvious questions therefore remain to be answered. What did Mowll say and do as Primate? What did it amount to? But, by way of evaluation, it also needs to be asked: was he ahead of or behind the times? Was he forward or backward looking? What did he contribute to the development of the Primateship? Does Mowll as Primate warrant celebration or neglect?

Primate of a Divided Church

When the Primate Henry Le Fanu, Archbishop of Perth, died in September 1946, Mowll's standing in the Australian Church was very different from what it had been in 1935 when he was a young and inexperienced newcomer. By this point he had behind him some twelve years of effective leadership of the Diocese of Sydney and the Province of New South Wales, as well as a strong record of participation in the life of the national church.[3] He was, moreover, easily the senior metropolitan bishop. Ostensibly his rivals were the other metropolitan bishops – Joseph Booth, Archbishop of Melbourne since 1942; Reginald Halse, Archbishop of Brisbane since 1943; and Robert Moline, recently appointed Le Fanu's successor as Archbishop of Perth in April 1947.[4] On the grounds of seniority alone it would have been a further affront not to elect Mowll a second time. Yet, in an atmosphere soured by the 'Red Book Case',[5] Halse and Moline as Anglo-Catholics seem to have had their supporters. The election was delayed until late in 1947 when a church congress to be held in Melbourne to mark the centenary of the foundation of the Dioceses of

---

itself has been little studied, but see Keith Rayner, 'The Primacy: Past, Present and Future,' The Sydney Smith Memorial Lecture, 18 November 1998, and Tom Frame, *Anglicans in Australia* (Sydney: UNSW Press, 2007), 86-99.

[3] Mowll frequently stood in as Chair of the Standing Committee because the distance of Perth prevented Le Fanu's regular attendance at the meetings in Sydney. General Synod Archives [cited hereafter as GSA] Series 43/18. Standing Committee Minute Books for the period 1935-1946.

[4] Mowll also benefited from the return to England in 1943 of the Anglo-Catholic Archbishop of Brisbane, William Wand, to become the Bishop of Bath and Wells. Wand, who had also come to office in 1934, would have been an appealing alternative to Mowll.

[5] On which, see Ruth Teale, 'The "Red Book" Case,' *Journal of Religious History* 12.1 (June 1982): 74-89 and Robert Tong in Chapter 6 above.

Adelaide, Melbourne and Newcastle would bring the bishops together. As Acting Primate Mowll opened the congress. In this setting he also delivered at Archbishop Booth's invitation the Moorhouse Lectures in which he argued for the need of the Australian church in the aftermath of World War II to be more outward looking and engaged with the wider world.[6] Intentionally or otherwise, Mowll made his pitch for election as Primate along these lines.

The bishops gathered for the election on November 22, 1947, in the Melbourne suburb of Cheltenham under the presidency of the senior bishop, William Elsey, the Bishop of Kalgoorlie. According to the account provided afterwards by the Bishop of Ballarat, William Johnson, after the archbishops had spoken and withdrawn from the meeting,

> the bishops entered upon deliberations which continued for several hours. Every bishop spoke, and the whole of the proceedings were on a very high level and were characterised by a spirit of deep solemnity and of true brotherhood.[7]

He also reported that 'the Archbishop of Sydney ... received an absolute majority in the ballot', so that 'the decision was a very decisive one'.[8] A somewhat different account was given later by the Anglo-Catholic James Housden, at the time the newly elected Bishop of Rockhampton, who recalled:

> My first meeting [of the Australian bishops] was a momentous one because it involved the election of a

---

[6] Howard Mowll, *Seeing All the World: a series of six lectures delivered in Saint Paul's Cathedral, Melbourne, during November, Nineteen hundred and forty-seven, together with two addresses given at the 1947 Melbourne Church Congress* (Melbourne: Ruskin Press, nd [1948]).

[7] 'Election of Primate,' *Church Standard* [cited hereafter as *CS*], 13 February 1948, 6-7.

[8] Judd and Cable, *Sydney Anglicans* (Sydney: Anglican Information Office, 1987), 251 say that the result was unanimous. I have found no evidence of this. In 1935 Mowll himself revealed that he had lost the election by only one vote. On this occasion he made no comment on the numbers.

Primate from among the four archbishops. We elected Abp Howard Mowll of Sydney after a long and difficult debate, for at that time there was deep feeling between so-called high Church and low Church.[9]

Even the Bishop of Ballarat noted that, when the result of the ballot was announced, 'There was a telling silence, after which the senior bishop declared the Archbishop of Sydney duly elected Primate of the Australian Church'.[10]

Not being wanted by all the bishops was Mowll's first problem on acceding to the Primacy. *The Church Standard* reflected the divisions within Australian Anglicanism when it reported Mowll's election:

> We may hope that Dr Mowll's election may effect happier relationships throughout the Australian Church. It will be a tragedy for Anglicanism in Australia if our comprehensiveness is lost by a regimentation of Churchmanship, whether of 'High' or 'Low', within certain dioceses.[11]

At stake was the inclusiveness of the Anglican tradition and the unity of the Australian church. At the time of the election it was not clear whether these fears were justified and whether the evangelical Mowll could hold the church together and preserve the integrity of Australian Anglicanism.

Mowll addressed this problem immediately. To the great surprise of the other bishops, when the result of the election was announced, he fell to his knees before the presiding bishop and asked for his blessing. His humility appears to have made a deep impression. Mowll's characteristic desire to serve is also the key to what Marcus Loane singles out as the outstanding feature of Mowll's primacy, viz. his frequent and extensive travels. Over the ensuing eleven years, he visited every diocese in the country. Greatly facilitated by recent

---

[9] James Housden, *Plus James: A Bishop Looks Back* (Melbourne: Anglican Media Melbourne, 1995), 68.

[10] 'Election of Primate,' *CS*, 13 February 1948, 6-7.

[11] 'The Primacy,' *CS*, 28 November 1947, 3.

improvements in communications and travel technologies, these journeys made Mowll the most widely travelled Primate to date. Mostly his visits were occasioned by special events such as consecrations and important anniversaries. Such occasions should have the dignity of the primatial presence, but they also provided both a new opening for the application of Mowll's cherished fellowship principle and an opportunity to embody the ideal of the Australian church. Effective in Sydney, personal contact was no less so beyond his own diocese. For it won over many Anglicans around the country by creating a sense of Mowll's authenticity and earnestness.[12] The solution to Mowll's first problem went a long way towards preserving the unity and comprehensiveness of the Church and provided the condition of his success as Primate. Mowll's travel and personal presence also set a new benchmark for the Primacy.

On taking up office, Mowll's second problem was knowing exactly what he had to do. For there was no clear statement of what was expected of the Primate. One indicator was the Church's constitution which had been adopted in 1872. Like the constitution itself, the provisions for the Primateship were minimal.[13] It gave the Primate power to summon, prorogue and dissolve a General Synod. He was also to preside over the General Synod and participate in its debates. But, reflecting the limitations of travel and communication in the colonial era, that was all. Inevitably the role grew as technology improved and both the church and the General Synod itself developed. As they emerged, its various committees and instrumentalities required the Primate's formal leadership. But the political reality was difficult. Although the Primate was little more than *primus inter pares* and the other bishops would not be dictated to, they still looked to the Primate for leadership. Expectations were high, and criticism could be strong and cutting.

---

[12] Looking back, Bishop Housden pronounced Mowll a success. Housden, *Plus James*, 68. See also the assessment after Mowll's death in *The Anglican*, 31 October 1958, 10 and the non-Sydney estimates in *The Anglican*, 7 November 1958, 1, 9.

[13] R.A. Giles, *The Constitutional History of the Australian Church* (London: Skeffington & Son, 1929), 272-3.

The other indicator was the example of the five previous Primates. This was uneven. The first Primate, Frederic Barker, having instigated the General Synod (which he regarded as one of his main achievements), appears to have shown little further active interest. However, his attendance at the 1878 Lambeth Conference established the representative dimension of the role. Barker's successor, Alfred Barry, a champion of Anglican comprehensiveness with a vision of global Anglicanism, might have provided imaginative leadership for the Australian Church, but he did not stay long enough to make a deep mark. In their own ways William Saumarez Smith and John Wright extended the largely symbolic representative side of the role. Le Fanu, Mowll's immediate predecessor, had been a popular and impressive leader of the church, his remoteness in Perth notwithstanding.[14] He was outspoken on major issues, a persistent worker for church unity, an effective chair of the General Synod when it met in 1937 and 1945, and a strong leader during the war. In 1947 it remained to be seen what Mowll would make of an expanding role.

Representation

Representation of the Australian church began almost immediately. Within days Mowll left the country for the 1948 Lambeth Conference. As Archbishop of Sydney, he would have gone anyway, but now he went as Primate of the Church of England in Australia. Mowll revelled in the dignity of his position and was no doubt gratified by recognition that he 'probably knows more quarters of the world more intimately than any other bishop'.[15] Apart from a report on *Dispensation in Theory and Practice*,[16] he played no great part in the deliberations of the conference, but he was a member of the 'Inner Circle' that advised the Archbishop of Canterbury and kept him informed of what was

---

[14] On Le Fanu, see J.H.M. Honniball, 'Archbishop and Primate: Henry Frewen Le Fanu,' in *Four Bishops and Their See: Perth, Western Australia 1857-1957*, ed. Fred Alexander (Nedlands, W.A.: University of Western Australia Press, 1957), 157-214.

[15] *The Handbook of the Lambeth Conference 1948* (London: SPCK, 1948), 45.

[16] *Lambeth Conference 1948. Report on Dispensation in Theory and Practice Prepared by the Committee Appointed by the Archbishop of Sydney Primate of Australia* (Saffron Walden: SPCK, nd [1948]).

happening in the committee discussions.[17] Mowll also gladly participated in the conference preaching program at weekends, the purpose of which was to propagate the vision of a world-wide church.[18]

The conference itself, the first in almost twenty years, had two main purposes.[19] One was to reconstitute the Anglican Communion following the disruption of the Second World War. The second, evident in the theme 'God in His World and in His Church', was to affirm the importance of the Christian message for the world as it underwent reconstruction and the place of the Anglican Church in presenting it.[20] Driven hard by the Archbishop of Canterbury, not the least of its achievements was to reactivate the Lambeth Conference as an Anglican instrumentality at a time when it might easily have fallen by the wayside. Fisher's de-emphasis of English leadership in favour of the idea of an association of national churches in communion with the See of Canterbury also impressed upon the bishops the reality of their Anglican identity and what they could contribute collectively to the post-war world. Of this development, fellow Australian participant, Bishop John Moyes of Armidale, observed:

> It was a new idea, a new conception, and the more we thought of it the more we knew this was a greater idea than previous Lambeths had known. There was coming into

---

[17] For the 'Inner Circle', Geoffrey Cantuar to the Archbishop of Sydney, January 1948. Sydney Diocesan Archives [cited hereafter as SDA] 1990/043/018: 'Archbishop of Sydney – Correspondence 1947-1948. Lambeth Conference'.

[18] Mowll gave a detailed account of his time in England in the *Sydney Diocesan Magazine* [cited hereafter as *SDM*] 20 November 1948, 211-14. R.T. Jourdain to R.C. Kerle, 7 November 1957. SDA 1991/008/028: 'Bishop Coadjutor Correspondence 1957-1958. Lambeth Conference 1958 Kerle'.

[19] On Fisher and the Lambeth Conference, see Edward Carpenter, *Archbishop Fisher – His Life and Times* (Norwich: The Canterbury Press, 1991), chap. 37, and Colin Podmore, 'The Development of the Instruments of Communion,' in *The Oxford History of Anglicanism. Volume IV. Global Western Anglicanism, c. 1910-Present*, ed. Jeremy Morris (Oxford: Oxford University Press, 2017), 283-90.

[20] *Handbook of the Lambeth Conference 1948.*

being a conception of an Anglican Communion, as wide as the world.[21]

Similarly moved by the occasion, Mowll was among those who embraced this new pan-Anglicanism, accepting its resolutions and recommendations, and commending the various reports and the 'Pastoral Letter of the Bishops' to the Australian Church.[22]

In attending the Lambeth Conference, Mowll followed in the footsteps of his primatial predecessors, but he broke new ground only a fortnight later when he went to Amsterdam for the inauguration of the World Council of Churches as a representative of the Australian churches. This had Mowll present at an epoch-making event which marked a new beginning in the history of world Christianity.[23] Already an enthusiastic ecumenist as a member of the International Missionary Council out of which the World Council had developed, Mowll was glad to be on hand to 'take counsel about the desperate need of the world and the strength and weakness of the Church to meet it'.[24] Here he encountered some of the leading figures of contemporary world Christianity – John Mott, Reinhold Niebuhr, Martin Niemöller, and Visser 't Hooft – and he was plainly inspired by their commitment and vision. Like the Lambeth Conference, the program was dominated by the need to respond to the devastation and confusion of the post-war world. Its theme, 'Man's Disorder and God's Design', was a clear

---

[21] John S. Moyes, *In Journeyings Often* (Melbourne: Oxford University Press, 1949), 55-6, with 61.

[22] See *The Christian Doctrine of Man and the Church in the Modern World. The Report of Two Committees of the Lambeth Conference, 1948, with the Resolutions Based Upon Them* (London: SPCK, 1948). *Summary of Proceedings of the ... Twenty-Eighth Synod of the Diocese of Sydney ... 1948*, 54-60 [mindful that the Synod Proceedings are always published in the Year Book of the following year, Mowll's addresses to the Sydney Synod are cited hereafter as 'Sydney Synod' with the year of the Synod's occurrence].

[23] Epoch-making in the sense that, for the first time since the first of its many splits in 1054, it gave *some* organisational expression to the proposition that the church is one. Based on David Thompson, 'Ecumenism,' in *The Cambridge History of Christianity. Volume 9. World Christianities c.1914-c.2000*, ed. Hugh McLeod (Cambridge: Cambridge University Press, 2006), 59-63, esp. 60-61.

[24] Sydney Synod 1948, 62.

indication of what the church thought it had to offer at such a time. Mowll was deeply impressed by the speeches and discussions, and readily embraced the ideals and proposals needed for 'the contribution we can and must make, as members of Christ's Church'.[25]

These meetings of 1948 left an indelible mark on the content and perspective of the Primacy to follow. In directly addressing the nature and work of the church in the setting of the needs of the post-war world, they furnished Mowll with a framework for understanding its mission in this era of its history. Certainly they reinforced and extended the perspective he had advanced in the Moorhouse Lectures of the previous year. More than ever, the Australian church needed to view itself in an international perspective. With ever increasing urgency, Mowll now countered the tendency to parochialism evident among church people in Australia who, like the populace at large, were anxious to return to an untroubled life after the traumas of the war. To the clergy assembled for the General Synod in 1950, he expressed the wish 'that we might arouse ourselves and, through us, the members of the Church, to the challenge of these days for our witness and service to the world around us'.[26] The underlying principle was ecclesiological:

> We have hardly begun to understand what it means to belong to a Church which is universal. We tend to think, plan and work within the narrow boundaries of our Parish, or even of our Diocese. The Church has to choose between living unto itself and living as a Mission to the world.[27]

But the immediate impulse was historical. Towards the end of his episcopate, Mowll was still emphasizing the importance of prioritising international obligations as a response to the times: 'The Church needs to face the urgency of the challenge of these days and to witness more effectively to our near neighbours overseas, even at the expense of our

---

[25] Sydney Synod 1948, 61-65.
[26] H.K.W. Mowll, 'President's Address to Synod,' *The Church of England in Australia and Tasmania. Summary of Proceedings of the General Synod of the Dioceses in Australia and Tasmania. Session 1950. Official Report* (Sydney, 1951) [cited hereafter as 'General Synod 1950'], 21.
[27] Sydney Synod 1954, 57.

own individual or parochial building schemes.'[28] Both principle and pressing need made connection with world Christianity a force to realise at the highest level the Church's calling to 'extend the field of Christian influence in human life'.[29]

The pursuit of this ideal in the circumstances of the post war world explains two important trajectories in Mowll's Primateship through the 1950s. As an avowed champion of the new pan-Anglicanism, he pressed the Australian church to take a fuller part in the Anglican Communion. He himself always made a point of welcoming visiting Anglican leaders – principally the Archbishop of Canterbury in 1950, but also the Archbishop of York in 1951 and others such as Stephen Neill and John Stott, both emerging figures in the English church – as symbols of its coherence and work. Above all, Mowll was glad to lead the Australian contingent to the Anglican Congress in Minneapolis in 1954, the first since 1910. As intended, the spectacle of almost 700 Anglicans from 327 dioceses around the world united in faith and worship served as a vivid representation of the pan-Anglicanism inaugurated six years earlier. Like others, Mowll was inspired by this demonstration of the dignity of Anglican identity and the claims of its mission.[30] Greatly uplifted by the occasion, he faithfully relayed the message arising from its theme, 'The Call of God and the Mission of the Anglican Communion', back to the Australian church.[31] At Minneapolis Mowll also took his place in the Advisory Council on Missionary Strategy, another of the institutions created to improve the continuity and organisation of the Communion between Lambeth Conferences. His main contribution was to chair a sub-committee which recommended the creation of Regional Councils of the Church in the South Pacific and in South-East Asia rather than establish a new province or provinces for those regions. Subsequently Mowll was

---

[28] Sydney Synod 1957, 228.
[29] *SDM*, 20 February 1955, 137.
[30] *SDM*, 20 September 1954, 53-9, for Mowll's account of the Congress. Cf. J.S. Moyes, *America Revisited: Minneapolis and Evanston, 1954* (Sydney: Church Publishing Company, 1955), chap. 3, and Joost de Blank, *Mighty River: An Informal Account of the Anglican Congress at Minneapolis, 1954* (London: Church Information Board, 1954).
[31] Sydney Synod 1954, 53-5.

deeply disappointed when ill health prevented participation in the review of a decade's work and preparation for the next decade at Lambeth 1958, for which he had been preparing as a member of the Consultative Committee.[32]

Mowll also returned as a champion of ecumenicalism in its latest iteration. Serving variously as President and Chairman of the Executive of the Australian Council for the World Council of Churches over the ensuing decade, he defended the WCC against its local critics, drew attention to its activities and put forward active support for reconstruction in Europe as a first step towards greater realisation of the ideal of the world church.[33] In the years that followed, he went on commending the operations of the WCC, not only because of its lofty ideal, but also because it made good practical sense.[34] Cooperative action by the churches was the only means available to the church of carrying out its work on the scale required. Mowll was also present at the next WCC assembly at Evanston, Illinois in 1954 where his vision of 'the reality of the Universal Church' was enriched.[35] In line with the hope of the conference itself, that its results would take root at the local level throughout the world, Mowll impressed its findings on the Australian church in the hope that it would be inspired and instructed as he had been.[36] Its theme, 'Jesus Christ as Lord is the only hope of

---

[32] Eg. R.C. Kerle to the Bishop of Coventry, 1 April 1958. SDA 1991/008/028: 'Bishop Coadjutor Correspondence 1957-1958. Lambeth Conference 1958 Kerle'.
[33] 'Message From Primate of Australia,' in the flier 'For Christian Reconstruction of Europe,' copy and related correspondence in SDA 1992/26/78: 'Archbishop's Office. World Council of Churches'.
[34] E.g. Sydney Synod 1955, 43.
[35] *SDM*, 20 October 1954, 73-9, 108-12 and *SDM*, 20 January 1955, 118-19. *SDM*, 20 October 1954, 73 for the quotation. On the Assembly itself, see W.A. Visser 't Hooft (ed.), *The Evanston Report: The Second Assembly of the World Council of Churches 1954* (London: SCM, 1955).
[36] Howard Sydney, 'Foreword,' to Victor C. Hayes, *We Came Together: A Report of the Second Assembly of the World Council of Churches Held at Evanston in August, 1954* (Melbourne, 1954), 3. Sydney Synod 1954, 53-7. H.W.K. Mowll, 'President's Address to General Synod, 1955,' *The Church of England in Australia and Tasmania. Proceedings of the General Synod of the Dioceses in*

both the Church and the world', was precisely his message. Having facilitated the visit, Mowll took particular pleasure in the work of the Council and the ecumenical movement becoming visible locally when he welcomed the Executive Committee to Sydney early in 1956 for its first meeting in the southern hemisphere.[37]

Of his duties as the representative of the Australian church, none gave Mowll greater pleasure than attending the coronation of Elizabeth II in June 1953. Always a devotee of the royal family, he was gratified by the invitation which he regarded as 'a great honour'.[38] The day itself he regarded as 'one of the great events of our time'.[39] Apart from the pageantry, 'the reality of the Queen's dedication was matched by the desire for a similar dedication of life and service on the part of those who joined in the service'.[40] Mowll's hope was that it would 'result in a rehallowing of all British people to the service of God and their fellow-men'.[41]

Having been made a Companion of the Most Distinguished Order of St Michael and St George in the meantime – another 'great honour' – no less exhilarating for Mowll was the royal visit to Australia seven months later. He enthused that Elizabeth would be the first reigning monarch ever to set foot on Australian soil and, as such, the first sovereign to attend a service in an Australian church.[42] Following the initial events of the tour in Sydney, Mowll travelled to Canberra as the guest of the federal government to represent the church in this part of the Queen's visit which included the opening of parliament. Throughout he attended welcomes, receptions, garden parties and banquets, with his own place and that of his church in the existing

Australia and Tasmania. Session 1955. Official Report (Sydney: Anglican Press, 1960) [cited hereafter as 'General Synod 1955], 30.

[37] Franklin Clark (President of the United Lutheran Church in America) to Mowll, 25 April 1955, and W.A. Visser 't Hooft to Mowll, 19 March 1956, in SDA 1992/26/78: 'Archbishop's Office. World Council of Churches'. *SDM*, 1 March 1956, 127-32.

[38] *SDM*, 20 April 1953, 195.

[39] *SDM*, 20 July 1953, 46.

[40] *SDM*, 20 July 1953, 46.

[41] *SDM*, 20 April 1953, 195.

[42] *SDM*, 20 October 1953, 83.

order on show, clearly loving it all. At the end of the tour he sent a message of farewell on behalf of the Church of England in Australia.[43] Of its effect, he observed: '"God Save the Queen" will be sung more wholeheartedly than ever. We have now seen the Queen herself, and we feel that we know her.' More importantly, he averred of the Queen: 'How fortunate we are to have a Queen who encourages Church-going in every place she visits, and who so obviously leads the Christian life herself, reminding us that we cannot progress in our national life without religion.'[44] With his perception of the monarchy as a force for Christian civilisation so triumphantly vindicated, Mowll's Britishness came into its own while he was Primate. If it appears to mark him as backward looking and conservative, it must be remembered that he regarded Britishness as a force for order and progress in the world.[45]

Mowll's pronounced anglophilia appears to set a limit to his internationalism. That this inference is mistaken is made clear by two re-orientations he urged upon the Australian church during the 1950s. The first was the need for increased engagement with the Pacific region, Africa and Asia. Mowll had long been mindful of the church's responsibility to the Pacific, and he nurtured the connection with the African church through the links of Sydney with the Diocese of Tanganyika.[46] In relation to Asia, his decade as a missionary in China had left an enduring concern for the well-being of the church in that country.[47] But, from around 1950, Mowll advocated wider involvement in Asia as a whole. To the General Synod of that year he observed: 'A unique opportunity has been given to us, as representatives of the British way of life and of the Christian faith, to influence 1160 million of the world's population living in close proximity to our shores.'[48] Yet

---

[43] *SDM*, 20 April 1954, 163.

[44] *SDM*, 20 May 1954, 187.

[45] For Mowll's Britishness, see chapter 4 above.

[46] For Mowll's perspective on the Pacific and Asia, see the two addresses he gave in Honolulu in February 1952. *SDM*, 20 September 1952, 107-109 and 20 October 1952, 122-124.

[47] Eg. Howard W.K. Mowll, 'West China Through the Eyes of a Westerner,' *East Asian History* 34 (2007): 117-132. This was the ninth annual Morrison Lecture delivered on 29 May 1940.

[48] General Synod 1950, 20-1.

Australians generally, he observed, did not grasp what this meant. As ever, Mowll's primary concern was the gospel and the need to strengthen the Asian churches while there was still opportunity.[49] However, he also maintained that there was great economic and material need which provided Australians with an opening to be good neighbours. Not only the church but also the nation would benefit: 'Australia has so much to give. If we give generously our horizon will be broadened and our economy strengthened.'[50] Here indeed was an opportunity for the church to lead the nation. Mowll himself showed the way by open support for Australia's participation in the Colombo Plan, travelling all around the country promoting 'the challenge of South East Asia' for the Australian Board of Missions and the Church Missionary Society, and representing the Australian church on numerous visits to Asian countries, especially India in 1952-3 and China in 1956.[51] Continually maintaining that 'We in Australia must be Asia minded,'[52] the need to be doing more for South-East Asia became a refrain of Mowll's primacy. He ranks with the most vocal contemporary advocates of this reorientation in the Australian outlook.[53]

The principal reason for this sense of urgency was communism. Amid the tensions of the Cold War, and in the wake of the Chinese Revolution of 1949, Mowll shared the widespread fear of the spread of communism as an ideology inimical to Christianity.[54] A problem throughout the entire Asia-Pacific region, the threat was now near to

---

[49] *SDM*, 20 November 1952, 132. General Synod 1955, 21.

[50] General Synod 1950, 21.

[51] 'Seven Weeks in South-East Asia,' *SDM*, 20 February 1953, 165-173; 20 March 1953, 185-191; 20 April 1953, 201-204. Loane, *Archbishop Mowll*, 242-246.

[52] *SDM*, 20 April 1952, 25.

[53] For the context, see Tomoko Akami and Anthony Milner 'Australia in the Asia-Pacific Region,' in *The Cambridge History of Australia. Volume 2: The Commonwealth of Australia* (Cambridge: Cambridge University Press, 2013), 537-560, esp. 549-552.

[54] H.W.K. Mowll, 'Christianity and Communism,' *SDM*, 20 December 1951, 156-160. For the context, Doris Le Roy, 'Anglicanism, Anti-communism and Cold War Australia,' PhD thesis; Victoria University, 2010.

home. As Mowll explained to the General Synod of 1950: 'Communism has spread its tentacles throughout Asia – especially in China – and a general feeling of tension exists in the countries of the Pacific.'[55] Mowll understood the appeal of communism in lands which were undeveloped and had been subject to rule by the colonial powers. In such circumstances, he maintained that the church had something important to offer. In 1949, he observed to the Sydney Synod that ministry sensitive to postcolonial sensibilities in South-East Asia presented an opportunity 'to strengthen the moderate elements among each of these peoples, enabling them to realise the great value of our Christian traditions and institutions.'[56] Mowll had always maintained that order, stability and freedom were among the benefits conferred by Christian civilization. They were greatly needed in contemporary Asia.

This outlook helps to make sense of the second reorientation Mowll advocated. Towards the end of his Primacy, he also encouraged the Australian church to look more towards America. He had long been impressed by the size and strength of the American church, which was clearly in evidence at both the Lambeth Conference and the World Council of Churches. His impressions were confirmed when he represented the Australian Church at the 58th General Convention of the Protestant Episcopal Church of the United States of America (PECUSA) at Honolulu in September 1955. Mowll was struck at this event by the manifest human and financial resources of the PECUSA and its strong commitment to the well-being of the church in the Pacific.[57] To impress his thinking on the Australian church, and to make visible what he claimed were strengthening ties with the American church, he invited Henry Sherrill, the presiding bishop of the PECUSA, to preach at the opening of the General Synod in the next month.[58] In the next couple of years, the 'Every Member' canvases of the American church seemed to show the way in the overt work of

---

[55] General Synod 1950, 20-1.
[56] Sydney Synod 1951, 6.
[57] Sydney Synod 1955, 42-3.
[58] General Synod 1955, 17.

church promotion, now a necessity in the life of the church.[59] Like other contemporaries, Mowll was also struck by the well-publicised evangelistic successes of Billy Graham in crusades in Los Angeles in 1949 and London in 1954. In July 1957, while a major crusade was in progress in New York, he invited Billy Graham to Australia.[60] While he insisted that the Australian church should remain essentially British, Mowll also maintained that, in a rapidly secularizing world, there was much to be gained for its prosperity and well-being by heeding American methods and practices.

Leadership

Throughout all the years Mowll represented the church in Australia and abroad, the work of domestic leadership went on unceasingly. It had begun as soon as Le Fanu died in 1946. As the senior metropolitan bishop, Mowll automatically became the Acting Primate and immediately took oversight of routine Church business. Once he acceded to the Primacy, leadership of this kind became a constant of his life. Usually hidden from public view, keeping the machinery of the Church ticking over formed a substantial part of his work which, as he freely acknowledged, was sustainable only because of the assistance of his coadjutor bishop in Sydney, W. G. Hilliard.

The focal point of Mowll's leadership activity was of course the General Synod. In addition to summoning and presiding over the periodic meetings, it fell to the Primate to manage its ongoing business. This included chairing its Standing Committee and many other committees and boards, such as the Australian College of Theology and the Australian Board of Missions. Meetings of the General Synod also involved a great deal of follow up work. The meeting of 1950, for example, required informing the dioceses of the Synod's decisions, launching appeals for financial assistance to such bodies as the Board

---

[59] Sydney Synod 1956, 44-6; 1957, 232-4. For the background, David Hilliard, 'God in the suburbs: the religious culture of Australian cities in the 1950s', *Australian Historical Studies* 24: 97 (1991): 399-419, esp., esp.414.
[60] S. Barton Babbage and Ian Siggins, *Light Beneath the Southern Cross: The Story of Billy Graham's Crusade in Australia* (Kingswood and Melbourne: The World's Work, 1960), 10-11.

of Religious Education and the Bush Church Aid Society, and congratulating the Church of South India on its inauguration and burgeoning work.[61] The constructive side of the work involved receiving draft determinations and garnering responses from the dioceses to those that were passed, and organizing the agenda and papers for the next meeting. It was a many-sided and demanding role to which, in line with his view of synods as essential administrative machinery, Mowll attended conscientiously to keep the church moving forward.

Of the ongoing business of the General Synod, the most important matter was the constitution of the church itself.[62] First raised in the early 1920s, it was still unresolved when Mowll became Primate. He was already fully aware of the issues, having been a member of the Constitution Committee *ex officio* as Archbishop of Sydney through the 1930s and 1940s. However, his chief concern during these years had been protecting the interests of the Diocese of Sydney. Indeed, in 1945 he had presented in conjunction with Broughton Knox and others a minority report of the Constitutional Committee.[63] As Primate, Mowll was now obliged to integrate the Sydney concerns with those of the church as a whole. He was disappointed when, following Sydney's provisional approval, other dioceses, against the background of the 'Red Book Case', rejected the revised draft of 1947. In an attempt to break the deadlock, Mowll reactivated the Constitution Committee in July 1950.[64] From that point he chaired several meetings a year as the church – spurred on by the intervention of the Archbishop of

---

[61] GSA Box 57.341/6/125, 128: 'Registrar of the Diocese of Sydney – General Synod Meeting. Correspondence and Related Papers 1944-1950'. It also required approaches to governments, for which see below.

[62] The standard account remains John Davis, *Australian Anglicans and Their Constitution* (Canberra: Acorn Press, 1993). For the Sydney perspective, see Cameron, *Phenomenal Sydney*, 53-64.

[63] 'Minority Report of the Constitution,' *The Church of England in Australia and Tasmania. Summary of Proceedings of the General Synod of the Dioceses in Australia and Tasmania. Session 1945. Official Report* (Sydney, 1948), 123 - 124.

[64] GSA, Box 101.448/1: 'Constitution Committee'.

Canterbury who supplied yet another draft constitution – endeavoured to resolve the issue.

In this new phase of negotiations, Mowll made four important contributions.[65] First, in another application of the fellowship principle, he made 'Gilbulla', the meeting centre of Sydney Diocese, available for the periodic meetings of the Constitution Committee. All agreed that enabling the Committee members to meet on a residential basis broke down barriers of distrust and misunderstanding by creating a setting for worship together and for informal and private conversations as a supplement to formal discussions. Second, influenced by the new pan-Anglicanism of the Lambeth Conference which was reinforced by the visit of the Archbishop of Canterbury to Australia in 1950, and satisfied that Sydney's interests were safeguarded in Fisher's draft constitution, Mowll pushed the church for a resolution of the matter. Third, he combined with T C Hammond to overcome the opposition of his own diocese to Fisher's proposal which intensified in the lead up to the 1955 General Synod meeting.[66] Finally, he overcame the resistance in Sydney to the revised constitution approved at this meeting for consideration by the dioceses. The turning point came at a special meeting of the Sydney Synod in 1957 when, again with the support of Hammond, Mowll persuaded his own diocese to accept the new draft.[67] While the arrangements had not been finalised by the time Mowll died in 1958, overcoming the opposition of Sydney to the new constitution at the same time as allaying the concerns of the other dioceses was among his most significant achievements as Primate.[68] When the constitution was finally adopted at the General Synod meeting of 1960 and came into

---

[65] For the course of the final phase of the negotiations, see Davis, *Australian Anglicans and Their Constitution*, chap. 6.
[66] Notice of a meeting for July 26, 1955, of the Anglican Church League and D.B. Knox to members of the General Synod, 6 September 1955, both in GSA, Box 101, 448/1/5: 'Constitution Committee'.
[67] 'Sydney Diocesan Synod, Special Meeting March 18, 1957,' GSA, Box 101. 448/1/4: 'Constitution Committee'.
[68] The letter of congratulation from the Bishop of Newcastle, Francis Batty, to Mowll, 23rd March 1957, GSA, Box 101. 448/1/4: 'Constitution Committee'.

operation in 1962, it owed a great deal to the statesmanship of Howard Mowll.[69]

An occasion to be seen to be leading the Australian Church by the wider Australian public did not come until 1950. In that year, Mowll carried out the one regular function assigned to the Primate by the Constitution, viz. to preside over the General Synod. He did so again five years later in 1955. Despite the opportunity to shine as a leader by casting a vision for the Australian church, Mowll's presidential addresses to the General Synod are less impressive than his charges to the Sydney Synod. Perhaps reflecting the more contested environment, before the General Synod Mowll was largely content to report on the life and work of the church since the last meeting and to foreshadow what now had to be done. This was why the presidential addresses mostly do not rise above reporting significant events in the Christian and wider worlds which helped to shape the church's responsibilities and mission. They also briefly canvas the interaction of the church with the Australian community, signalling events and occasions which warranted particular attention, reminding the church of the primacy of its missionary task in a setting where the great majority of people had no connection with any church, and exhorting church people to look to their laurels to ensure its character and spirituality did nothing to thwart its mission. Yet, while generally prosaic and transactional, in two matters Mowll's presidential addresses were more visionary and prophetic.

Of specific developments affecting contemporary Australian society, none was more important in Mowll's outlook than immigration. Like other contemporary leaders, he could not but be impressed by the scale and speed of the post war inflow of migrants. The obvious challenge was the substantial increase in the size of the Australian population and consequent expansion of settlement, especially in the capital cities. Mowll's review of the facilities of the dioceses at the General Synod of

---

[69] Briefly acknowledged in the Report of the Constitution Continuation Committee to General Synod in 1960. *The Church of England in Australia and Tasmania. Proceedings of the General Synod of the Dioceses in Australia and Tasmania. Session 1960. Official Report* (Sydney: Anglican Press Ltd, 1960), 36.

1955 was intended to stir the church at large to confront its diminishing capacity to minister effectively to a changing community. Less obvious but more important was the impact of migrants on the character of the Australian people. Recognising that many migrants were not from a British background, Mowll expected that they would readily accept the British heritage and way of life and be absorbed into the prevailing culture. The responsibility he pressed upon the Australian church was active support for this process: 'Whatever the Church can do to relate itself to these newcomers, to offer them friendship and to facilitate their full assimilation, will be of great value in helping them to become part of the life of Australia and participants in our British heritage.'[70] On this view, the church should be assisting society to grow numerically while maintaining the status quo culturally.

If demography was the fundamental social issue, the most urgent was the advent of television. A new medium of mass communication already widely available in Britain and America, it was to be inaugurated as a public service in Australia in 1956. Lest anybody underestimate its significance, Mowll identified television at the General Synod of 1955 as 'the most important invention since printing'.[71] He was apprehensive about its possible effect on the moral and spiritual standards of the Australian people. At the same time, he recognized that it presented the church with a great opportunity. As an example of what might be achieved, he reminded the Synod of the church's successful lobbying of the federal government for a Royal Commission into the implications of television which had delivered the same rules for the new medium as applied to radio broadcasting. However, this 'watchdog' function needed to be sustained because the legislation governing television had yet to be passed and licences would initially be provisional. Mowll also commended to the wider church the example of Sydney Diocese which had purchased a large shareholding in Television Corporation New South Wales (TCN) in order to have representation on the board. It had in addition formed a production company to generate quality material which would ensure that the Christian message would be well expressed and establish the church's

---

[70] General Synod 1955, 21.
[71] General Synod 1955, 26-8. Quotation on 26.

credibility in the new medium. Television was but a new facet of the perennial task of utilising 'all facets of truth and knowledge, in the service of the Kingdom of God',[72] and much remained to be learned before its full scope for the work of the church was understood. But Mowll urged the church to delay its response no longer.

The advent of television illustrated how the church's place in Australian society broadened Mowll's political activity as head of the Church of England to include involvement with the Commonwealth and all state governments. At one level this was procedural, addressing the arrangements by which Australian society functioned. In this respect most important were the steps taken to ensure that the pre-eminence of the Church of England was duly recognised on public occasions.[73] Other matters affecting the standing and operations of the church included taxation exemptions for donations to church buildings and facilities.[74] From the states the church sought proper religious instruction in schools and inclusion of the work of the ministry in publications providing vocational guidance.[75] More broadly, the church lobbied to safeguard the emblems of Christian Australia. One such matter was the restoration of 'F.D.' to the coinage,[76] while another was the treatment of the colours of regiments in the armed forces.[77] Through 'the long 1950s', it became necessary increasingly for Mowll

---

[72] General Synod 1955, 28.

[73] General Synod 1955, 46, Resolution 8. Minutes of Standing Committee: 16 July 1951, 6-7; 10 February 1950, 3; 28 July 1950, 2; 18 February1950, 1-2; 7 October 1955; in GSA Series 43/18: 'Standing Committee Minute Book 1944 – 1962'.

[74] General Synod 1950, 49, Resolution 23. General Synod 1955, 49, Resolution 23. Minutes of Standing Committee, 22 July 1949, 2, in GSA Series 43/18: 'Standing Committee Minute Book 1944-1962'.

[75] General Synod 1950, 53-5. General Synod 1955, 47, Resolution 12. Minutes of Standing Committee: 28 July 1950, 3; 16 July 1951, 2; 14 November 1952, 3; in GSA Series 43/18: 'Standing Committee Minute Book 1944-1962'.

[76] Standing for *Fidei Defensor*, 'Defender of the Faith'. Minutes of Standing Committee, 29 July 1955, 3, in GSA Series 43/18: 'Standing Committee Minute Book 1944-1962'.

[77] The issue is discussed in Le Roy, 'Anglicanism, Anti-communism and Cold War Australia,' 137-139. It arose from a protest against the Anglican character of the service by Melbourne's Roman Catholic Archbishop Mannix.

and the church to act politically to prevent erosion of its place, and more fundamentally the place of Christianity, in Australian society.

A second level of political engagement arose from the church's perennial concern for the moral and material well-being of the Australian people. In a society recovering from the disruption of the war, the church retained a strong interest in matters that made for order and stability – marriage and divorce law, liquor reform and the provision of suitable housing.[78] The special interests of two groups were also advanced. Reflecting a new hopefulness for the future of indigenous peoples, the church lobbied the Commonwealth for a more equitable distribution of social services to indigenous people and the removal of 'gross injustice to aborigines and half-castes'.[79] For the aged the church campaigned for adequate pensions, seeking in particular the abolition of the means test on Commonwealth age pensions.[80] This concern embraced the clergy, whose material condition after retiring was felt to be especially precarious. Representations were therefore made with some success to exclude their superannuation payments from the calculation of state pensions.[81] As Primate Mowll readily accepted responsibility for the church's role in society to work generally for the conditions of healthful living and specifically to protect the weak and marginalized.

---

[78] Minutes of Standing Committee, 22 July 1949, 4-5, in GSA Series 43/18: 'Standing Committee Minute Book 1944-1962'.

[79] Minutes of Standing Committee, 16 July 1951, 2 (with the letter of Robert Menzies of 14 May 1951 defending the Government's handling of Aboriginal affairs) and 7 October 1955, 2 & 3, in GSA Series 43/18: 'Standing Committee Minute Book 1944-1962'. For the context, John Harris, 'Anglicanism and Indigenous Peoples,' in Kaye, *Anglicanism in Australia*, 223-246, esp. 238 - 241.

[80] General Synod 1950, 48, Resolution 19. General Synod 1955, 48, Resolution 19. Correspondence in March-April 1951, GSA, Box 57, 341/6/125: 'Registrar of the Diocese of Sydney, General Synod Meeting, Correspondence and Related Papers 1944-1950'.

[81] Minutes of Standing Committee, 10 February 1950, 3; 28 July 1950, 2; and 28 July 1955, 4, in GSA Series 43/18: 'Standing Committee Minute Book 1944-1962'. The Church also sought Social Service Benefits for missionaries. 7 October 1955, 3.

At a third level Mowll as leader of the church was concerned about the direction of Australian society. Amid the ideological struggle of the first post-war decade, most worrying were the strikes and agitation of the trade unions.[82] In 1950 Mowll condemned a movement 'built on the assumption that a man need not do a full day's work to receive a full day's pay'.[83] Yet he could see both sides of the issue. He attributed the unions' outlook to an understandable response to a long history of labour relations characterised by exploitation and consequent distrust. It was nevertheless a threat both to the material prosperity of the nation and, in its tendency to promote laziness and selfishness, to the moral fibre of the Australian people. At such a time of social division and moral crisis, Mowll discerned an important role for the church. He cast the unions' position as contrary to the principle that a person's work was an aspect of Christian service which should be done 'with all his might'. His response was to press the necessity of teaching and example: 'We as a Church have a solemn responsibility to make all men see that the Christian life can be lived both by individuals and a communion.'[84] By its all-important witness, the church was to be a leader of society as well as its moral guardian.

Mowll's position on these social and political questions presumed that the church was a major institution in Australian society. Yet, ever alert to secularising trends, he was by no means complacent in this presumption. Again in 1950, Mowll noted the degree of irreligion among the Australian people and the missionary task it imposed on the church: 'Around us in Australia there are 70% of the population who are completely out of touch with any of the Churches. The call comes to us all to face the task of bringing them into the life of the Church and to win them for Christ and His service, showing by our own attitude and actions the reality of our Christian faith.'[85] This was the key to Mowll's review five years later of church buildings, schools

---

[82] On this period, see Judith Brett, 'The Menzies Era, 1950-66' in *Cambridge History of Australia*, ed. Alison Bashford and Stuart Macintyre (Cambridge: Cambridge University Press, 2013), vol. 2, 112-134, esp. 115-121.

[83] General Synod 1950, 21-22.

[84] General Synod 1950, 21.

[85] General Synod 1950, 21-22.

and youth work and social ministry. On the one hand, he had observed 'the vigour and development of the church in this Commonwealth'.[86] Yet, on the other, he now emphasized the need for the church to husband its resources and develop the instruments most likely on his understanding for it to remain a formative influence on the beliefs and values of contemporary Australia.

Above all in this respect, Mowll now advocated on a broader front than Sydney Diocese the need to mobilize the laity 'to exercise a conscientious and an informed part in the administration of their Church, more especially in its work and witness to the Community'.[87] While always necessary in principle, in the ideological context of 1950s Australia, the deployment of the laity was essential and urgent. Without acknowledgement of the source, Mowll quoted the observation: 'The real battles of the Faith today are being fought in factories, shops, offices and farms; in political parties and Government agencies; in countless homes; in the Press, Radio, and on Television; and in the relationships of Nations.' He pointed out the corollary: 'The Church is already in these fields of action, in the persons of its Laity – let us help them to make their work effective.' Enabling the laity, always important for Mowll, was now presented as a condition of the church's retaining its place in the social order of Robert Menzies' Australia.

Conclusion

Mowll's political and social praxis stamp him and the Australian church under his leadership as manifestly conservative. In retrospect it is clear that his outlook and assumptions belonged to a world that was passing away. In the following decades, Australia moved decisively away from the British and Christian heritage Mowll took as axiomatic.[88] But this should not detract from the part he had played in 'the long 1950s'. During these years, Mowll was a very active Primate,

---

[86] General Synod 1955, 21.

[87] All quotations in this paragraph are from General Synod 1955, 30.

[88] Documented broadly by Hugh McLeod, *The Religious Crisis of the 1960s* (Oxford: Oxford University Press, 2007) and traced in the Australian setting by Hugh Chilton, *Evangelicals and the End of Christendom: Religion, Australia, and the Crises of the 1960s* (London: Routledge, 2020).

leading and representing the Australian church with deep commitment and exemplary diligence. In the process he developed the Primacy in new ways, particularly by making it a more palpable presence throughout Australia and abroad. While he did not have the same impact on the wider church that he had in Sydney, these innovations were the basis of a very considerable achievement as Primate. Not only did Mowll lead the church through its adjustment to peace as the world emerged from the turmoil of total war. By the personal ministry now enabled by easy air travel, his willingness to put aside the Protestantism that governed his administration in Sydney and work with Anglicans of all traditions, and by his contribution to the adoption of the new constitution, he maintained the integrity and unity of the Australian church in an era of deep division. Writing about this period of Australian Anglican history, Tom Frame observes that the church 'struggled to be outward rather than inward looking'.[89] This was a struggle Mowll as Primate recognized and countered in word and deed, succeeding to a considerable extent in aligning the church of the 1950s with the aspirations and ideals of the Anglican Communion and the ecumenical hopes of the world church. He also pushed to the forefront of the concerns of the Australian church its particular responsibilities to South-East Asia and the Pacific, while recognizing at the same time the value of connecting with the capacity of the American church. As an activist evangelical, his primary motivation was always the imperative of the gospel, but Mowll was also responding to the post-1945 church and world settings, especially the spectre of rampant communism. In Australia, this malign force combined with the effects of increasing secularization to motivate Mowll to contend politically for both Christianity as the basis of civilization and also the pre-eminence of the Church of England as the primary representative of that Britishness which he believed offered so much to the contemporary world. As a conservative Mowll appreciated the changes taking place in Australian society no better than others with the same outlook, and he evinces a weak grasp of the decline of British power in the new world order, although his successors as Primate similarly

---

[89] Frame, 'Local Differences, Social and National Identity,' in Kaye, *Anglicanism in Australia*, 101.

clung to the importance of the church's British identity down to the 1980s. Whatever his limitations, as Primate of the Church of England Mowll takes his place among the church leaders of the 1950s who stood for the Christianity that still underpinned the values of Australian society. Despite his conservatism, he was neither *behind* nor *ahead* of the times but very much *of* the times, well suited to leading the Church of England in Robert Menzies' Australia. As Mowll's contribution comes to be better understood, he will warrant greater consideration in future accounts of the Anglican Church in Australia than he has hitherto received.

11. Dorothy Mowll: A Woman of Courage

Jane M Tooher

"The frontiers of the Kingdom of God were never advanced by men and women of caution." (Dorothy Mowll, 1957 Diary)

Introduction

Dorothy Anne[1] Mowll (nee Martin) (OBE, FRGS) (1890-1957) was born to reformed evangelical parents, both of whom had a deep commitment to worldwide mission, with a focus on the indigenous church. Her family also prioritised serving others above worldly comforts. This chapter will focus on how we see those two priorities – a commitment to worldwide mission and service of others – in Dorothy's life.[2]

Dorothy's Early Years and Influences

Dorothy's Parents: Rev John Martin (1857-1921) & Eliza Anne Martin (née Goldie) (1850-1894)

Both of Dorothy's parents left England for China in 1881 to serve as single missionaries. Her father went with the Church Missionary Society (CMS)[3], and her mother with the Society for Promoting Education in the East (FES). Two years after arriving in China, John Martin and Eliza Goldie married in January 1884.[4] The ministries they

---

[1] Dorothy's baptismal certificate lists her as Dorothy Anne, but her family may have called her, at least initially, by her middle name as the 1891 England Census lists her as 'Anne D. Martin'.
[2] Dorothy kept diaries of her time in China and in Sydney. See Loane, *Archbishop Mowll*, 10, 255-257.
[3] Register of missionaries (clerical, lay & female) and native clergy from 1804 to 1904, Church Missionary Society, 1905, List I, 940: John Martin; A special thank you to Ivana Frian, Archivist, Cadbury Research Library, University of Birmingham, and to Roderick J. Benson, Research Support Officer, Moore Theological Library, for their help in accessing the CMS archives.
[4] This is contra Eugene Stock who suggests John and Eliza Martin were already married in 1881. See Eugene Stock, *For Christ in Fuh-kien: The Story*

were involved in included: theological education; a Bible school for Chinese women; ministry training; people affected by leprosy; a boarding school for Chinese girls, and a boarding school for Chinese boys. We see evidence for all of these in John's annual missionary letters.[5]

Eliza died suddenly in January 1894. One of the things written after her death, reflects her priorities: 'During her twelve years' service [...] she laboured devotedly for the salvation of the Chinese women and girls.'[6] Although Dorothy was only three years old when her mother died, she would go on to have the same concerns her mother had.

In his 1894 annual missionary letter, John writes of his devastation but also his trust in God following Eliza's death.[7] John's sister initially helped care for his six children. However, she had to leave China due to ill health. Eliza's sister Emma Goldie, also a CMS missionary in China, then spent much of her time caring for her nieces and nephews.[8] Emma wrote:

---

of the Mission of the Church Missionary Society (4th ed.; London: CMS, 1904), 75. This seems unlikely as Stock himself had stated earlier on page 34 that Eliza departed England in 1881 with FES as a single woman. FES records state that John and Eliza married in January 1884. See, https://www.researchsource.amdigital.co.uk/Documents/Images/CMS_II_P art1_Reel10_Vol1/100, 13. CMS records that John Martin left England on 26 October 1881 for China.

[5] E.g. 'From Rev. J. Martin Lo-ngwong, Fuh-kien Mission 23/12/1893', *Church Missionary Society Extracts From The Annual Letters of the Missionaries For The Year 1893-1894* (CMS III Part 4 Reel 35 Vol 1), 302-304.

[6] Eugene Stock, *For Christ in Fuh-Kien*, 34.

[7] 'From Rev. J. Martin, Lo-ngwong, South China, 27/12/1894', *Church Missionary Society Extracts From The Annual Letters of the Missionaries For The Year 1894-1895* (CMS III Part 4 Reel 35 Vol 1), 308.

[8] See, 'From Rev. J. Martin, Lo-ngwong, South China, 27/12/1894', *Church Missionary Society Extracts From The Annual Letters of the Missionaries For The Year 1894-1895* (CMS III Part 4 Reel 35 Vol 1), 310; 'From Miss E. S. Goldie, Lo-ngwong, December 1894', *Church Missionary Society Extracts From The Annual Letters of the Missionaries For The Year 1893-1894* (CMS III Part 4 Reel 35 Vol 1), 311.

It pleased God early in this year to call home my beloved sister, and from that time I have felt that my first duty was the care of her motherless little ones. What time I could spare I have devoted to the woman's [Bible] school. This school was very dear to my sister, and earnestly she laboured amongst these women [...].[9]

We assume Emma ended up having a great influence on her niece since Dorothy spent so much of her formative years with her aunt, both in China and in England (when Emma was back on furlough).

Tragedy struck again when John's youngest daughter Olive died on 1 August 1894. Following the deaths of his wife and youngest daughter, the initial plan was for John to return to England with Emma and all five children, but as Emma notes, things changed:

From the beginning of this year, until March, I was at Lo-ngwong. Having Mr Martin's five children under my care for education as well as everything else, I was not able to give much time to Mission work. Still I was able to teach every day in the women's school, which was under my charge, and also did some visiting in the city. The last months spent at Lo-ngwong were very sad ones. It seemed as if the path of duty was leading me to leave my work in China for a time, to accompany Mr Martin to England in charge of his children. However, having arrived at Fuh-chow ready to start for England, plans were changed, and it was agreed that Mr Martin should only take home his three eldest children, and I remain out here with the two youngest [Dorothy and Cyril]. This arrangement was a great comfort to me. I felt the work so dear to my heart was given back to me once more.[10]

---

[9] 'From Miss E. S. Goldie, Lo-ngwong, December 1894', *Church Missionary Society Extracts From The Annual Letters of the Missionaries For The Year 1893-1894* (CMS III Part 4 Reel 35 Vol I), 310.
[10] 'From Miss E.S. Goldie, Fuh-chow, South China', 31/12/1895' *Church Missionary Society Extracts From The Annual Letters of the Missionaries For The Year 1895-96* (CMS III Part 7 Reel 36 Vol I), 315-316.

John went back to England on 29 March 1895 with his three oldest children, where they were looked after by relatives and continued their education. He returned to China by himself on 5 October 1895 to begin mission work in Ku-cheng (Gutian County). In March 1896, five-year-old Dorothy and four-year-old Cyril were reunited with their father when Emma Goldie brought them from Lo-ngwong (Luoyang) to Ku-cheng.[11]

John going to Ku-cheng at that time is striking enough, but having his two youngest children arrive six months later spoke volumes. Why was this? On 1 August 1895 in Ku-cheng, one male and eight female missionaries, along with the five-year-old son and the one-year-old daughter of two of the victims, had been viciously murdered by a group of Chinese men.[12] The presence of young Dorothy and Cyril eight months after the massacre made a great impression:

> Some of the CEZMS ladies returned to Ku-cheng city in March, and Miss Goldie, with my two youngest children, arrived about the same time. The presence of the children made a favourable impression on the people, the Christians being specially pleased. Not very long after their arrival, I heard it was reported that the Heathen and Christians had been heard to say, 'The missionaries were not afraid to live in Ku-cheng again, and they indicated by bringing up the two children they were willing to entrust themselves to us.'[13]

---

[11] 'From the Rev. J. Martin, Ku-cheng, South China, 28/12/1896', *Church Missionary Society Extracts From The Annual Letters of the Missionaries For The Year 1896* (CMS III Part 4 Reel 36 Vol 1), 328.

[12] Those murdered included Australian C.M.S. Victoria missionaries, Harriette (Nellie) Elinor Saunders (17/04/1871 - 01/08/1895) and Elizabeth (Topsy) Maud Saunders (30/07/1873 - 01/08/1895). See, *The Sydney Morning Herald*, August 1895, (https://trove.nla.gov.au/newspaper/article/13977480). John Martin was back in England when the massacre occurred. He had met Nellie and Topsy after they arrived in China in December 1893.

[13] 'From the Rev. J. Martin, Ku-cheng, South China, 28/12/1896', *Church Missionary Society Extracts From The Annual Letters of the Missionaries For The Year 1896* (CMS III Part 4 Reel 36 Vol 1), 328.

We would assume living in Ku-cheng, and the local people's surprise and encouragement about that, made a lasting impression on five-year old Dorothy. It is easy to think that John might have been more cautious in what ministry he chose to do, but his actions proved the complete opposite. Her father's willingness to live and minister in Ku-cheng reflects some of the influences that inevitably shaped Dorothy from such a young age.

In March 1897, the shape of John Martin's ministry changed again when he began as the Principal of the CMS Theological College in Fuh-chow (Fuzhou).[14] This college had been opened in 1883 to train and equip Chinese men for ministry. John remarried in 1910 and continued to serve with CMS in China until his resignation in 1916, one year after Dorothy herself began as a missionary with CMS in China. John returned to England in 1916 where he served in parish ministry until his death on 26 May 1921.

Dorothy's Childhood and Teenage Years

John and Eliza Martin's first three children, Sarah Elizabeth (1885-1924), John Aston (1887-1965), and Francis Henry (1888-1917) were all born in China.[15] During a furlough back in England Dorothy was born at her grandmother's home in Bath on 18 June 1890.[16] One month later she was baptised by her father at St Stephen's, Bath, on 18 July 1890.[17] John and Eliza returned to China with their children when

---

[14] 'From the Rev. J. Martin, Fuh-chow, South China, 29/12/1897 and 12/01/1898'. *Church Missionary Society Extracts From The Annual Letters of the Missionaries For The Year 1896* (CMS III Part 4 Reel 37 Vol 1), 391, 394. See also, Stock, *For Christ in Fuh-kien*, 28, 180.

[15] 1901 England Census, (https://www.ancestry.com.au/imageviewer/collections/7814/images/SOM RG13_2343_2344-0202?pId=12646098).

[16] *The Sydney Diocesan Magazine* (cited hereafter as *SDM*), Vol. 10-No.12, February, 1958 192; See also 1901 England Census, (https://www.ancestry.com.au/imageviewer/collections/7814/images/SOM RG13_2343_2344-0202?pId=12646098).

[17] 1880-1913 Church of England Baptisms, St Stephen, Bath, Somerset, England, (https://www.ancestry.com.au/imageviewer/collections/60857/images/engl 78030_d-p-ba-st-2-1-1_m_00033?pId=301495509).

Dorothy was six months old.[18] In the following year her brother Cyril Gordon (1891-1980) was born, and one year later her younger sister Olive Goldie (1892-1894).

During her time as a missionary Emma Goldie made several trips back to England, and one such trip was in 1899. By at least 1901, Dorothy and the rest of her siblings were living with her in Bath. It is not known how long Dorothy lived with her aunt at that time, nor the exact influence and impact Emma had on the young Dorothy. But it is certain that Emma had a lot of contact with Dorothy in her early years, both in China and in England.

Education and Missionary Service Preparation

Dorothy attended Bath High School for Girls where she excelled in the classroom and in hockey.[19] After the completion of her secondary studies aged 18, Dorothy followed in the footsteps of both her parents and aunt. She had long desired to return to China to be a missionary herself[20], and so to equip herself for the task, she took cookery classes, studied teaching[21], nursing[22], and missionary studies.[23]

Missionary Service as a Single Woman

Dorothy arrived in China in 1915 with advantages that most missionaries do not have. She was the daughter of missionary parents who had served in China, and all her siblings had been born there. She herself had previously lived in China, and so she was familiar with

---

[18] Loane, *Archbishop Mowll*, 189.

[19] *SDM,* Vol. 10-No.12, February 1958, 192.

[20] Dorothy Martin, 'Annual letter 1918' in, *East Asia Missions Part 20: Annual Letters for Japan, China and Canada 1917-1934, GI AL, Missionaries MA-MD,* C.M.S. Archives,
(https://www.researchsource.amdigital.co.uk/Documents/Images/CMS_I_P art20_Reel431_Vol1/165).

[21] Dorothy studied at the Froebel College and received the Kindergarten Certificate and the Training Diploma.
(https://www.roehampton.ac.uk/colleges/froebel-college/froebel-history/).

[22] *SDM,* Vol. 10-No.12, February 1958, 192.

[23] Dorothy trained at the C.M.S. Highbury Hostel for her missionary studies which was one of three female training centres that C.M.S. operated.

aspects of the culture and the language. Added to these attributes was her physical appearance of dark brown eyes and hair, all of which helped the Chinese feel confident in her.[24] Dorothy did not return to the areas where her parents and aunt had served, rather she went to serve in Western China, which was more remote. It was also mountainous, which Dorothy absolutely loved. 'She had all the qualities of a pioneer with her zest for hardship and her ardent pursuit of the new and unknown.'[25]

Dorothy's Annual Letters

Each CMS missionary was expected to write an annual letter and the CMS archives have four letters from Dorothy. These letters prove to be an invaluable source in helping us to get to know the woman that Dorothy was, especially since the location of her extensive diaries is not presently known.[26] Dorothy's letters reveal, among other things, her evangelistic zeal; her love and concern for the local people's physical and spiritual needs; her desire to train people in ministry; the priority she saw in educating others; her lack of complaining despite facing very difficult and trying circumstances; her fearlessness; and her love of the mountains.

1917

In her brief 1917 letter, Dorothy writes that she has focussed on language study over the course of the year. She has however also been able to teach in the girl's school, helped with the women's work, and visited some of the out-stations. We hear of her love of the mountains, but we also see her growing awareness of the spiritual and physical needs of the Chinese people.[27]

---

[24] *SDM,* Vol. 10-No.12, February 1958, 192.

[25] Loane, *Archbishop Mowll,* 189.

[26] Loane, *Archbishop Mowll,* 10. Following the death of Howard Mowll, Dorothy's diaries were given to her brother, Dr John Aston Martin.

[27] Dorothy Martin, 'Annual letter 1917' in, *East Asia Missions Part 20: Annual Letters for Japan, China and Canada 1917-1934, GI AL, Missionaries MA-MD,* C.M.S. Archives, (https://www.researchsource.amdigital.co.uk/Documents/Images/CMS_I_Part20_Reel431_Vol1/163).

1918

Dorothy's 1918 letter is longer and more serious in tone than her 1917 letter. She writes that there has been a lot of looting, and as a result, they were locked in the city for two months, and this had caused stress for both the local people and the missionaries. Dorothy also says that after two years of language learning, her move to the outpost of Longan was unexpected. But she also notes that she felt it was a definite call, and that as a child she had always hoped to do pioneer work:

> The idea of 'pioneer' work on the borders of 'Unknown Territory' always appealed to me [...]. I have had no lack of experiences, and although our hopes of evangelistic tours, and visits to outstations, have not fully been realised, owing to the disturbed state of the district, my two trips have made me long for more opportunities.[28]

> I felt highly privileged to be called to such a work, to preach the Gospel to so many who have never heard before – the sort of pioneer work I had dreamt of, as a girl at home. To realise my dream seemed wonderful and I hope to have similar experiences in the future. I hope I shall always remain as enthusiastic, but know I wish that I were more qualified for the work. I long for a bigger grasp of the language – to understand more of the lives and thoughts of the people, and to grow in my own spiritual life – I want a greater love for these women – and a greater yearning to win them to Christ.[29]

---

[28] Dorothy Martin, 'Annual letter 1918' in, *East Asia Missions Part 20: Annual Letters for Japan, China and Canada 1917-1934, GI AL, Missionaries MA-MD,* C.M.S. Archives,
(https://www.researchsource.amdigital.co.uk/Documents/Images/CMS_I_P art20_Reel431_Vol1/165).

[29] Dorothy Martin, 'Annual letter 1918' in, *East Asia Missions Part 20: Annual Letters for Japan, China and Canada 1917-1934, GI AL, Missionaries MA-MD,* C.M.S. Archives,
(https://www.researchsource.amdigital.co.uk/Documents/Images/CMS_I_P art20_Reel431_Vol1/167).

Dorothy goes to places that no missionary had ever been previously, and amongst the more overall serious tone of the letter, she also wrote of her love of the area because of the mountains, and of her desire to go to Mount Xuebaoding, Songpan County, the 'Tibetan mount, [...] which is the height of my ambition!'[30]

1919

Out of the four letters, this is the hardest one for Dorothy to write. Dorothy mentions several times that she is alone in a lot of the work. It seems they were very short of missionaries, and that Dorothy felt hurt that she seemed to be blamed for something which was outside of her control. By all accounts she worked very hard, but her having to stay at the school – since a foreigner needed to always be there – meant that the outstations were neglected. [31]

Between letters 3 and 4, Dorothy returned to England for furlough where two interesting events happened. She went to the consecration of Howard Mowll at Westminster Abbey on 22 June 1922, since he would soon be the new assistant bishop of West China. Six months later on 9 January 1923 she also went to his farewell at Church House, Westminster. She did not imagine at the time, that in the following year she would become his wife.[32]

---

[30] Dorothy Martin, 'Annual letter 1918' in, *East Asia Missions Part 20: Annual Letters for Japan, China and Canada 1917-1934, GI AL, Missionaries MA-MD,* C.M.S. Archives, (https://www.researchsource.amdigital.co.uk/Documents/Images/CMS_I_P art20_Reel431_Vol1/167).

[31] Dorothy Martin, 'Annual letter 1919' in, *East Asia Missions Part 20: Annual Letters for Japan, China and Canada 1917-1934, GI AL, Missionaries MA-MD,* C.M.S. Archives, (https://www.researchsource.amdigital.co.uk/Documents/Images/CMS_I_P art20_Reel431_Vol1/168).

[32] Marcus L. Loane, 'Dorothy Anne Mowll', Australian Dictionary of Evangelical Biography (https://sites.google.com/view/australian-dictionary-of-evang/m/mowll-dorothy-anne-1890-1957). The Australian Dictionary of Evangelical Biography suggests that Loane says it is October 1923 when Howard and Dorothy married not October 1924, but we would suggest this is

1923

In Dorothy's final letter we read that once again she was moved, this time to Hanchow (Hangzhou), for women's work. She was also appointed the supervisor of the primary schools, and teaches temporarily in a boy's school. Tragically two male missionaries, Mr Watt and Mr Whiteside, had been shot dead by a local gang, and when the deaths occurred, Dorothy was staying with Mr Watt's wife.

Dorothy wrote:

> We have started holding a Women's Evangelistic Meeting every week, looking to the [Chinese] Christian women to bring their neighbours and friends [...] and the attendance has been excellent. This effort is giving the Christian women a definite share in the work, a share which they can all take – and it is bringing us in touch with a larger circle of women.
>
> Mrs Whiteside has a unique opportunity of appealing to these women. She tells them how she has suffered with them – [...] yet, in these days of sorrow, anxiety, and fear [...] they may have peace – the peace which she possesses in her great sorrow.[33]

Dorothy also writes of one of their first ordained Chinese deacons and the work he was doing, and how well he and Dorothy worked together. She recognises that the station is fortunate in having some keen Chinese Christian male leaders. But she finishes her letter with a note that is interesting, since we know what happens to her. Dorothy says her travelling is limited because of the presence of gangs, and that the gangs also mean she doesn't know what her future ministry will look like.

---

typo on the Dictionary's part, not an error on Loane's part, as Loane makes clear in *Archbishop Mowll*, 92, that Howard and Dorothy married in 1924.

[33] Dorothy Martin, 'Annual letter 1923' in, *East Asia Missions Part 20: Annual Letters for Japan, China and Canada 1917-1934*, GI AL, Missionaries MA-MD, CMS Archives,
(https://www.researchsource.amdigital.co.uk/Documents/Images/CMS_I_P art20_Reel431_Vol1/171).

Fellowship of the Royal Geographical Society

It is not certain which areas of China Dorothy mapped, or how she was trained for such a task, but she charted some of the country she journeyed in. In recognition of her contribution to mapping previously uncharted areas, the Royal Geographical Society elected her as a Fellow.

Dorothy was interested in maps throughout her whole life. Yet how this love was fostered is not sure. This love of maps went along with a love of mountain scenery and mountain climbing.[34] In August 1917, Dorothy and a friend set out to climb the 19 000 feet Chin-ting-shan or Nine Pinnacle Mountain. Her friend had to stop, but Dorothy and her local guide reached the peak. No other foreigner had previously managed this feat.[35]

Missionary and Ministry Service as a Married Woman

Howard West Kilvinton Mowll was the Assistant Bishop of West China from 1922 to 1926, Bishop of West China from 1926 to 1933, and then Archbishop of Sydney from 1934 to 1958. On 27 August 1924 Howard announced his engagement to Dorothy. 'They had met in London and in Shanghai, and he had seen her from time to time in Szechwan. He had soon found out how much she was in demand, and had made up his mind to win her hand.'[36]

An insight into Dorothy's mind up to and during their engagement is seen in a letter she wrote two weeks before they married:

> I feel in a dream, and can hardly believe it is really me –
> although I am very happy. He is a dear and we are awfully
> fond of each other. It was just suggested in May but I was
> so anxious to be quite sure it was God's will, from every
> point of view, that we waited three months to pray about it

---

[34] *SDM*, Vol. 10-No.12, February 1958, 193-194.
[35] Loane, 'Dorothy Anne Mowll', Australian Dictionary of Evangelical Biography, https://sites.google.com/view/australian-dictionary-of-evang/m/mowll-dorothy-anne-1890-1957.
[36] Loane, *Archbishop Mowll*, 92.

[...] Sintu folk foreign and Chinese are very sad at my going! I am very sorry to leave the work here.

Please continue to pray for me as I start along this new path. It will be different from the past – life in Chenghu, a big house – entertaining etc., also long journeys through the Diocese which I shall enjoy, I could never have faced the new duties etc. unless I felt confident that it is God's will and he will supply my need.

Lots of love from yours as ever, Dorothy A Martin.

Thank you, I have a CSSM chorus book & use it often.[37]

Their engagement came as a surprise to many as their friendship was discreet, and for the three months Dorothy considered Howard's proposal, she actively chose to avoid much contact with him. Her heart was in China and she was worried Howard would not want to remain there. Although many of her fellow missionaries did not expect her to get married, they were delighted with the news. Bishop William Wharton Cassels, one of the Cambridge Seven, was Howard's bishop from 1922-1926 and he married them on 23 October 1924 in Mienchu.[38]

Dorothy as a Partner of Howard

Dorothy's warmth, openness, and a strong desire to make people feel welcome, meant people loved experiencing hospitality from the Mowlls in both China and Sydney. Loane sums up beautifully how Howard and Dorothy complemented each other, and how much he was dependent on her:

---

[37] Letter from Dorothy A. Martin to Miss Pym, 9 October 1924, Sintu, Szechuan, W. China, (CMS Archives, CMS_ACC_1015_F1, Letter from Dorothy Martin with invitation). See also Loane, *Archbishop Mowll*, 190-194.
[38] Their marriage on 23 October 1924 was according to Anglican rites and then on the 17 December 1924 it was further solemnized by the British Consulate General. See,
(https://www.ancestry.com.au/imageviewer/collections/60911/images/4559 6_635001_0342-00031?pId=15773).

Marriage brought to Bishop Mowll the great joy of an ideal partner, though there were so many contrasts in their life and manners. He was solemn and she was gay; he was dignified, courteous and shy while she was full of merriment, adventure and vitality; he was slow and deliberate in thought, speech and movement, while she was fond of games and loved walking and gloried in the mountains; he was tall and handsome while she had those direct and disconcerting eyes. He was always in need of an intimate companion in whom he could wholly confide, and he was to lean on her with absolute confidence. She was ready to play her role as his interpreter, and set out to win for him the trust and goodwill of the Chinese; and he relied on her without reserve in all questions of language and travel quite as much in all the details of judgment and action. Their minds were drawn into one mould of thought and plan, and the passage of years only increased this deep sense of absolute harmony. The pattern in China was to repeat itself in Sydney, where their lives were completely organised around the pivot of the diocesan activities. Their happiness and their fellowship with each other had no limitation, except in the absence of child-life from their home.[39]

Dorothy was known to be able to keep a cool head in stressful situations, and this was no doubt extremely helpful for Howard both in China and in Sydney, given the many complexities of life and ministry that they faced in both countries. The Mowlls were victims in China of robberies, assaults, they were shot at (fortunately the gunmen missed) and at least one kidnapping. In one robbery, Dorothy helped bandage Howard after he had been clubbed and stabbed in his back, and she did this while having herself just been clubbed in the head. The scar from that injury would remain with her the rest of her life, such was the cut. As Loane says about Dorothy during that incident, 'But her presence of mind never left her, and she tried to persuade

---

39 Loane, *Archbishop Mowll*, 195 and 196.

them [the robbers] to sit down and drink a cup of tea.'[40] Her
fearlessness helped Howard in many awful situations.

Dorothy's writings

Dorothy kept diaries of her time in both China and Sydney, but
unfortunately, we do not know where they are, or if they still exist.

In 1938 Dorothy authored a short study book called *China To-day*.[41] Her
purpose in writing was to help readers understand what changes had
happened in China, so they would not have a mistaken view of what
China was like. Dorothy outlines a number of ways Christianity has
influenced China, and how CMS has been a part of this. She includes
stories from different dioceses, illustrations, maps, and photos of
Chinese Christian men and women who were involved in various
ministries.

Ever concerned to train, equip, and educate others in ministry, Dorothy
included at the end of each chapter questions that are '... designed to
test the knowledge gained from reading ... and to encourage
further study'.[42]

Mowll Village: Dorothy's concern for aged care[43]

Dorothy got to know many women in the Sydney diocese during WWII
as they served alongside her in the ministries of the Church of England
National Emergency Fund (CENEF), which provided for the needs of
service men and women[44], and also in the work of the Sydney Diocesan
Churchwomen's Association. As Dorothy heard more of these
women's stories, she became aware that some of them did not have
adequate means to provide for their future. Many of them had lived
through two world wars, and the depression of the 1920's and 1930's.
While Dorothy was concerned for church members, Howard was

---

[40] Loane, *Archbishop Mowll*, 121.
[41] No publisher details are given.
[42] Dorothy Mowll, *China To-day*, 6.
[43] A special thank you to Robin Wood and Elisabeth Arnett in accessing
archival information about Mowll Village.
[44] See previous chapters by Colin Bale and Ruth Lukabyo for further
information on CENEF.

worried for how clergy and missionaries would face life after retirement, since they were on limited incomes.[45]

How did the vision of aged care that Dorothy so desired eventuate? In God's providence, the wife of the Prime Minister, Dame Patti Menzies, shared a similar concern to the Mowlls for the housing situation of older Australians in their retirement. Dame Patti influenced her husband, and he, the Australian government:

> ... in March 1955 the Minutes of CENEF Board of Management Meeting contained the following paragraph:

> "His Grace the Archbishop mentioned the suggestion of Mrs Mowll that homes for retired Clergy and Church Workers might be built and suggested Menangle as the site. The Archbishop's announcement was prompted by the Commonwealth Government having recently passed the 'Aged Persons Homes Act'."

This Act arose from a speech made in Sydney by the then Right Honourable R. G. Menzies:

> "One night at dinner back in 1953 my wife[46] said to me, 'You know, I'm tremendously troubled about one problem in this country, and this is how old people get on when they have no home of their own. I know there are institutions, and I know there are all sorts of rules and regulations, but more than anything else is that they should have their own home, their own room and their own friends. Why couldn't you – start some sort of fund which would enable the Commonwealth to help build such places?'"

> And it was out of this conversation there grew the Aged Person's Homes Act. This Act allowed a 2 for 1 pound

---

[45] Gwen Davidge, 'What was Mrs Mowll's Vision?' (Unpublished paper). Notes for a talk to be given at Tuesday Barton Hall Fellowship (late 1980's, ARV Archives.)
[46] See also 'Foundation for Hope', *Daily Telegraph*, December 1965.

subsidy to be made by the Federal Government to Churches and Recognised Charitable Organisations for the purpose of assisting them to provide Homes for the Aged. [...].

Early 1956 the Archbishop advised he had constituted a Board [...] to make further enquiries. The Board was to consist of: The Archbishop and Mrs Mowll, Bishop Hilliard, the then Archdeacon Kerle and Reverends C Goodwin, R G Fillingham, W Deasey and Mr W Lober. [...].[47]

When the board was deciding on a site for the proposal, three properties ultimately came before them: Menangle, Bowral, and later Castle Hill. No-one except Dorothy was keen on Menangle. Archdeacon Goodwin recalled:

She visualized a place, there was only one place she'd consider having it, and that out by Gilbulla conference centre at Menangle. Those of us on the board who didn't like this I'm afraid stonewalled, and the next couple of years was a period of a battle of wits between the archbishop's wife and certain members of the board, sometimes to the considerable embarrassment of the archbishop, who I think was more on our side, in most cases, than that of his wife. [...].

During Mrs Mowll's illness, of course, nothing was done, and then unfortunately, not long after her death, the archbishop himself became unwell and, being rector of the parish he lived, I saw him every day frequently, and he

[47] Gwen Davidge, 'What was Mrs Mowll's Vision?' (Unpublished paper). Notes for a talk to be given at Tuesday Barton Hall Fellowship (late 1980's, Information gathered from ARV Archives).

said to me one night "Clive, I want you to do something about Dorothy's unfinished task."[48]

Following Dorothy's death, the Menangle site was not pursued since no-one on the board was convinced it was a good proposition. Howard was very keen on the 30-acre property Retford Park in Bowral. When the board were meeting to finalise its purchase, the Rev R G Fillingham asked Goodwin if he had seen the 120-acre property Elwatan at Castle Hill. Though he had not seen Elwatan at this point, Howard did not want it. Goodwin however said to him that there was no comparison between the two properties for their purpose. Howard, surprised by Goodwin no longer being interested in Retford Park, spoke to Mrs Goodwin in order that she might be able to change Goodwin's mind. These conversations all happened on a Saturday, and the following Monday the three of them went to Bowral.[49]

On the way home from Bowral, Goodwin surprised Howard by announcing that they would go home via Elwatan. Howard made clear to Goodwin that he knew that Castle Hill was not on the way to Darling Point!

> He didn't take very kindly to it but he gave in as I was the driver, and he worked on the wife all the way home, if I remember, to try and talk me out of it; but anyway, he did come and view the place, and his last words were, after he had seen it, "Well if you and the committee are convinced this is right, I suppose it is right", and that was on the Monday, and he was dead before the end of the week.[50]

> Three days later on 27th October, Bishop Kerle called an urgent meeting. The Trustees of Elwatan had been made another offer and required an answer by the 28th. At the

---

[48] Clive Andrew Goodwin (De Berg Tapes: Tape 222, National Library) 4 May 1967. See also, 'Ven. C. Goodwin, 'Purchase of "Elwatan" for the Church of England Retirement Villages', Unpublished paper, 1977.

[49] Clive Andrew Goodwin (De Berg Tapes: Tape 222, National Library) 4 May 1967.

[50] Clive Andrew Goodwin (De Berg Tapes: Tape 222, National Library) 4 May 1967.

meeting Mr GA Lloyd - Lord Nuffield's personal representative in Australia for the Nuffield Foundation - was asked to negotiate for an extension of time for a few days, to make further financial arrangements." [...]. Mr Lloyd's negotiations were successful [...].

On 15th November 1958, the Standing Committee of the Diocese passed an ordinance entitled "Church of England National Emergency Fund Constitution Ordinance 1958." [...]. Clause 8 of the Ordinance includes a provision that the land and premises described be used as a "Church Veterans Village". [...].

The contract was completed in May 1959 [...]."[51]

Dorothy had excellent foresight and vision to recognise the importance to promote a way of life for retired people, not just to provide them housing.[52] This is a highly significant contribution Dorothy has made to the Anglican diocese of Sydney.

What we are doing at Castle Hill, or rather what we have achieved there, has to our delight attracted both national and international attention. [...] We had the pleasure recently of spending time with one of the Canadian senators who is chairman of the committee setting up an organization or rather, charged with the responsibility of drafting a bill similar to our Aged Persons Home Act, and she was most interested and took copious notes of the way things are worked here. Then, of course, there are other

---

[51] Gwen Davidge, 'What was Mrs Mowll's Vision?', Unpublished notes for a talk to be given at Tuesday Barton Hall Fellowship (late 1980's). Information gathered from Anglican Retirement Village Archives.
[52] 'Mowll Memorial Village', In Focus, 24 November 1984, 2. See also, Ven. C. Goodwin, 'Purchase of "Elwatan" for the Church of England Retirement Villages', Unpublished paper, 1977.

dioceses in Australia who are looking to us for guidance [...].[53]

Mowll Village was opened on 24 October 1959, exactly one year after Howard's death. All but one of the Australian bishops attended the ceremony. [54]

Portrait paintings of Howard and Dorothy Mowll at Mowll Village

The Rev Alfred G Reynolds was a clergyman, missionary, and artist. His portrait paintings include Bishop Alfred Stanway of Tanganyika, the Rev Dr Leon Morris, and Howard and Dorothy Mowll.[55] Several decades after completing his portraits of the Mowlls, Reynolds reflected on the differences he experienced in painting Howard in contrast to Dorothy. He was much happier with his portrait of Howard and he explains this was because he knew his subject much better. Reynolds had been in meetings with Howard over the course of 25 years, and in those meetings, he took notes about Howard's appearance. As soon as Howard died, Reynolds began a life-size painting of him. After Bishop Clive Kerle saw the painting, he asked Reynolds if they could have it for Mowll Village. He was then commissioned to paint a portrait of Dorothy, yet he did not know her, and he was very disappointed with the end result.[56] He had relied on photos and comments from Dorothy's bridesmaid who lived in Tasmania where Reynolds also lived. But this was very different to the detailed study he had made of Howard over 25 years. Reynolds came to Sydney for the opening of Mowll Village where many others were able to see his portraits for the first time. The portraits currently hang in the entrance foyer of Lober House, Mowll Village.

---

[53] Clive Andrew Goodwin (De Berg Tapes: Tape 222, National Library) 4 May 1967.
[54] Village Origins: Our History (Anglican Retirement Villages, Diocese of Sydney, 1999), 5, 9.
[55] A.G. Reynolds, *Variations in a Varied Life*, 3rd ed. (Melbourne: Rochester Engineering, 2008 [1989]) 158.
[56] Reynolds, *Variations in a Varied Life*, 158.

Speaking ministry

As the wife of the Archbishop, President of the Mother's Union[57], and a former missionary, Dorothy had ample opportunities to give talks to women. In one such talk, that she gave in Armidale in 1934 not long after moving from China to Sydney, we see her desire to train up local women into positions of ministry leadership. This talk reflects clearly her philosophy of ministry. Despite both her parents and her aunt having died a number of years earlier, and despite Dorothy having ministry experience herself as a single and married woman, her philosophy of ministry had not changed over the years, and she shared the same ministry philosophy as her parents and aunt.

We are fortunate that a local Armidale journalist thought her talk important enough to write a story about it in their newspaper:

> [...] The Chinese Christians were always looking to others [missionaries] for leadership.

> Mrs. Mowll said she was always asking these young women what would happen if the missionaries left the country, and she endeavoured to stir them up to realise their responsibilities.

> In 1927 [...]

> Communism spread and the missionaries were compelled to leave. [...]

> They were away for 12 months, and the Christian Chinese women had to decide whether they had become Christians from conviction or merely because they were keen on the foreigners. It was a time of testing.

> When they returned 12 months later the missionaries found that the timid Bible women had risen to the occasion and had gone to the temples and preached to the

---

[57] MU archives held at Moore College Library.

crowds. As a result of being left alone they had shown their colours and carried on.

There was no longer any need for leadership and the missionaries were enabled to devote their time to training others. [...]

The women were working in a wonderful way and all were linked together to show their love for the Lord.[58]

Dorothy's death

Dorothy died aged 67 on 23 December 1957 in Sydney from Hodgkin's disease. Her funeral was at 2pm at St Andrew's Cathedral on 27 December 1957 and was attended by 2000 people.[59] The Archbishop of Brisbane read Psalm 90 and the Archbishop of Armidale read 1 Corinthians 15:20. Bishop W G Hilliard preached and Bishop Kerle led in prayer. The Mother's Union also held a service of thanksgiving at the cathedral for Dorothy's life on 25 March 1958. Howard died within a year of Dorothy on 24 October 1958.

Following the news of Dorothy's death, tributes flowed in from around the world, testifying to people's great love and admiration of her, and their thankfulness to God for the woman he made her. In the weeks after her death, Howard received thousands of letters of condolence. A more formal tribute was also made with the entire *The Sydney Diocesan Magazine* (Vol. 10, No. 12 February 1958) being dedicated to Dorothy's life and ministries. Even before her death, Dorothy was recognised in 1956 with her being appointed an Officer of the Order of the British Empire (OBE) for her service of others during WWII and in the years following.

---

[58] Author unknown, 'Spreading the gospel: Mission work in West China', *The Armidale Express*, 28 September, 1934.
(https://trove.nla.gov.au/newspaper/article/192897499/22125716#)
[59] *The "Four Streams". Newsletter of the Diocesan Association for Western China No. 1. (New Series)* (February 1958), 13.
(https://www.churchmissionarysociety.amdigital.co.uk/Documents/Images/CMS_CRL_Four_China_Feb_1958_01/0#Articles).

Howard and Dorothy Mowll had no children that took the Mowll name, but they had many spiritual children because they had invested in so many people's lives for the cause of Jesus Christ.[60] Like her parents and aunt before her, Dorothy's life – both as a single woman and as a married woman – was characterised by a commitment to worldwide mission and service of others.

[60] See other chapters in this volume for details on Howard Mowll's ministry. See also Loane, *Archbishop Mowll* for further comments on the ministries of Howard and Dorothy Mowll.

12. Howard Mowll's Bible

Stuart Piggin

How do biographers access the deepest thoughts of their subjects and how do they identify what their subjects think it is most important for us to know? In the biography of Archbishop Harry Goodhew, released in 2021,[1] I suggested that in his diaries we find his deepest thoughts; in his sermons, the thoughts he considers most important to share with the people of God. For Howard Mowll, both are found in his Bible. His copious annotations map his intimacy with God and also his plans of many a sermon. It is a major resource for identifying his theology, his devotional life, and his homiletical practice. In this chapter, I will focus on one of his Bibles, but Archbishop Peter Jensen has kindly lent me two of Howard Mowll's New Testaments,[2] which should also be analysed in the search for his thoughts *coram deo*.

The Parallel New Testament 1882

The first of these New Testaments is the Parallel New Testament of 1882, the 1611 Authorised Version in parallel with the 1881 Revised Version. Mowll has written his own name at the front and under that: 'K S C' which I take it refers to the King's School, Canterbury, and the date 20 February 1907. He was at the King's School from 1903 to 1909. There he was a regular prizewinner; the last prize he won was the Marshall Wild Divinity Prize in 1907 for form VA.[3] This parallel Bible may have been the prize. It is not extensively annotated, but in the first 9 chapters of Mark's gospel he has underlined numerous words and in the margin written the equivalent Greek word. Individual words are underlined in Ephesians, but with no further annotations, except in one verse. In Ephesians 5:4, the word 'filthiness' is underlined and the

---

[1] Stuart Piggin, *Harry Goodhew: Archbishop, Godly Radical, Dynamic Anglican* (Sydney: Morning Star Publishing, 2021).
[2] Editor's note: these two Bibles have also been donated to the Moore College Library.
[3] Loane, *Archbishop Mowll*, 32.

Greek written in the margin. In Philippians 3 and 4, and Colossians 3 and 4, some words are underlined. Then in I Thessalonians and in 2 Thessalonians chapter one many words are underlined, and their Greek words written in the margin. He also notes that I Thessalonians was written in the winter of 53-4 AD. Some words are underlined in Philemon, and there are two marginalia in 1 John, and that's it!

Greek New Testament 1904

The second of Mowll's New Testaments which Dr Jensen has lent me is Mowll's Greek New Testament, the BFBS 1904 edition. It was given to him on 2 February 1911 on his 21st birthday by his 'affect[tionat]e Uncle, W R Mowll'. This is the Rev. William Rutley Mowll of whom Loane observes that in 1902 he was 'at the height of a splendid soul-winning ministry'.[4] There follows the text 1 Cor 16:13 in Greek: 'Watch ye, stand fast in the faith, quit you like men, be strong.' He needed to hear and heed that text. Just two weeks before he had been appointed president of the Cambridge Inter-Collegiate Christian Union (CICCU), then in its first year of disaffiliation from the Student Christian Movement (SCM), and just 10 months later came the famous 1911 Reuben Torrey Cambridge Mission which Torrey thought the 'most fruitful' in which he had ever engaged.[5]

This New Testament is not extensively annotated either. It has very wide margins on each page and lots of space at the bottom of each page – so it is designed to accept heavy notation. Mowll wrestles with four Greek words in Matthew 3 and one word in Matthew 9, three words or phrases in Mark 1, two of which he observes are 'peculiar to St Mark', two words in Mark 5, and then nothing until Luke, the first six chapters of which he annotates very heavily. The first 4 chapters of John are lightly annotated, and chapter 11 rates a comment on one word, as does Romans 5, and the last annotations in his Greek NT are in Galatians chapter one which, however, is very heavily annotated. The annotations often mention grammatical issues as you would expect in a Greek NT,

---

[4] Loane, *Archbishop Mowll*, 24.
[5] Loane, *Archbishop Mowll*, 49.

but not invariably. The needs of the preacher seem to have generated some of the entries.

Mowll's Chaldercot Bible

I have called it his Chaldercot Bible because in the inside cover a name plate reads: 'H. W. K. Mowll, Chaldercot, [D]over.' It used to be in the possession of Mary Andrews, who three decades ago gave it to me, and I have now passed it on to the possession of the Moore College Library.

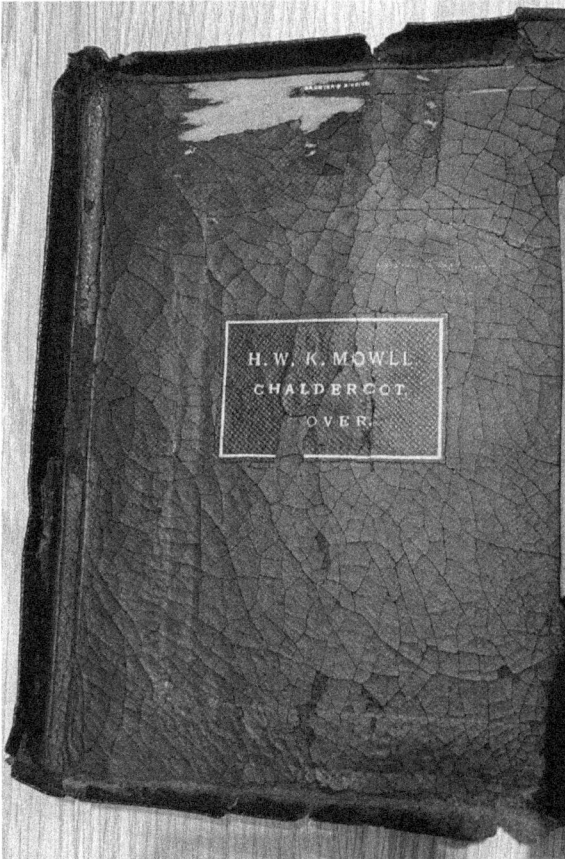

Figure 2: Label inside front cover of Mowll's Chaldercot Bible

We do not know when he acquired it, and the Bible itself is undated. Chaldercot, Dover, was the family home of his earliest memories, and when in 1945 the Home Mission Society purchased the lovely property in Port Hacking as a centre for youth work, he had it dedicated with the name of Chaldercot.[6] That this Bible is identified with Chaldercot suggests Mowll acquired it early in his life.

On the spine, the words 'Holy Bible' occur and, at the bottom of the spine, the single word 'Bagster'. At the top the inside cover, gilt-stamped, about 1 mm high, are the words 'Bagster's binding'. On the undated title page, the publisher is identified as Samuel Bagster and Sons. This was a Bagster Bible: expensive, morocco bound (goatskin), rice paper. I first came across Bagster Bibles when studying Florence Young, the revered missionary with the South Sea Evangelical Mission. When she turned 18 and professed conversion, her father, in celebration of her conversion as much as her 18th birthday, presented his daughter with a Bagster's Bible.[7]

The well-known motto of the firm, *pollai men thnētois glōttai, mia d'athanatoisin* (The inhabitants of earth have many tongues, those of heaven have but one), is attributed to the Rev Henry Francis Cary, assistant librarian of the British Museum who is buried in poet's corner, Westminster Abbey. The Bagster family said the Latin version, *multæ terricolis linguæ, cœlestibus una*, was composed by William Greenfield. His father was a missionary with the London Missionary Society (LMS) who drowned on a voyage of the Duff which had brought the first LMS missionaries to the South Seas. William was a linguistic prodigy employed on Bible translation by the Bible Society and was working on a grammar in 30 languages when he died at the age of 32 of 'brain fever'.

On the title page itself, Mowll has written a number of sentiments on the nature of Scripture. It is *Cor Dei in verbis Dei*, the heart of God in the words of God (Gregory). 'The Holy Scriptures are to believing souls what the meadow is to the ox, what the home is to the man, what the

---

[6] Loane, *Archbishop Mowll*, 217.

[7] Stuart Piggin and Robert D. Linder, *The Fountain of Public Prosperity: Evangelical Christians in Australian History, 1740-1914* (Melbourne: Monash University Publishing, 2018), 423.

nest is to the bird, the stream to the fish, and the cleft of the rock to the seafowl.' (Martin Luther).

Loose enclosures

There are 19 loose papers or cards in the Bible presently. The loose papers have been preserved *in situ* and described on the Library catalogue record. They are certainly part of the Mowll story. The second such piece is an invitation in French to assist at the service to pray for the repose of the soul of Monsieur Jules Coiret, a Croix de Guerre winner, who had died, three months earlier, on 29 September 1918. This was during Mowll's six-month tour of duty as a chaplain in France. He had taken many funerals and, says Loane, 'to his own surprise sometimes heard a Confession'.[8] What does it mean that he kept this very Catholic invitation in his Bible? That he was a Protestant, but not a bigot? I think on the grounds of other evidence that this is true of him. The next loose paper is his own 2-page confession. It is sacred ground, beginning: 'I have not given enough time to Intercessory Prayer and to Bible Study'. He confesses to his 'Lack of control' over his thoughts, to 'Irritability of temper', to 'lethargy and indifference', to 'lack of spiritual freshness'. He prays for 'sound judgment', 'control of speech', for 'increased sympathy' and 'lessened sensitiveness'. When was it written? One of his petitions reads 'That my Chinese fellow workers may feel that I seek at all times to understand their viewpoint'. So, it was written sometime between 1922 and 1933 when he was in West China, first as assistant bishop and then bishop. There is a page from *China's Millions,* the magazine of the China Inland Mission. It is dated November 1923.

---

[8] Loane, *Archbishop Mowll*, 79.

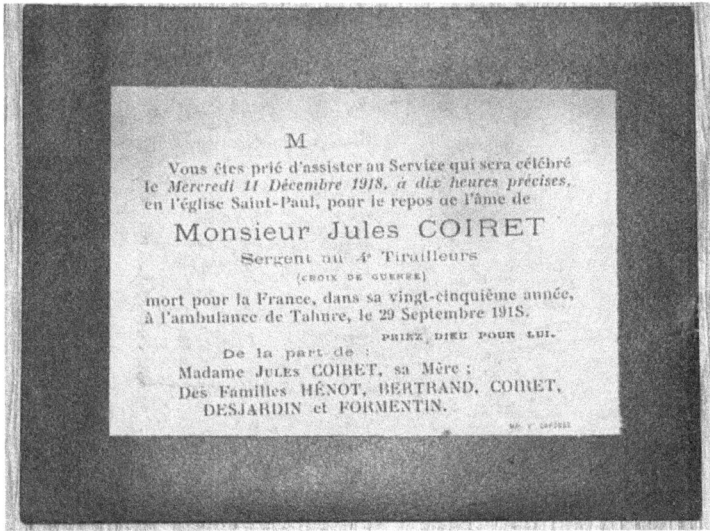

Figure 3: Memorial card for Monsieur Jules Coiret

There are also sermon summaries, poems and prayers. Loane tells us of Mowll's preaching:

> He was not a remarkable preacher, but his sermons were all immensely practical and down to earth. ... He would take a verse, or chapter, or whole book of Scripture, and draw out its leading message with direct and forceful application.[9]

One of the sermon summaries is four pages long and covers the whole book of Ruth; a second, Romans 6-8.

One of the devotional thoughts found in these papers Mowll has attributed to Maréchale (field marshall). This was Catherine Booth-Clibborn who fell out with the Salvation Army over her fondness for the extravagances of Alexander Dowie. But John Ridley, the Baptist evangelist, thought highly of her, and it is revealing that Mowll may have thought so too. Catherine wrote a hymn about Australia's role in furthering the gospel among the nations:

---

9 Loane, *Makers of our Heritage*, 177.

Go and tell of His redemption,
Let Australia set the pace;
Christ alone brings full salvation,
Reaching every tribe and race.[10]

Two of the loose items are blotting paper: his annotations in the Bible are in ink written with a fountain pen. He must have been careful: there is no ink blot anywhere in all the annotations. But the Bible is water damaged: the ink has not run, but it has faded. Moore College Library will receive it just in time.

Notes written on the front and back blank pages

Front and back blank pages of the Bible are covered with copious quotations. Consistent with the afore-mentioned two-fold purpose of resourcing personal devotion and public proclamation, the front pages are evidence of his white-hot Keswick spirituality; the back pages illustrations taken from his wider reading. The first entry in the Bible reads:

God never would send you the darkness
If he felt you could bear the light.
But you would not cling to his guiding hand
If the way was always bright.
And you would not care to walk by faith
Could you always walk by sight.

Then:

Life is a mission. Its end is service. Its law is self-sacrifice. Its strength is fellowship with God.

Stirring stuff, but also cutting to the quick in the most practical of matters:

---

[10] Piggin, *Attending to the National Soul,* 176.

I am saved, but is my home life
What the Lord would have it be
Is it seen in every action
Jesus has control of me?

Facing the title page are prayers for divine assistance in either preaching or studying the Word.

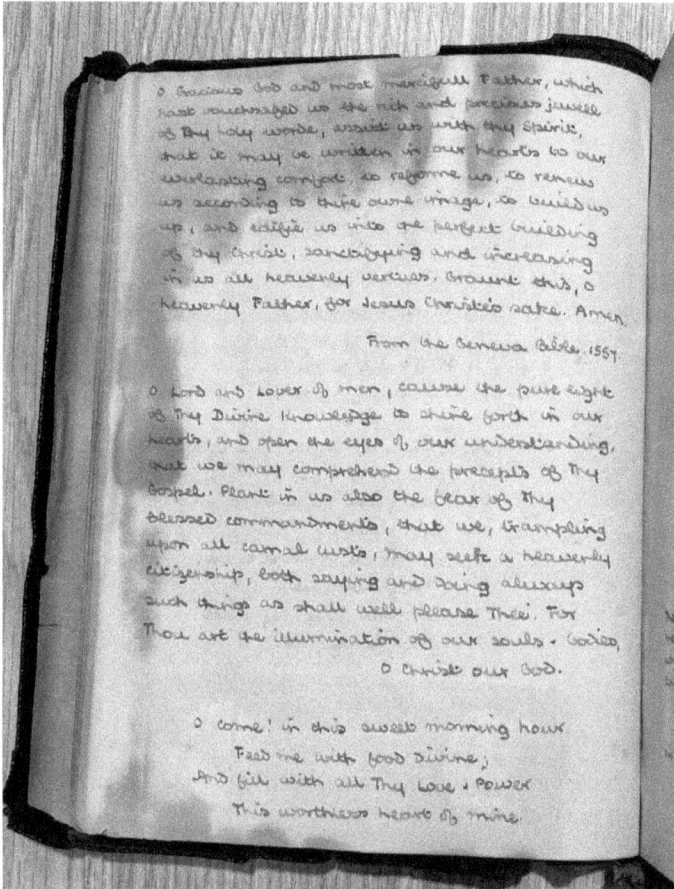

Figure 4: Notes on a blank page

Loane tells us 'He was a great lover of books and his table always seemed to groan with recent publications. Friends were enjoined to let him know when a new book appeared.'[11] Here is the source, in the rear of the Bible, of some 133 sermon illustrations. For example:

'What must I do to be lost ... nothing'

'F.A.I.T.H. Forsaking all I take him.'

'Are you a Christian
No! Oh! No! I'm a member of the C of E.
Told by Lord Grey'

Peasant in N.W. Canada to Lord Grey. "I could speak to the Lord Jesus easier than I could speak to you." "Of course you could, you speak to him every day and you've never seen me before."

Textual Marginalia

Coming (at long last) to the text of the Bible itself, easily the commonest notation is a 3-fold summary, I assume for homiletical purposes. Normally just three lines, one line for each point, but occasionally much fuller, as in the case of his sermon notation on Jonah 1, with many verses under three headings: i. The Sender of the Storm; ii. The Effect of the Storm; iii. The Calming of the Storm.

The first Scriptural verse attracting a marginal comment is Genesis 1:3 'And God said', on which Mowll wrote 'The agent of change, life and power is always the Word of God.' Mowll is far more interested in drawing spiritual truths out of the Bible than historical facts. On Genesis 2:2 God resting on the seventh day, he notes: 'The Lord may work in many a house. He can rest in very few.' As befits his Dover origins, Mowll is intrigued by Noah's ark. There are three sermon summaries on Noah. On 5:22 'And Noah walked with God':

> Thoughtless said, "Ship miles from water. Noah crazy"
> Clever said, "Too big to navigate"
> Practical said, "Spend money on better housing"

---

[11] Loane, *Heritage,* 179.

Angry said, [indecipherable – Mowll must have been in a paroxysm when he wrote it!].

The sermon summaries, if indeed that is what they are, are strong on alliteration:

> Men who said "No" to God
> Esau the man of Pleasure
> Balaam the man of Profit
> Jonah the man of Prejudice
> Pharaoh the man of Pride.

Old Testament marginalia is consistently Christological. On Exodus 33:21-22, 'And the Lord said, "Behold there is a place by me, and thou shalt stand upon a rock: And it shall come to pass, while my glory passeth by, that I will put thee in a clift [sic] of the rock"',

Mowll comments:

> It is one thing to know Christ is the Rock
> It is another thing to be standing on the Rock
> It is a further blessing to be hid in the cleft of the Rock.

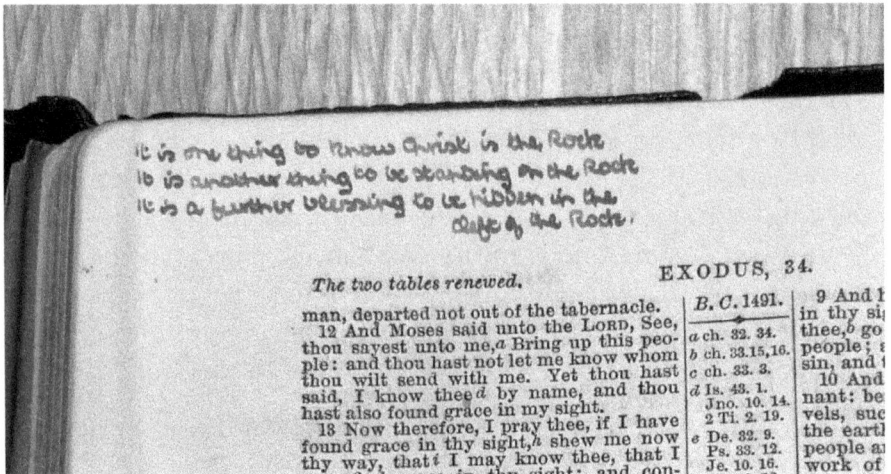

Figure 5: Marginal notes for Exodus 34

Some marginalia read like sermon perorations, such as these words of Saul's ruin in 1 Samuel 28, and which I can imagine Mowll saying to his eyes-agog CICCU fellow students:

> It was a dark and sad hour when Saul, before his last and losing battle, looked upon the shade of Samuel. It is not less dark and sad when the shade of our boyhood meets us in manhood and in tones more of sorrow than anger tells us that we are kings who have lost our crowns.

He was a man of his times, of course, capable of sentiments no longer considered acceptable. For example, on Psalm 105:44, 'He gave them the lands of the heathen: and they inherited the labour of the people', he comments: 'Cf. Deut. 6:11 Not like colonists who inherit with much toil.'

Mowll clearly read the Old Testament in the light of the New, especially in its archetypes of redemption. There is an elaborate meditation on Mephibosheth in 2 Samuel 9:

> Mephibosheth (The Reproach) – A picture of the wondrous grace of God in Redemption:
>
> 1. Dwelt in Lo-Debar the place of loneliness. 4.
> 2. Lame in both feet so could not come of himself. 3.
> 3. Kings sought him out. 1.
> 4. Brought to King through the instrumentality of another.2.
> 5. Received a 3-fold promise of the royal provision. 7.[12]
> 6. Provision was to be continuous according to his needs. 7.
> 7. Adopted into the King's family. 11.

---

[12] 'And David said unto him, Fear not: for I will surely shew thee kindness for Jonathan thy father's sake, and will restore thee all the land of Saul thy father; and thou shalt eat bread at my table continually.'

8. When promises fulfilled. He never got beyond needing the King's strength. Of himself he could do nothing 13.

9. It was all for Jonathan's sake 1. Jonathan a gift of God. John 3:16.

This is not an academic's Bible; there is nothing here which is controversial, calling for debate. But his spirituality is neither emotionalism nor moralism[13] nor experientialism.[14] Clear thinking is required as well as good living: Proverbs 23:7 'As he thinketh in his heart, so is he'. And yet it is not rationalism either. He was not in pursuit of knowledge only but, quoting Paul, making 'manifest the savour of his knowledge', as though the knowledge alone would not suffice.[15]

It was an understanding which made him attractive and encouraging to those who were being saved. Let us take an example from his days in China. Unlike Dorothy, Howard never acquired Chinese and had no sense of tone values, a drawback which he always regretted. Yet the Chinese thought of him as a great man and he won their hearts[16] – perhaps because his own was so healthy? On 29 December 1932, he returned from an extensive visitation to his home in Chengtu (Chengdu) in West China to find it had been ransacked following a 'savage battle' on the Chengtu compound. In his wrecked study one text looked down from the wall, 2 Chronicles 20:15 'The battle is not yours, but God's.' Loane tells us that this text 'spoke to his heart with great encouragement'.[17] In his Bible, this verse along with four others in the chapter, is underlined, and the chapter itself he has labelled 'The

---

[13] Mowll emphasizes salvation not ethics in the Book of Proverbs. On Proverbs 14:12 he notes that 'The Believer's End' is 'Peaceful, Hopeful, Desirable, Accompanied, Loved, Confirmed, Saved.'

[14] On Job 4:12 he notes: 'Eliphaz had remarkable experience and so considered he had a right to judge and correct Job.'

[15] 'Fragrance', China's Millions, November 1923, 164.

[16] Loane, Heritage, 165.

[17] Loane, Heritage, 154 (note that, because of a publisher's error, the page number is printed as 154 but should be 164).

Soldier's Chapter'.[18] Those words are prefaced in 2 Chronicles 20:15 with the words 'Be not afraid or dismayed by reason of this great multitude; for the battle is not yours, but God's'. In this season of rampant secularisation and exponential decline in church going, I had become dismayed by reason of the great multitude of those who stood against us – so 90 years after Mowll's heart was encouraged, mine was too by the same verse.

Mowll emphasises that we are soldiers in a battle, we are workmen in fields. For him, the Bible is a training manual for labourers to plant the seed and bring in the harvest. In Isaiah 32 he finds '3 Conditions for Effectual Sowing: 1. The King must have his rightful place. 15 The Spirit Effectual Sowing: The King must have his rightful place. 15 The Spirit must be received in his fullness 17, 18. The Soul must maintain the rest of Faith.' There are striking references to 'backsliders' in his notations (e.g. Ps 78; Jer 2 and 3; Ezek 16:15-34; Zeph 1:6). Because 'backsliding' is Scriptural at least in the AV, it does not seem to worry him that this was a conspicuous element in Wesleyan Arminianism to which he would not have adhered, being a Reformed Calvinist.

The soteriological interpretation of the Old Testament is made explicit in the New, of course, beginning with:

---

[18] Similarly, he identifies Psalm 139:8 "If I ascend up into heaven, thou art there", as "The Airman's Text". He has already listed from I Chronicles 12 the:
  Qualifications for the Christian Soldier
  Ver. 2 Offensive weapons
  8. Defensive weapons
  33. Discipline
  38. Watchword "Make Jesus King"
  40. Spirit – Joy.
Again at the beginning of 2 Timothy he gives a list of the qualities of the good soldier:
  A Good Soldier of Jesus Christ
    Must keep under his body 1 Cor 9:26,27.
    Must use spiritual weapons 2 Cor 10:3-5.
    Must put on the whole armour of God Eph 6:10-18.
    Must endure hardness 2 Tim 2:3.
    Must put aside the things of the world 2 Tim 2:4.

Has Christ fulfilled in you the meaning of His names? He is –

1:21. Jesus – to save you from sin

23. Emmanuel – to bring God to you and you to God

2:6 Governor – to rule your heart and life.[19]

The two most heavily annotated books in the whole Bible are John's Gospel and Romans. The notation on John's Gospel begins with:

Look at Christ

1. To be saved, John 3:14,15.
2. To be renewed 2 Cor 3:18
3. To be glorified 1 John 3:2

John the Baptist preached Jesus Christ as

Judge Matt 3:2-10.
Sinbearer John 1:29
Bridegroom John 3:29

The strong emphasis on saved to serve continues. For example, on John 20:

20:16 When Mary knew Him as 'My Master'
It dried her tears 13.
It corrected her mistakes 15.
It made her a messenger 18.

One is saved to serve as an evangelist and therefore an apologist. On 20:31 'these are written, that ye might believe ...', he observes:

That Christ is 'The Truth' is recommended to men by various forms of witness.

1. The witness of the Father 5:32-37.
2. The witness of Christ Himself 8:14, 18:37.
3. The witness of works 5:36.
4. The witness of Scripture 5:39-40.

---

[19] In the book of Matthew.

5. The witness of the forerunners 1:7.
6. The witness of the Disciples 15:27.
7. The witness of the Spirit 15:26.

He clearly thought of the Acts of the Apostles as the Acts of the Spirit. He heads it with 'Five Reasons why men were not filled with the Holy Ghost'[20] and on Acts 19:2 he gives 'Conditions for Receiving the Holy Ghost'.[21]

Conclusion

We have here the Bible of one who is unequivocally evangelical in doctrine, evangelical in the preacher's public proclamation and evangelical in personal devotion. It is the Bible of one who has enlisted in the Lord's army as well as in the British army, and is therefore the Bible of a soldier of Jesus Christ. It is the Bible of one with a constraining desire to serve, specifically to serve the Gospel. It is the Bible of one with a heart for evangelism, and therefore it is replete with mini-sermon summaries addressed, not to academic debates, but to reflections on why some reject Jesus as Saviour, on reasons with apologetic intent for accepting Jesus, on the fullness of the work of Jesus and the need to be filled with the Holy Spirit, and on the theme of saved to serve, and the need for the servant of Jesus and his Gospel to guard his soul, lest having preached to others, he should himself backslide and become a castaway.[22] Howard Mowll's Bible is a treasure trove, chockers with the precious gems which adorned the prince of Sydney's archbishops. It deserves to be studied far more closely than

---

[20] 1. Lack of Conviction. The Twelve. 1
2. Desire of Power. Simon. 8
3. Need of Instruction. Cornelius. 10
4. Lack of Seeking. Ephesus 19
5. Love of Sin. Epistle? Whitsunday.
The numbers after 1-4 refer to chapters in Acts, so this opening sermon summarises the whole book.
[21] 1. Repentant Faith Acts 2:38.
2. Earnest Prayer Acts 2:1, 4:31.
3. Definite Acceptance Acts 19:2.
4. Obedient Walk. Acts 5:32.
[22] 1 Corinthians 9:27.

has been done here and will repay any such student a handsome dividend.

Other recommendations

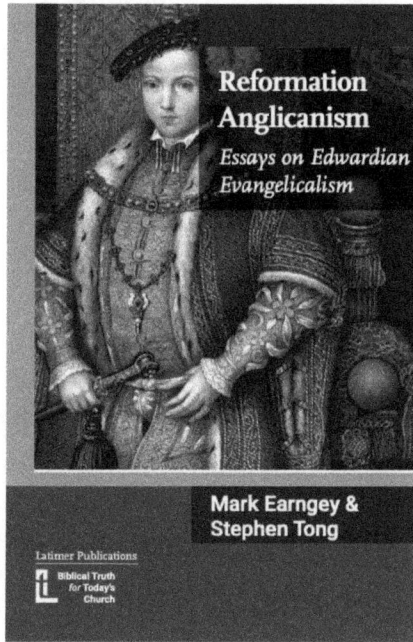

Reformation Anglicanism: Essays on Edwardian Evangelicalism is a superb set of essays arising from the Moore Theological College symposium on Reformation Anglicanism held in 2019. Featuring essays from various reformation scholars, this collection of articles focuses on some foundational documents (e.g. *Book of Homilies, Articles of Religion*) and foundational reformers (e.g. Thomas Cranmer, Martin Bucer, Heinrich Bullinger) involved with the English Reformation, and its Edwardian phase in particular. This edited volume not only offers a sustained focus on the often-neglected mid-Tudor phase of the Reformation but explores new avenues of research on overlooked subjects such as the *45 Articles of Religion*, John Ponet's *Short Catechism,* the *Reformatio Legum Ecclesiasticarum,* the ministry of John Hooper, and the memory of Martin Bucer. Students and scholars alike will benefit from this fresh examination of these anchors of Anglicanism which were hotly contested both then, and now.

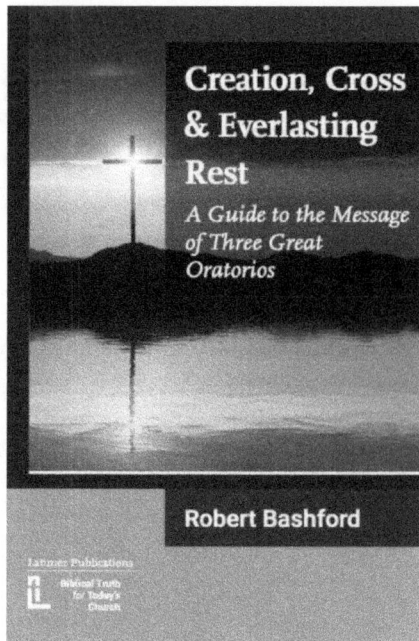

This book is a study of three great oratorios: Haydn's *The Creation*, Bach's St Matthew *Passion*, and Brahms' *Requiem*. They can be called 'great' because they excel both as musical masterpieces and as clear expressions of biblical truth. The study has as its aim to increase enjoyment of these works and to deepen understanding of their message.

The three selected oratorios, individually, open a window on major doctrines of the Bible. Collectively, they present a panorama of a considerable expanse of the message of Scripture. Joseph Haydn's *The Creation* takes us to the beginning of all things in the physical domain. We are invited to marvel at God's creative power displayed in the heavens and the earth and culminating in the creation of humankind. Ominously, the oratorio ends with a strong hint of the tragic Fall of Genesis 3.

Redemption is the theme of J.S. Bach's moving St Matthew *Passion*. We come to the heart of God's great plan of salvation. Bach's work takes us through the Passion of the Lord Jesus Christ, as it unfolds in chapters 26 and 27 of Matthew's Gospel. Johannes Brahms' *Requiem* is very different from other 'requiems.' By means of a selection of Bible texts, our gaze is directed repeatedly away from the sorrows and frustrations of this life towards the solid and lasting joys of heaven to come.

The 'What to Listen out for' sections in this book provide comments on the music in a user-friendly way.

In our Christian Leadership series

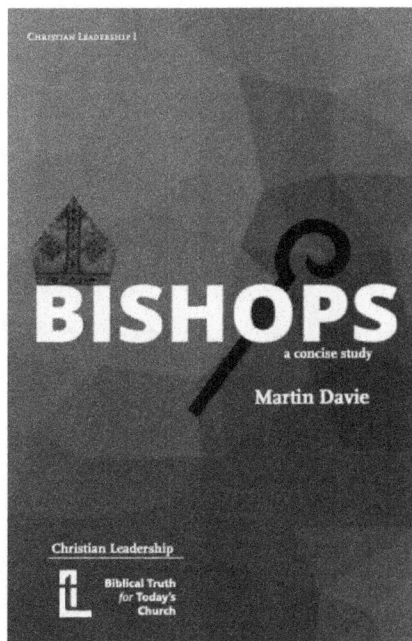

Bishops Past, Present and Future: A Concise Study summarises the key points of the argument of Martin's major study *Bishops Past, Present and Future* (Gilead Books, 2022). It is designed to meet the needs of those who would like to know about the role and importance of bishops in the Church of England, but who would baulk at tackling the 800+ pages of the original book.

This concise study is published in the hope that it will help many in the Church of England, both ordained and lay, to think in a more informed fashion about how bishops should respond to the challenges facing the Church of England at this critical point in its history as it considers how to move forward following the publication of the Living in Love and Faith material.

In our St Antholin Lecture series

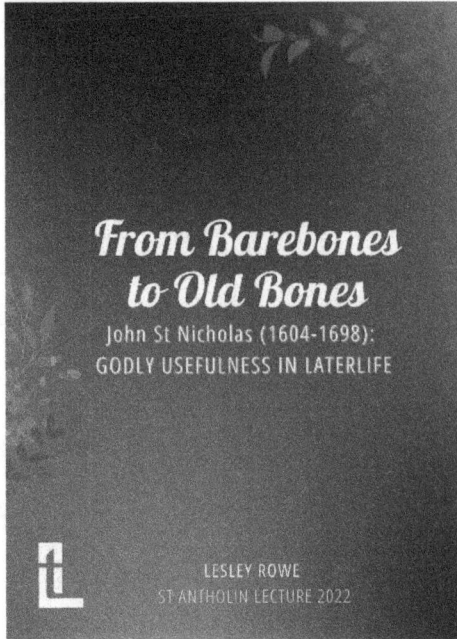

*From Barebones
to Old Bones*
John St Nicholas (1604-1698):
GODLY USEFULNESS IN LATERLIFE

LESLEY ROWE
ST ANTHOLIN LECTURE 2022

John St Nicholas was a Leicestershire puritan minister, ejected after the Restoration in 1660. Subsequent to his ejection, he lived on for a further 38 years. How he used his time during his lengthy 'retirement' provides a helpful model for today's Christians seeking to continue serving God as they get older.

www.ingramcontent.com/pod-product-compliance
Lightning Source LLC
Chambersburg PA
CBHW031127090426
42738CB00008B/997